<small>PRAISE FOR</small>

THE HOLY VOTE

"Suarez is at his most eloquent when discussing religion and American national security. By writing with passion and clarity about our holy wars, Suarez, one of our best journalists, may have given us a Cronkite moment of his own."
— *Washington Post*

"A balanced account of the issues in question. This is a journalist's journey worthy of comparison with Dan Wakefield's classic, *Supernation at Peace and War*."
— *Library Journal* (starred review)

"It's darn good colloquy about the Religious Right, separation of church and state, and old and new issues."
— *Booklist*

Don Perdue

About the Author

RAY SUAREZ has been a senior correspondent with *The NewsHour with Jim Lehrer* since 1999, where he is responsible for conducting news-making interviews, hosting studio discussions and debates, reporting from the field, and serving as a backup anchor. He came to the *NewsHour* from NPR's *Talk of the Nation*, and before that, he spent seven years covering local, national, and international news for an NBC-owned station in Chicago.

ALSO BY RAY SUAREZ

The Old Neighborhood:
What We Lost in the Great
Suburban Migration, 1966–1999

The
HOLY
VOTE

The Politics of
Faith in America

RAY SUAREZ

HARPER

NEW YORK • LONDON • TORONTO • SYDNEY

For Carole
with me every step of the way

HARPER

A hardcover edition of this book was published in 2006 by Rayo, an imprint of HarperCollins Publishers.

HarperCollins books may be purchased for educational, business, or sales promotional use. For information please write: Special Markets Department, HarperCollins Publishers, 10 East 53rd Street, New York, NY 10022.

FIRST HARPER PAPERBACK PUBLISHED 2007.

Designed by Christine Weathersbee

Library of Congress Cataloging-in-Publication Data has been applied for.

ISBN: 978-0-06-082998-8
ISBN-10: 0-06-082998-2

07 08 09 10 11   DIX/RRD   10 9 8 7 6 5 4 3 2 1

CONTENTS

Contents

PROLOGUE

Let love be genuine; hate what is evil, hold fast to what is good; love one another with mutual affection; outdo one another in showing honor.

Do not lag in zeal, be ardent in spirit, serve the Lord.

Rejoice in hope, be patient in suffering, persevere in prayer.

Contribute to the needs of the saints; extend hospitality to strangers.

Bless those who persecute you; bless and do not curse them.

Rejoice with those who rejoice, weep with those who weep.

Live in harmony with one another; do not be haughty, but associate with the lowly; do not claim to be wiser than you are.

Do not repay anyone evil for evil, but take thought for what is noble in the sight of all.

If it is possible, so far as it depends on you, live peaceably with all.

Beloved, never avenge yourselves, but leave room for the wrath of God; for it is written, "Vengeance is mine, I will repay, says the Lord." No, "if your enemies are hungry, feed them; if they are thirsty, give them something to drink; for by doing this you will heap burning coals upon their heads."

Do not be overcome by evil, but overcome evil with good.

—From the letter of Saint Paul to the Romans, 12:9–21

ONE

Credo . . . I Believe

I LOVE MY COUNTRY. I love my church.

I love the land itself in its stunning beauty, and my 300 million countrymen and -women. I even love the ones that make me crazy.

I love my *church,* the small-*c* place in a corner of Washington, D.C., where I sing and pray and teach Sunday school. And I love my *Church,* the teeming, globe-straddling capital-*C* place that I've given my lifelong devotion and trust to, along with my affection.

I am thrilled to see what looks like wisdom and kindness from my country and its people. I cringe when I see my country going off course. I think I am a patriot. At the same time I wrestle constantly with myself over what the country at its best ought to be, and how the things we do will affect the rest of the world.

In every corner of the world, I've gained strength and consolation sharing bread and wine with fellow Christians, and watched as the church has tried to live up to the encouragement from Jesus in the Gospel of Matthew, to feed the hungry, welcome the stranger, clothe the naked, visit the sick and the imprisoned.[1]

I pray often, and nobody knows I'm doing it. I have prayed in school all my life, but it never caused a fuss, because I didn't need official sanction, a loudly announced time at the school's flagpole, or a mandated moment of silence in order to accomplish the task: a few words between me and God.

I say the Pledge of Allegiance without coercion or irony, and don't drop the "under God." But I do wonder how I'd feel about the whole exercise if I didn't believe in God, and was being made to recite the Pledge.

I revere the Constitution and its attempts to speak to every generation of Americans, and the hundreds still to come. I also recognize that the Constitution is a political document, not a sacred one. It was crafted by politicians as a handbook to get us through the rough spots in American daily life. It was crafted in response to the particular grievances against the British monarchy and the fresh memory of failing self-government under the Articles of Confederation.

While it was very much a product of one hot summer in Philadelphia in the infancy of a fragile and insecure country, the national charter has aged magnificently. The Constitution helps maintain a voluntary consensus, a submission to the rules of a shared enterprise, in a country not defined by blood, clan, land origin, or religious belief.

The adaptability of the Constitution has gotten our country through uncomfortable and conflict-filled ages, including a blood-soaked spasm that saw one vast section of the country pull away from that consensus umbrella to save human slavery. When the Civil War began, slavery enjoyed recognition under the Constitution. When the smoke from millions of rifle rounds and cannonballs cleared, over a million people were dead, and that same Constitution forbade the ownership of one human being by another.

Whenever it is called for at a public occasion, I sing the national anthem, even though it must be the hardest national anthem to sing on this anthem-filled planet. And I'm especially fond of the final, frankly religious, stanza.[2]

Why tell you all this?

I tell you this because, until recently, I thought of all of the above as pretty normal. However, today, I feel as if I'm no longer living in the country I was raised in. Something valuable in the accommodation we made for one another is gone, and getting it back will take something more than just groping our way forward.

I tell you all this also because trying to discern the secret agendas of American journalists (I am one) has become something of a parlor game. One of the most offensive markers of our era is the implied division of our citizens, by our citizens, into Real Americans and everyone else, Patriots and everyone else, and Christians and everyone else. Of all the assumptions a reader might make about me, Christian Patriot might not have readily come to mind. Northeasterners, Latinos, reporters, and Christians outside certain denominations have, to some people, been traditionally suspect: someone who is all those things is only more so.

Ours was not founded as a Christian country. In the 230 years since then that label has only become less appropriate. We do have a unique status as the wealthy, industrialized country with the largest numbers of religious believers, active congregants, and people who merely say they believe in God. The gross numbers visible from a cruising-altitude-look at the country hide a complex mosaic of belief and a broad continuum of conviction as to what belief in a Creator means to our country today.

Our national life is cobbled together from a mix of noble dreams and grubby politics. That is no shame, but rather a realistic combination of the forces that move us as a people. Yet, more and more Americans, in full backlash against one another, want purity of purpose in the sausage-making of policy. And when they don't get it, they often identify the culprit as religion: there is both too much of it, and too little of it, in our shared civic life.

These are strange days.

I grew up at a time when it seemed every second adult had a cross of ashes on his or her forehead on Ash Wednesday, the first day of the Christian penitential season of Lent. I grew up at a time when half my schoolmates would open up their lunches for a week in the spring, to inspect the version of a "sandwich" their mothers had cobbled together from various fillings and matzoh. Passover days were part of the heartbeat of the neighborhood, keeping time for everyone as we moved through the year.

Also in spring, hundreds of other kids were dragged to department stores for their Easter clothes, and on that Sunday the streets were filled with surprisingly cleaned-up-looking kids, some with Brylcreemed hair, coming back from church and heading to relatives' for dinner.

In the fall came Sukkoth, a Jewish harvest festival, and makeshift shelters sprouted on fire escapes, in alleys and backyards and driveways, as the Jews of the neighborhood gathered outside on the last few nice nights of the fall for a festive dinner.

I tell you this for a reason. Not to hit your bloodstream with a sudden jolt of saccharine about the good old days. Not to flood your eyes with sepia-toned images of girls in frilly first communion dresses and boys in yarmulkes heading to religious instruction before handball and stickball.

It's something much more basic than that.

From life in a world soaked in religious imagery and practice, where the seasons of the year were punctuated by public displays of piety, I learned that the best distance to keep between church and state was a broad and respectful one. The Lord's Prayer wasn't said at school. There were no crèche displays in our public parks. There was no agitation for scripture readings at school. When a clergyman (and they were all men then) was at school for a major occasion, he could be relied upon to deliver a broad, bland, and monotheistic prayer.

On one fairly routine day covering the Chicago City Council, I watched as the aldermen stood for an invocation, delivered on this day by the late George Hagopian. The request for divine help in the work of the city council started innocently enough, with praise for God and thanks for his kindness. Then it veered away from the kind of prayers the council's four Jewish aldermen might include in their private devotions, ending in the name of "Your Blessed Son, Our Lord and Savior, Jesus Christ, and Mary, His Ever-Blessed Virgin Mother."

Was the prayer appropriate? I asked two of the council members during a break in the session later that day. One said, "Oh, that's just George. There's certainly nothing hostile about it. It's something you get used to."

I asked if they should have to get used to it. The other member chimed in. "You're too young to remember public school beginning every day with a Bible reading. Over the loudspeaker system. And the Lord's Prayer! And my school was heavily Jewish. It's Chicago. That's just the way it is."

It is, granted, a small thing. But in the moment of recalling youthful exclusion, a successful American Jew became almost rueful, trying to explain to a reporter what the constant reminder of his differentness, even as an elected member of a governing body, really means.

By the time I started school, in 1962, American public schools were changing. We learned to pray, if we prayed, at home. We learned about the

Bible, if we did, on our own and our family's time. Nobody felt that anything was missing.

I was born into what I've since been told was the decaying and fallen world after Supreme Court decisions like *Abington Township School District v. Schempp*. Talk to older Americans and they'll routinely date the decline of American morals from the series of Supreme Court decisions that severely restricted school prayer.

School prayer is still a topical issue and an important component of the political and cultural wars of this young century. Until 1963, Pennsylvania had a requirement that ten Bible verses be read to begin the day in the state's public schools.[3] In finding for the Schempp family—Unitarians who found that the readings both contradicted their own beliefs and isolated their children—Justice Tom Clark wrote, "The very purpose of a Bill of Rights was to withdraw certain subjects from the vicissitudes of political controversy, to place them beyond the reach of majorities and officials and to establish them as legal principles to be applied by the courts. One's right to . . . freedom of worship . . . and other fundamental rights may not be submitted to vote; they depend on the outcome of no elections."[4] When you write a phrase like that, you might be forgiven for thinking you are locking in a legal view for the ages. Yet the fight continues.

I was in kindergarten when Schempp was handed down, and am the middle-aged father of a first grader as I write this today. In the decades since that 1963 court decision and others that followed, the country has become not only more religious but more religiously diverse at the same time. Today, our national family now includes tens of millions who profess no religion at all.

However, those same years saw, first, the construction of a workable consensus around the place of religion in the public sphere, and then a militant backlash against that consensus. The United States is now contested terrain, a place where many of the commonplace ideas of the postwar decades are now reopened for negotiation—and battle.

The battle over the place of religion in public life has pushed more people to the poles of the debate. We are whipsawing between bare-knuckled partisan combat waged with all the tools of modern communication—satellite teleconferences and e-mails, blast faxes and pressure campaigns—and a contest of psychobabble: a world where people are, moment by moment, "insensitive," "hurt," "oppressed," and "marginalized."

This is a battle fought by gesture, sign, and signal. This is a fight in which symbolic acts are given deep significance. The acts are significant to those who carry them out for an audience of TV cameras, and assigned great importance by the people who see them.

Look. There's a man lying facedown on the steps of the Alabama Supreme Court. He's got an enormous black-leather-covered Bible in his hand. He's weeping. He's waiting to be carried away by uniformed officers who have ordered the court steps cleared.

Quick! What's the man doing?

Careful. Your answer may force you into joining a group you may not be sure you want to join. Will the weeping man's prayers prevent the two-and-a-half-ton monument from being moved from the court rotunda? Does the man believe his prayers will encourage a God who has so far taken no direct action to smite the moving men?

Or is this man and many others like him, shouting and predicting doom for the State of Alabama, involved in a very modern kind of public theater meant to force us, the distant audience in a continent-sized country, to take sides in a fight over a religious monument? However, this pious and very public support for public displays of the laws handed down on Mount Sinai sits very uncomfortably alongside the persistent public opinion research that shows most Americans can't name all ten, never mind in order.

The charm of that one datum is this: it may prove both sides' points. Depending on where you sit when you read the poll numbers about biblical ignorance, it may show that all the bellowing about the Commandments' public display is just so much hypocrisy, or it may demonstrate exactly why the ancient laws should be posted in every public building in America. (I will get back to the Ten Commandments in chapter six.)

Along with all the other changes in American political life came a change in the way we see each other. We Americans do not go into battle crediting the other side of the argument with operating out of goodwill. Increasingly, your opponent is not merely wrong, or mistaken, but bad. In the eyes of many fighting to insert more religion into the public sphere, their opponents hate America, hate religion, and will not stop until all signs of religion are chased from the public realm. In the eyes of many fighting for strict separation, the religious will not stop until there is a theocracy in America, until it becomes a conservative Christian state.

The stereotyping is nonstop. The allegations are often laughable. But the visions of America from the two poles are mutually exclusive, and—at first glance—irreconcilable. The large and growing number of Americans who profess no faith at all may make tough and unsentimental critiques of American political life and the national culture, and yet find displays of American religiosity damaging affronts to their liberty.

Then big religious voices in the culture reply in an equally laughable way. Despite their wealth, influence, power, and reach (not to mention their power in the political party that currently controls both houses of Congress and the White House), these institutions cry out that a hostile popular culture, academia, and "activist judges," among other members of a vast rogues gallery, have persecuted religion in general, and Christianity in particular.

Both sides submit for your judgment an America that simply does not exist. One side suggests there is the oppressive establishment of a confessional state, where people who take seriously the First Amendment's free-exercise clause are a hounded and dwindling population. The other sees a dark and scary world where American entertainers, journalists, professors, and liberal politicians are enforcing an anti-Christian worldview.

You might say, "That isn't politics. It's church-state separation." Or, "That isn't politics. It's culture." The public square is the place where culture becomes politics. When we come together to negotiate the terms under which the institutions we hold and support in common are managed and ordered, politics are the tools we use. We use politics to persuade boards and commissions, we use it to elect leaders, and the leaders seek to persuade one another using the calculus of public support and the power it conveys. If I put the Ten Commandments over my bed, it is a matter of personal taste. When I decide I love the commands handed down on Mount Sinai so much, I want it on the facade of city hall, that's politics.

Political tools are the ones we use to try to turn a point of view into law. That way it moves from one person's or one group's conviction to a rule that applies to many, or all.

That leap, from the purely private realm to the public one, where some individuals can have power over the choices and life conditions of others, is where the intimate relationship between God and a human being becomes political. It's the spiritual corollary to the pugilist-political cliché: "Your rights end, and my rights begin, where *your* fist meets *my* nose."

Deciding where to draw the line between my nose and your fist will not be easy because the terms of engagement have changed. American evangelicals will no longer accept at face value the notion that religious persuasion belongs at home and out of the public way. Richard Cizik, leader of the National Association of Evangelicals, told the PBS documentary series *Frontline,* "What we're talking about is an evangelical view that you can't compartmentalize religion and civil government. If Christ is redeemer, over not just the private (the church) but the public (the state), then the state itself can be redeemed in a positive sense. You cannot, to the evangelical, relegate faith to the private arena only. You simply can't do that.

"Right behavior coming from right beliefs are two sides of the same spiritual coin. But that challenges the modern fundamental assumptions about Western political values that, 'Well, religion is private. Politics is public. And never the twain shall meet.' So by our very pietistic influence, evangelicals are challenging, I would say, the biases of Western political foundation."

Not even all evangelicals agree. The Reverend C. Welton Gaddy is pastor of a Baptist church in Louisiana and executive director of the Interfaith Alliance, a national religious group in Washington, D.C. When asked about where that subtle line is between private devotion and public duty, he said, "Yes, thankfully, he [President George Bush] has a profound religious faith, and I hope that he draws on that faith—I think he does—

for personal sustenance, for strength, for courage. But no elected political leader has a right to try and use public office to advance his or her particular faith tradition. That's where I get real nervous, sometimes, with the way the president uses religious language."

I FIND MYSELF WISHING my two loves, my church and my country, would find some different ground rules for their relationship, because their current intertwined embrace has nothing particularly good in store for either of them. The politicization of religion has led us to strange outcomes, such as one congregation's expelling members who voted for John Kerry.

The "religionization" of politics has also led us to some odd places, such as battles over whether taxpayers' money can and should be given to religious organizations for natural-disaster relief.

We can't get American religion out of politics, or politics out of religion. It's too late for that. It would be like trying to get the sugar out of a cup of coffee. But finding a way these two behemoth institutions in American life can coexist, while respecting the convictions of believers and protecting the rights of nonbelievers and those who disagree, is the riddle we must solve.

It's hard, looking back, to remember the moment when I realized everything I grew up with had changed. Maybe it was when George H.W. Bush, a lifelong Episcopalian unschooled in the fine points of modern evangelical testimony, struggled to define exactly when he was born again.[5] Or maybe it was Bill Clinton's deeply odd *mea culpa* at the National Prayer Breakfast after the Monica Lewinsky scandal broke.

There are plenty of candidates: three-star general Boykin's denunciations of Islam, in uniform, in churches; the brandishing of a Bible by an American president telling a congregation, "This is the handbook of the Faith-Based Initiative"; the public assertion of Harriet Miers's membership in a conservative evangelical church in Texas as if it were a qualification for a seat on the nation's highest court.

By the time flags on American public buildings were flying at half staff for the recently deceased Vicar of Christ on Earth, the Supreme Pontiff of the Roman Catholic Church, Pope John Paul II . . . well, something had certainly changed. In just over forty years we had gone from Senator John Kennedy, a Roman Catholic candidate for president, carefully distancing himself from one pope, to a "born again" Protestant president ordering national, *public* recognition of the death of another.[6]

American public life is shot through with religion: religious sentiment, prayer, "God talk" of all kinds, is now part of our civic debate in a way that would have made an earlier generation of politicians downright uncomfortable and still trips up political candidates today. If only it stopped there.

The politics of gesture is in fall cry, particularly suited as it is to the symbolically freighted world of religion and politics. Take as one modest example the confrontation in Guilford, North Carolina, over courtroom oaths and the Koran. Recently a local Muslim association offered to make a gift of Korans to courtrooms where they might be needed to swear in witnesses from North Carolina's growing Muslim population. A local jurist, senior resident judge W. Douglas Albright, refused to accept copies of the book Muslims believe was dictated by God, via an angel, to the Prophet Muhammad. "An oath on the Quran is not a lawful oath under our law," declared Judge Albright, who runs the county courts. State law mandates laying a hand on the "Holy Scriptures"—which Albright limits to the Bible. "Everybody understands what the holy scriptures are," he contends. "If they don't, we're in a mess."

You might have assumed that oaths are taken in court as a way to remind witnesses they are expected to tell the truth when they testify. You might also wonder what is more important to the judge: to make a point about the centrality of Christianity to North Carolina's history or to get non-Christian witnesses to affirm their intention to tell the truth in open court. In this case, symbol trumps substance when a judge decides that "holy scriptures" means the same thing to all people. For Judge Albright, if that fuzzy phrase doesn't mean the Holy Bible, and preferably a King James Version, "We're in a mess."

His Honor and I agree, we *are* in a mess. But we two, American-born Christian citizens, probably disagree about plenty, as well. I'm just "relativist" enough to think that the best document for a witness to swear on is the one that will yield a public oath most meaningful to the swearer. He or she is standing in a public place, the court, and looking out at fellow citizens and engaging in a symbolic act.

Anyone taking the oath can decide to lie, no matter where his or her hand is resting. A decree that members of any non-Christian religion must swear a public oath on a book that might carry little meaning for them, or one that might contain repugnant ideas, is not a ringing endorsement for pluralist democracy.

The message here is not that of the Constitution's article 6, section 3, "No religious test shall ever be required, as a qualification to any office or public trust, under the United States." On the contrary, the message is more like, "We run the show, pal. Better get used to it."

IN AN ERA of nonstop political combat, the addition of religion only tends to make the fighting more ferocious, the winning and losing more personal. Injecting religion into debates over public policy guarantees you'll have willing foot soldiers on your side and angry opponents fighting you every inch of the way.

The majority decision in *Roe v. Wade,* the Supreme Court ruling that made abortion legal in all fifty states, said little about religious concerns. The justice writing the opinion, Harry Blackmun, brought up traditional religious teachings on abortion only to demonstrate, in his view, that there was diversity of opinion, and that it leaned to the view that life began at birth.

Then, after patiently laying out the groundwork presented in argument and citing precedent to reinforce his rationale, Blackmun located abortion securely in medical and legal decision-making, not in religious conviction, "The abortion decision in all its aspects is inherently, and primarily, a medical decision, and basic responsibility for it must rest with the physician."[7]

One of the little-cited aspects of the *Roe* decision is the attempt to fix the beginning of life, as part of a general inquiry into when a state interest in the life of a fetus might rise to rival or equal the unquestioned interest in the life of the mother. Religion's claims to speak in this matter of personal conviction, like so many others, is said to rest on tradition and centuries of teaching. However, the Blackmun opinion identifies many different teachings over time and a preponderance of legal and religious codes that elevate the safety of the mother over the safety of the fetus and treat early abortion as a less serious matter than late abortion.

The never-ending battle over *Roe* (to which I'll return in chapter eight) is a perfect distillation of the way twenty-first-century religious concern seeks to pressure secular government, which is law made on behalf of all the members of a society, and allow only one conclusion. Not all Americans oppose legal abortions. Not all Americans who identify themselves as religious believers oppose legal abortions. Not all Americans who oppose legal abortion do so out of religious belief. Yet the unrelenting pressure to end legal abortions not only comes from religious believers but presumes to assert the antiabortion case as the only possible one to be reached from a position of integrity, faith, and logic.

The fight over *Roe* leaves that moral high ground wide open for the side that calls itself pro-life. The side calling itself pro-choice has left morality out of the debate, choosing to stress the legal arguments instead. What both sides share is the lamentable decision by the majority of their participants—though not necessarily their leaders—not to cooperate with their adversaries to reduce the number of abortions. By stressing above all the correctness of their positions, neither side has reliably chosen to act for what both sides say they really want: fewer abortions in America.

The pro-lifers elevate principle above politics and leave abortion intact, if less available, across the country. Pro-choicers elevate politics above principle, and play right into their opponent's hands. Both sides say the principle at the core of their respective arguments is too precious to surrender to mere tactical advantage.

Those who would make abortion illegal in the United States cannot or will not admit that most Americans do not consider a small cluster of cells shortly after fertilization to have the same rights as a fetus in the thirty-eighth week of gestation.

Those who would keep abortion legal in almost all circumstances cannot or will not concede that a large number of Americans grow more uncomfortable with abortion with each new scientific threshold in fetal diagnostics, and with every passing week in an individual pregnancy after the first trimester.

The structure of their confrontation can be seen in many issues that divide Americans in religious and political terms. There is a reluctance to find the functional heart of the matter. There seems to be an unwillingness to find a victory, short of total victory, if it means getting plenty of what you want, but without ideological purity.

But more telling, there is also a reluctance to build coalitions with other activists who are driven to the same issue by other motivations. Some evangelical Christians are fueled by scriptural mandates to be good stewards of the earth, but have a terrible time forming coalitions with environmentalists who may have no religious motivation at all.

As a reporter, as a citizen, as a Christian, I no longer have much interest in the question, Does religion belong in American politics? The two are intertwined and have been since the first days of European settlement in North America. For twenty-first-century Americans the real question is, How is it there? When does it play an informative role? When does it reflect distilled public will about an issue?

I was at a panel discussion on religion and society at the World Economic Forum in Davos, Switzerland. Europeans were teeing off on America, convinced that the United States is well on the way to theocracy. I raised my hand, and pointed out that the president saying "God bless the United States" at the end of a speech is such a common feature of American life that it is transparent to most of us. Even unchurched people tell public opinion researchers that a president being a person of faith reassures them. Imagine if, instead of giving a vague benediction, the president explained his view of what happens to bread and wine at communion. That would be a different thing altogether.

If an American president channels a broad, theistic sentiment that represents the faith of most Americans, it is barely noticed. But those same listeners would not want to hear that same person go into detail about the content of that faith in a public way. There is a difference between a chief executive and a theologian in chief.

It has been interesting watching the evolution of gay marriage as an issue. The way we talk about personal conviction, religiously based notions of propriety, and government regulation of a civic institution are all mixed up with one another. George Bush has repeatedly cited public opinion in his insistence that all legal paths to gay marriage should be slammed shut.

One thing the president has not done is trust Americans to air the issues raised by support or opposition to gay marriage. By harnessing religious arguments, many politicians have purposely ignored the existence of marriage as a civil institution quite apart from the religious sanction given marriage.

If I believe that something like gay marriage is wrong for religious reasons, does the government have an obligation to draft the laws regulating marriage in a way that matches my religious convictions?

There is little question that a straightforward reading of the Bible is tough on homosexuality. From the distance of tens of centuries, we can debate why both the Hebrew and Christian scriptures say what they do; more nuanced interpretations can be less harsh, but nonetheless there is condemnation of sexual relations between people of the same sex.

So far, the power in the argument remains in that unremarkable reading of ancient texts. We are, as a society, having a hard time getting to what relevance those verses from the Bible might have to making law in a diverse society. Millions are not married. Millions are neither Christians nor Jews. Millions more are homosexual. So far, we have decided as a society that heterosexuals own marriage by the power of their superior numbers.

Yet we do not allow states to deviate from other forms of equal protection under law just because a majority of citizens might decide they would like to do so. In fact, that notion was specifically attacked by Justice Wiley B. Rutledge in his concurrent opinion in *Abington . . . v. Schempp:* "While the Free Exercise Clause clearly prohibits the use of State action to deny the rights of free exercise to anyone, it has never meant that a majority could use the machinery of the State to practice its beliefs."

Got that? A majority cannot use the machinery of the state to practice its beliefs. Though the prospect for some is truly frightening, the religious and civic debate on gay marriage is far from over. We will take a closer look in chapter five.

No matter where your own opinions lie on any of these issues, I want this book to alternately infuriate and intrigue you. After a long look at the history of mixing religion with politics in the United States and more detailed examinations of specific issues where American politics, culture, and religion collide, I will close with a look at the future based on today's political and religious landscape.

TWO

How Did We Get Here?

ONE OF THE MOST frequently cited ideas about American origins, and contemporary religious and political debates, is this: "America is a Christian nation." As it happens, this is also one of the most frequently refuted ideas. Who is right? Is anybody right? Is America a Christian nation, or just a nation with a lot of Christians?

In the way that we debate these questions in modern America, to embrace one story is to reject the other. To highlight the absence of the word "God" in the United States Constitution (don't bother . . . it's not there) is to reject the stirring retelling of the Christian origins of our modern state: from John Winthrop's shivering Christian dissenters on one coast, to Brother Junipero Serra's Catholic missions strung all along the other coast, converting Indians and naming the western-division cities of major league sports.

It's not *either or.* It's *both and.* The United States, from its earliest days, has been a country that gathered in people fleeing religious oppression, leaving them free to flourish, and occasionally persecute others. The United States has also been a place where there also lived, sometimes quietly, sometimes boldly, people convinced that God, if there was one in the first place, took no interest in the petty details and daily lives of his creation.

So you, twenty-first-century American, are free to cherry-pick. On one side of the table, build a pile of quotations, anecdotes, and citations that demonstrate how deeply religious early Americans were, and how their convictions shaped the country's early history. Just be sure that sitting right across from you are those gathering a formidable collection of citations for the secular origins of American culture and the American way of politics. Otherwise, you will get only half the story.

Father Martin Smith, an Episcopal theologian and writer, reminds audiences that this country's claim to religious distinction is sound. "America's separation of church and state is a unique event in the history of the world. Recall that most of the people who have ever lived, lived in states where the myth of creation established the existence of the people as a unique group, and married that to the authority structure of the state.

"Untethering those two lines of authority from each other was a revolutionary act as significant as separating from England, and created the Petri dish in which a nationhood not based on clan and religion could flourish." That's strong stuff. It is a recognition of the centrality of religious faith to millions of Americans. It is at the same time an endorsement of America's secular approach to governance, *untethered from religion,* fostering a fertile religious environment.

During the 2004 national election, Americans argued over whether they lived in two Americas or not. The Red State–Blue State dichotomy that was a gift of the 2000 race was still very much with us, overlaid with other "twonesses": the Americas of black and white, rich and poor, urban and suburban, churched and unchurched.

While they rose in 2004 to grab even more real estate in the popular consciousness, many of those two-Americas questions are simply a part of everyday life in a continent-sized country with three hundred million people.

I remember one morning appearance on C-SPAN's morning news roundup program. I was nursing a cup of coffee while running through the newspapers with Brian Lamb, and he presented me with an unexpected topic of morning chitchat, Thomas Jefferson. I talked about the just-passed anniversary of his birth, the rehab job just completed on his memorial in Washington, D.C., and almost as an aside, given the religious fervor with which Bill Clinton's moral failings were being debated in the Capitol, how the Sage of Monticello would match few members of the Christian Coalition's definition of a Christian.

A caller from South Carolina dismissed my opinion of the third president's religiosity from the secure bunker of ignorance, calling it, "sickening," and "typical anti-Christian, NPR propaganda." Well, ma'am, as we survey the cavalcade of American history, there are many presidents whose religious convictions might be called a mystery, but Jefferson is not on that list. The prolific Virginian sometimes seems scarcely to have had a thought in his long and active life that he didn't commit to paper.

One of my Jefferson favorites is a letter to his nephew Peter Carr, in 1787. His nephew is moving ahead with a demanding course of study, which Jefferson heartily approves. He endorses the study of Spanish over Italian, and speculates on astronomy and math. When he comes to the subject of religion, Jefferson suggests, "Question with boldness even the existence of a god, because, if there be one, he must more approve the homage of reason than that of blindfolded fear."

This isn't bad advice even for the twenty-first-century Christian. If that approach leads you to faith, it gets you there from conviction rather than from intellectual laziness. If it leads you to unbelief, you get there with integrity, rather than with a shrug. Jefferson continues, "Read the bible then, as you would Livy or Tacitus." Now we're treading on dangerous ground. The word of God, even his very existence, held up to the same kind of analysis and consideration as a work of literature, or a philosophical treatise?

Then Jefferson "outs" himself as a son of the Enlightenment, "For example in the book of Joshua we are told the sun stood still for several hours. . . . The pretension is entitled to your enquiry, because millions believe it. On the other hand you are Astronomer enough to know how contrary that is to the law of nature that a body revolving on its axis, as the earth does, should have stopped, should not by that sudden stoppage have prostrated animals, trees, buildings, and should after a certain time resumed its revolution, and that without a second general prostration. Is this arrest of the earth's motion, or the evidence which affirms it, most within the law of probabilities?"

In a final riff of advice to young Carr, the future president delivers what would be the final blow to his chances for election in 2008 instead of 1802. "You will next read the new testament. It is the history of a personage called Jesus. Keep in your eye the opposite pretensions. 1. Of those who say he was begotten by god, born of a virgin, suspended and reversed the law of nature at will, and ascended bodily into heaven; and 2. Of those who say he was a man of illegitimate birth, of a benevolent heart, enthusiastic mind, who set out without pretensions to divinity, ended in believing them, and was punished capitally." Though the then-ambassador to Paris doesn't come right out and say it in this letter, he's siding with the second bunch. Jefferson's Jesus was a moral teacher of modest birth, who did not call himself God.

Above all Jefferson, this exquisitely educated man, counseled an even-handedness in assessing the world that we don't see much in evidence in the modern political class. He asks his nephew to keep an open mind and never rely on the beliefs of others to make up his mind for him, "I repeat that you must lay aside all prejudice on both sides, and neither believe nor respect any thing because any other person or description of persons have rejected it or believed it." [1]

It is frequently declared in the current debates over religion in public life, the separation of church and state, and the use of publicly owned land and buildings for religious purposes that America was founded as a Christian nation. The people who say it in speeches or write it in essays often use the phrase with full and serene confidence that the listener or reader knows what that might be. What is a Christian nation? Is the United States one of them? If the majority of Americans really wanted to aspire to the lofty boast of this being a "Christian nation," what obligations, if any, would they have to undertake?

Author and Christian layman Bill McKibben notes that 75 percent of Americans believe, as evidenced in a recent survey, that the adage, "God helps those who help themselves," comes from the Bible. Its actual author was none other than that crusty old skeptic, Benjamin Franklin. Maybe you have heard that saying your whole life without thinking too much about where it comes from. The distinction is crucial. "God helps those who help themselves" is a very *American* notion, and one that flies directly in the face of almost everything Jesus taught.

Being a Christian nation would mean finding a way to stop being the wealthy, industrialized nation with the highest rates of murder and violent crime on the planet. Being a Christian nation would mean finding a way to climb up from the bottom of the chart of government giving by wealthy nations to the world's poor.[2]

Both the very secular and the very religious make key errors in looking back at American history: the very secular almost erase the impact of religion or ascribe only negative effects to its profound presence in the daily lives of many Americans; the very religious exaggerate its place in America's founding documents, among its Founding Fathers, and in charting the course of the country's growth, from an insecure archipelago of former colonies to a globe-straddling commercial and military power.

The people we now call the Pilgrims, Anabaptist dissenters from England's established church who came to the northern Atlantic coast of what is now the United States in the early seventeenth century, were indeed deeply religious. To merely look back and note their search for religious freedom and take that as proof of America's religious foundations is to purposely ignore the brand of religion they practiced, and the kind of society they made.

The characteristics of the settlements that spread into New England from Plymouth Rock were the antithesis of what would become our national aspirations, and what we value about being American. The theocratic settlements were rigid, intolerant, racist, dishonest, and occasionally murderous in their dealings with the Indians. Can you take your Pilgrims *à la carte*? Can you vaguely endorse their religiosity and then close your eyes to its impact on the kind of place it made early New England?

That naïve, purposeful mistelling of American history has its uses on both sides of the cultural divide. However, if you are willing to present only some parts of the lives of early Americans as admirable and worthy of imitation, you reveal much when you draw the line. There is a certain intellectual dishonesty in quoting the Mayflower Compact, finding the roots of modern Thanksgiving in Plymouth Plantation, but then quietly erasing the mass murder of Pequots a few decades later.

One of early America's most prominent preachers and theologians, Cotton Mather, was not shocked by the massacre of hundreds of men, women, and children. He did not peer into the Gospels for ammunition to condemn wholesale murder. Instead, he noted with some satisfaction that some six hundred Indian "souls had been sent down into hell," where they belonged.

No doubt early New Englanders were frightened of Indian reprisal. Invaders often are. But these early American Christians also exhibited an all-too-human failing. They denied the humanity of their enemies in order to make killing them easier. Because the Pequots, the Wampanoags, and many other tribes that were hunted to near-extinction were not Christian, in the eyes of early New Englanders they failed to meet a baseline test for compassion.

Down the coast in Virginia, sons and daughters of England were embarking on a very different kind of experiment. They had few pretensions to creating "a citty on a Hill," as longed for by John Winthrop. They longed for gold, and found it not in mines, but in tobacco. Virginia was a tough place to live. Its new inhabitants did not seek a higher power as much as the power of the sword and the purse. Named for Elizabeth I, the Virgin Queen, it divvied up the vast lands into estates for a transplanted English aristocracy. The muscle to exploit the land came from indentured servants and slaves, and the frontier threat came from Indians roughly pushed inland by the new British dominion.

The church, as institution, in much of English-speaking America did not have the far-reaching power it had back in Europe. The established, that is, government-supported, churches kept their doors open with state subsidy and commanded an uneven loyalty from Massachusetts to Georgia. Roman Catholics were fully free in Maryland, and for much of the early story of the United States, Baltimore exerted a tremendous influence on American Catholicism.

Jews lived in small communities along the seaboard. They could be found from Newport, Rhode Island, to Savannah, Georgia. In early America the Sephardim, the Jews who spread through the Mediterranean world after the Portuguese and Spanish expulsions, gave American Jewry a very different flavor from that of its later nineteenth-century incarnations. The German Reformed Jews and the Yiddish-speaking Ashkenazim of Eastern Europe would lay the demographic foundations for the twenty-first-century Jewish community.

The thinly settled western edges of British America, bumping up against French Louisiana, were places where "church" was an informal thing: a community leader holding group prayer in his home, or a more formal liturgy when a clergyman came through town as he rode a "circuit" that passed through networks of small settlements.

For many early Americans, religious life was a loosely structured, episodic affair. Popular preachers were the pop stars of their era, before mass communication and easy transportation. Meetings in clearings and barns resembled competitions, with traveling preachers showing their best stuff in front of enthusiastic crowds hungry for stimulation and news of the outside world.

Then as now, the religious life of Americans was one of stunning contrasts and bewildering variety. The largely self-taught preachers of the slave quarters kept the hope of freedom alive with the promises of the Psalms and the liberation of Israel. The theological debates of Protestant Europe ricocheted through the still-young colleges in Cambridge, New Haven, Princeton, and New York, and found an American iteration in the pulpits of Unitarian, Congregational, Anglican, and Methodist churches.

Some colonists translated the New Testament from the original Greek. Others learned chapters by rote in the light of a flickering fire, after long days of backbreaking labor. That same variety of religious conviction was on display in the taverns and coffeehouses of the port cities, in the artisans' societies that sprang up everywhere, and eventually in the state assemblies and the Continental Congress that met to invent the United States.

There is a funny little paradox that becomes evident when trying to understand America's Christian roots and whether and how they lead us to the yeasty diversity and bitter debates of today. In eighteenth-century America, church attendance was very low compared to today. Yet any literate person knew the Bible well, both the Old and New Testament. Even the semiliterate and illiterate knew whole hunks of the Bible by heart: the Psalms; the Beatitudes; the foundational stories of Adam and Eve, Job, and the passion of Jesus.

Today, with the highest level of church attendance in the wealthy world and one of the highest rates of self-declared god-belief in all the world, scriptural illiteracy in the U.S. is widespread. I have already mentioned the revealing assignment of "God helps those who help themselves" to Scripture instead of *Poor Richard's Almanack*. Even as battles over Ten Commandments monuments in courthouses and copies nailed to schoolhouse walls reach the nation's highest court, a sizable majority of Americans can't name the laws handed to Moses on Mount Sinai, even out of order.

Let's head to Philadelphia in the mid-1770s. Historians have noted the sizable presence of Deists among the delegates to the Continental Congress. Deists were skeptics. They were unsure of the Divine hand in the daily workings of the world and wondered about the involvement of the Creator even in the watershed events of humankind. They assumed a Creator, but differed on his continued involvement in his handiwork, their opinions falling along a continuum that ranged from a Creator with profound, high-impact interest in the affairs of people, to something more like a watchmaker who sends his creation off to whirr and spin, tick and count the hours, without any further effort from the watchmaker.

When that first Congress ratified and signed the Declaration of Independence, it contained ringing and inspirational language from the twin fonts of American thought: Christian theology and classical philosophy. The two were well represented in the Declaration's main author, Thomas Jefferson, a man who revered Jesus of Nazareth and Epicurus, the pre-Christian Greek philosopher, with near-equal fervor.[3]

"We hold these truths to be self-evident, that all men are created equal, and are endowed by their creator with certain inalienable rights. That among these are life, liberty, and the pursuit of happiness." Jefferson was already a successful politician in his home colony of Virginia and a successful drafter of laws when he penned those words. They are as close to secular scripture as Americans get, invoked along with the preamble to the Constitution and parts of the Bill of Rights and the words of Lincoln like a well-remembered psalm or parable.

During the long gelling of the United States as a functioning political and economic system, roughly from the first Continental Congress to the end of George Washington's presidency, more than twenty years, there were plenty of debates about the role religion was going to play in the life of the new country. Newly independent colonies had to decide, and in some cases headed to court to hash out, the status of their once-established, government-supported churches.

While the stirring, persuasive, and rhetorical Declaration of Independence mentions God at many points, the Constitution hardly mentions a Creator at all. Their functions are quite different: the Declaration is both an indictment and a "Dear John" letter (a "Dear George letter," perhaps?) from an entire subcontinent to a distant monarch. Written more than a decade later, the Constitution is a schematic diagram and operator's manual for the running of a state. In the few places religion is mentioned in the Constitution, it is there by subtraction, forbidding a religious test for public office, and in the Bill of Rights, guaranteeing there could be no state church and that people would be free to worship as they choose.

In the run-up to the ratification of the Constitution by the states, literate America was treated to a public hashing out of the arguments for the new compact. The series of essays and commentaries by James Madison, Alexander Hamilton, and John Jay, now called the Federalist Papers, walked the public through what the constitution could and could not do.

In Federalist Number 10, Madison sets out a theory of factions; as he sees it, a zero-sum idea of competing desires held by different parts of a divided public: "By a faction I understand a number of citizens, whether amounting to a majority or minority of the whole, who are united and actuated by some common impulse or passion, or of interest, adverse to the rights of other citizens, or to the permanent and aggregate interests of the community." It might work to insert the word *denomination* here in place of *faction*.

Madison finds a parallel between freedom of thought in politics and the natural world: "Liberty is to faction what air is to fire, an aliment without which it instantly expires." That is a concrete, and stirring, example of how freedom inevitably leads to differing convictions. It is a strength, and for the foreseeable future, a signal of man's imperfection: "As long as the reason of man continues fallible, and he is at liberty to exercise it, different opinions will be formed."

For Madison, the mechanics of the Constitution will help a naturally divided people find common ground. This Virginian is a religious man who finds it hard to believe that God did not take a hand in the creation of the new United States: "It is impossible for the man of pious reflection not to perceive in it a finger of that Almighty hand which has been so frequently and signally extended to our relief in the critical stages of the revolution."[4] At the same time, he finds no special place of honor for the faithful in the structure of the new country: ". . . the door of this part of our federal government is open to merit of every description, whether native or adoptive, whether young or old, and without regard to poverty or wealth, or to any particular profession of religious faith."[5]

It may be true of all people, but it is particularly true of Americans that they habitually compare the morals, day-to-day life, and values of past generations and find them superior to those of today. The imagined American past is particularly open to this kind of speculation. It is common to find in the statements of the most religious Americans a yearning for a long-ago America that is a better place than this one.

The profane, violent, and rough world of eighteenth- and nineteenth-century America is thought to be a less immoral place than our own country. Unfortunately, a moral calculus that exalts sexual morality above all things finds a long-ago America of chronic poverty, disease, starvation, and the exploitation of the weak by the strong to be a more admirable place than the America where a man can ask another one out on a date and the central government demands income taxes. It is common to imagine that the immortal prose of the Declaration and the visionary wisdom of the Constitution resulted in a place where both were respected as law.

One phrase that appears nowhere in either document is "wall of separation between church and state." It is an oft-repeated article of faith among today's conservative Christians that because that phrase is only a quotation from an 1802 letter to a Connecticut church from Thomas Jefferson, it should hold no claim on our view of America today.

Writing to a congregation from the famously separationist Baptist

Church in Danbury, Jefferson said, "Believing with you that religion is a matter which lies solely between man and his God, that he owes account to none other for his faith and worship, that the legislative powers of government reach actions only, and not opinions, I contemplate with sovereign reverence that act of the whole American people which declared that their legislature should 'make no law . . . free exercise thereof,' thus building a wall of separation between Church and State."

Though the quote has no force of law, it does anticipate a diverse and multifaceted nation that lies far in the future, long after Jefferson's death. He goes on to write, "I see with sincere satisfaction the progress of those sentiments which tend to restore to man all his natural rights, convinced he has no natural right in opposition to his social duties."

Jefferson's idea of human beings acting in the marketplace out of private conviction, restrained by law and "social duties," is a good approximation of how a secular state that is home to religious citizens may happily function. What remains for us in twenty-first-century America is to decide how true to our actual roots in free exercise and rigorously secular government we are going to decide to be.

Rabbi David Saperstein sees the genius of the founders in the secular design of a state by often deeply religious men. Furthermore, in its radical departure from the nation-states of Europe, defined by blood and clan, religious identity and class, America became a great place, a safe place, to be a Jew. "The genius of America was for the first time in human history to create a political order in which your rights and opportunities as a citizen would not depend upon your religious identity, beliefs, or practices. That was an extraordinary, revolutionary idea. To minority religions, particularly, who so often had been the victims of discrimination and persecution, it made all the difference. And this was a land in which Jews have known more freedoms, more rights, more opportunities, than we have known in 2000 years of Diaspora, Jewish life.

"It was precisely during the war and postwar era that asserted the rights of women and minorities—Jews, Catholics, dissenters, disabled, agnostics, atheists—against the whim of white males in the majority, that Jews were able to move from the peripheries of American society to the very center of American academic, professional, political, economical life, in a way that had never been, with opportunities never accorded to us anywhere before in our history. It happens precisely because of that revolutionary vision of the relationship of the political order and religion in American life."

Rabbi Saperstein also sees a parallel founding ethos, that of the New England religious settlements, Manifest Destiny, and countless settlers who hoped to establish a social order following God's laws rather than man's. "They really believed that they were creating an order in which the coercive of power of government could and should be used to implement God's law here on earth. So what we are seeing played out today was played out in the two founding narratives of our nation and has been with us ever since in this regard." Needless to say, the rabbi sides with the framers, but concedes that America's story is shot through with this parallel ideal.

The long century from the first presidency and the infancy of the Constitution in the 1790s to the Gilded Age of a continent-sized, rich, and increasingly powerful America is one of great secular thought and significant religious foment. To say the country was all one thing or all another is to seriously misread our history.

Men like Ralph Waldo Emerson and William Lloyd Garrison blazed an intellectual trail across the mid-century that perhaps owed its inspiration to religious thinking and texts, but was rigorously church-free. As adults both men rejected organized religion, and both men saw the individual as the source of reform. Filling lyceums and tents and auditoriums across the young country, Emerson told Americans that the power to tame and perfect the self lay in the self, rather than in the will of God. After following his father into the ordained ministry, Emerson had broken with the church, and spent much of his long life moving further and further from it. He said, "In the matter of religion, people eagerly fasten their eyes on the difference between their own creed and yours; whilst the charm of the study is in finding the agreements and identities in all the religions of humanity."

Garrison did not start with Emerson's advantages of good name and exquisite education. His restless and self-cultivated intellect, and his willingness to ceaselessly pound the powerful and influential, mark him as a particularly nineteenth-century character. In an age of what were called "enthusiasms," his angry war on slavery, hatred of drink, and suspicion of organized religion made him a passionate standout in a passionate age. Garrison wrote, "Tell a man whose house is on fire to give a moderate alarm; tell him to moderately rescue his wife from the hands of the ravisher; tell the mother to gradually extricate her babe from the fire into which it has fallen; but urge me not to use moderation."

Remember, the country was on fire with campaigns for political reform, westward expansion, abolition, temperance, women's suffrage, socialism. The loose grip of denominational religion made possible by the eighteenth-century gift of no established church allowed these movements to rise up in an almost rain-forest-like natural frenzy.

In the same era, the social inventiveness of Americans gave rise to tremendous religious adaptation, shape-shifting, and invention. The singing and shouting of revivalism might have attracted the condescension of the clergy learned in Hebrew, Greek, and Latin back in the east, but a new American religious continuum was hammered together in the nineteenth century. It glowed in torchlight and was cooled by mass baptism at the riverbank. There was a religious scene like Ptolemy's universe, fixed and orderly, back in Boston, Baltimore, and Savannah.

Beyond the reach of the denominations were American originals like Joseph Smith, whose visions in upstate New York began the Church of Jesus Christ of Latter-Day Saints, the Mormons. In the same cluster of years, William Miller began the preaching about the Second Coming, which would lead to the creation of the Seventh-Day Adventist Church. As the Millerites were winning converts and Joseph Smith was writing down what would become known as the Book of Mormon, Mary Baker Eddy was a little girl in New Hampshire. In an America struggling to recover from the Civil War, her ideas about prayer and Scripture would begin the foundation of the Christian Science Church.

Frantic, brutal, bloody nineteenth-century America was a place where military men became "heroes" by slaughtering Indians. It was a place where treaties were routinely broken with indigenous nations shortly after the ink on them was dry. It was a place where black women were property, and casually raped after dessert. It was a place where a dustup as phony as the Gulf of Tonkin incident could be cooked up for nineteenth-century consumption and used as the justification for a war of conquest against Mexico that was meant to push the Stars and Stripes, and slavery, to the Pacific.

For a "Christian country," it was not an era covered in glory, or a time easily dressed up for later consumption. It was a time of sparse church attendance, situational ethics, and incidents needing plenty of sugarcoating to make a history worth singing about. But the decades of expansion, Civil War, Reconstruction and turmoil, industrialization and immigration, also set the table for the rise of religion and its embrace of politics more than a century later.

In America in 2006, a persistent idea peddled is that the country is a fallen one, far less religious than in more pious times past. This creates twin imperatives: recapture a lost past and reject the customs and common life of your own time. That American tendency is not serving us well in the twenty-first century. We will return to this theme later on.

The Reverend Barry Lynn is a United Church of Christ minister and the head of Americans United for the Separation of Church and State. His reading of American history leads him to a strict separationist stance. "I would say the majority of the framers of the Constitution, for example, were people who believe fundamentally in private religious expression. Now, they used religious language like politicians do today for a variety of reasons, but they were not people who felt that the essential nature of America was as a religious country."

Lynn sees an American operator's manual meant for a young country to grow into. Which is why, he insists, the framers were specific when they needed to be, and vague when they wanted to be. "We know general principles only because these were written in what subsequent jurists have often called majestic generalities, because clearly the Bill of Rights was designed unlike other provisions in the Constitution with considerable vagueness, deliberately so. When the Congress wanted, when the drafters of the original Constitution wanted to be real specific, they'd say you have to be thirty years old in order to serve office in the House of Representatives. However, when they didn't want to be specific, then they used these kinds of phrases, and they're pretty clear, I think, as you read enough of founding documents, that they knew they were writing for a future that they assumed would be long in duration—that this was the beginning of a governance structure. It was not the end of it. They clearly knew that. They provided multiple methods for amending the Constitution precisely because they knew that as the country grew, as the government became more complex, people would say that we have to think about this and that and you guys didn't."

That idea of continued revelation in a civic sense mirrors Lynn's view of sacred texts as well. "I do believe that the Bible is an important source of information, advice, but it is not the final word. God still communicates with us through the act of prayer and that as a consequence we have kind of an ongoing revelation of God in our lives."

It should come as no surprise that over the course of my research and interviews, a general rule prevailed: those Americans who saw the Constitution as a document whose modern meanings had changed from its origins and throughout American history also saw the Bible as a document open to new interpretation, to unfolding revelation. In general, those whose theology tended toward biblical inerrancy and a literal meaning of Jewish and Christian scripture also endorsed what is often called "strict constructionism," a reading of the Constitution that attempts to understand what the men who wrote it meant and intended.

One marked contrast between the men who wrote the New Testament, whether you believe it was from their own imagination or divine inspiration, is that many of them thought they were writing toward the end of time. Those who fought over, amended, and ratified the Constitution framed it with the hope that their handiwork would last far into an unimaginable future.

The Constitution includes specific instructions for changing it. It is a tribute to the structure of the document that only a little more than two dozen times in more than two centuries has our basic law needed modification. The Bible, for better or worse, is fixed, and beyond our ability to know the motivations of its writers.

The writers of the Bible could not have imagined the U.S. Constitution. What Americans of all religious persuasions now think of both of those texts, and their intersections, has created conflict. An increasingly assertive evangelical movement is banging up against a resistant secularist faction, guaranteeing fights in the legislatures and courts for years to come.

America came roaring out of victory in World War II ready to make up for lost time. There were weddings to be thrown, babies to be had, houses to build. A broad religious consensus had been reached that saw religion, not as a divisive institution, but one that could serve as social glue, according to Professor R. Scott Appleby of the Joan B. Kroc Institute for International Peace Studies at Notre Dame University: "Will Herberg wrote *Protestant, Catholic, Jew: An Essay in American Religious Sociology,* which argued, okay, we're no longer WASPs. We're certainly not Catholic fully; we're not Jewish in terms of a dominant religious culture.

"But we've kind of achieved a comfortable amalgam. And that signaled something new on the American horizon. And that book was well received in scholarly circles and also kind of quasi-popularly. And that thesis was part of the 1950s on one level. The idea that, okay, we have religion. It's a similar religion. It's in these three denominations. It doesn't threaten the political order. It's comfortable. It's part of the American character. It's not going to be decisive politically, but it's there and we respect it and recognize it.

"By the '60s that had changed. In the early '60s for all kinds of complicated reasons, you get what, as far as the fundamentalists and the evangelicals are concerned, and what the Catholics refer to as 'a disastrous decade,' the long 1960s. From prayer in public schools being outlawed by the Supreme Court to 1973, *Roe v. Wade.* That long '60s is a time that those people see, people on the religious right see, as the dark period in which a Protestant-Catholic-Jew affirmation is undermined, first by the irrelevance of religion in public life, and this more insidious assault on religion in public life."

It is easy to see why the quiet embers of religious politics in the South would finally be blown into flame by the postwar decades. What Richard Land of the Southern Baptist Convention calls "the sin of segregation" was in full rout, with its legal consequences about to remake the daily lives of people across a large swath of the country.

There is a lot of agreement across the political spectrum about the evangelical foray into politics. Albert Mohler is president of the Southern Baptist Theological Seminary. Like many other Christian conservatives, he saw the glimmerings of the movement in the large vote among evangelicals for Jimmy Carter in 1976. "There was an enormous transition between 1976 and 1980; you can roughly equate that with the years of the Carter administration. For the Southern Baptists there came an enormous shift in consciousness in 1980, when we became more involved in marriage, family, and a host of related issues. The development of a new Christian right came in with the campaign for Ronald Reagan. It became a new cause.

"Candidly, there had been tremendous disappointment in Jimmy Carter. Remember, at that time the South was still largely Democratic. A large share of Democratic congressmen and senators were elected from the South. We thought of Carter as one of our own, and he was a huge disappointment. And in 1980 that new sense of urgency led to a movement. The movement preceded Ronald Reagan. Some people think he created it. In fact the concern was already there. What was lacking was a leader whom we could approach with those concerns."

The Reverend Dr. C. Welton Gaddy is the president of the Interfaith Alliance, which describes itself as "the faith-based voice countering the radical right and promoting the positive role of religion." He is hardly what you would call a screaming liberal. He still serves a Southern Baptist Church in Louisiana while doing his advocacy work in Washington, D.C. Back in the Nixon years, he took a high-profile post with the Southern Baptist Convention: "In 1971 I went to work at what was called the Christian Life Commission of the Southern Baptist Convention. It was the social ethics agency in Southern Baptist life. My title was director of Christian Citizenship Development.

"My challenge was that Southern Baptists had never really motivated its church members to be good citizens. The challenge that I faced at that time was cliché-ish in nature. It was the regular response, 'politics and religion don't mix.' Politics is a field that is dirty, and if you get involved in it, it's going to pull you down more than you'd pull it up.

"I'm saying to you, somewhat tongue in cheek, I'm sorry we did such a good job on that, because what happened was we began to see around 1975, 1976 much greater involvement on the part of Christian evangelicals in the political process. I kind of go back to that gathering call to the Religious Roundtable, in Reunion Arena in Dallas just prior to the Reagan campaign, as the place where the evangelical Christian community kind of came together and said, we're going to get on board, behind what was a fairly partisan political agenda."

Today Dr. Gaddy thinks he did not change as much as his denomination did, and he thinks he knows why: "I think I saw many of my colleagues in the evangelical tradition watch with admiration the way in which mainstream Protestantism had success in the civil rights movement, had success in probably cutting short the war in Vietnam, and several of the leaders began to think, here is an avenue of power for us. Here is a way for us to express ourself in society and perhaps even to garner more political power than we ever thought we might have on a national basis. And I think that's what happened. And unfortunately in some instances, not in all, but in some instances the driving force was not about the discovery of a new means of serving the nation, but it was about a new means of controlling the nation. So it was about power more than service."

The Reverend Richard Land, working as a pastor in those same years, has a very different story of who was moving away from whom. He portrays rising Christian political activity as all in a day's work in the American marketplace of ideas. "Because some things are good for folks, and some things aren't. And if we're a person of faith, our religious faith informs our moral values. And we have a right to bring our religiously informed moral values into the public marketplace of ideas, just like those who are without significant religious faith have a right to bring their moral values to bear, and hopefully through vigorous debate, those with the better ideas, the ideas that work, win."

But Land also has a strong disagreement with the Gaddy version of the conservative Christian foray into politics. Southern Baptists and other organized evangelicals were not getting into politics because of the power. They were, in his memory, frightened of what was happening to the country. "You had, growing up in the '60s and the '70s in this country, a feeling that among the various elites in our culture—and I hope this doesn't come as a shock to you that we do have elites in this culture—that the various elites, the legal elite, the educational elite, the social elite, and even to some degree the religious elite, did everything they could to trivialize religion and marginalize religious faith from the public-policy square."

When it's portrayed that way, it is hard to disagree, and hard to separate the new conservative evangelical activism from any political movement of the last two hundred years. Engaged citizens organize around a cause and agitate until they win. What could be wrong with that?

"I think it leads them to be unrealistic about their government," the Reverend Gaddy told me. "Because if you expect the government of the United States to be the instrument for ushering in the morals, visions, and relationships of the realm of God, I think you're going to be sorely disappointed. Because that's not the purpose of this government."

The 1980s were a good time for the conservative evangelical movement. As Ronald Reagan told the National Association of Religious Broadcasters, "I know you can't endorse me. But I endorse you." A slice of the American culture that had felt locked out of the action for more than a century was suddenly parlaying with the president of the United States. Conservative Christians might have still been treated with condescension and scorn by elements of the culture, but it didn't matter. They were going to remake the culture in their own image, with statehouses, the national legislature, and state boards of education behind them. Or, at least, that is how it looks from the secular side.

Albert Mohler is not convinced. He rejects the notion that taking a more active role in politics has meant a surrender of precious moral capital: "I don't think anything's been given away. In terms of partisan identification, back in the 1960s evangelicals were as solidly identified with Democrats as they are with Republicans today. So over our history there has been no real neutrality."

I asked the pastor and educator if the solid backing of the Republican Party has been worth it for Southern Baptists and other conservative Christians. "I think it's a mixed bag. You can look at it this way. Twenty-five years after the election of Ronald Reagan, *Roe v. Wade* is still ruling precedent. Just to continue with that one issue of abortion, we have made headway in the culture. Young people are less likely to be pro-abortion, but the gains have been incremental."

From the secular side looking over at the politically active religious, you see a movement at the top of its powers, with significant influence, if not control, of major power centers in Washington, D.C., and across the country. Yet one of the best-known Christian conservatives is not even sure his side has won much. At least not yet. "With the judiciary as a whole, we've made some considerable and incremental gains. And the nation really faced a judiciary that was hostile to the political and religious convictions of a lot of Christians. The other big issue is where we would otherwise be . . . that's a continuing question that requires a lot of reflection. If evangelicals hadn't been a countervailing force, what kind of shape would we find the country in today?"

Rabbi Saperstein sees this as a battle where one side, inexplicably, has been able to capture and hold all the high ground. "You know, I look on Capitol Hill, and 90 percent of the people I know who are Republicans or Democrats really are seriously religious people. And yet if they're not talking the fundamentalist rhetoric, it just doesn't count.

"I was invited to address the Democratic retreat, the annual retreat for the House of Representatives, the Democratic caucus, down in Williamsburg, on the issue of religion, morality, and values. You know, so many of these people believe in their hearts, but they're kind of frustrated and chagrined that the right has abrogated religion itself. They feel this way not just for political reasons but because it affronts their entire religious worldview. But they don't quite know how to comfortably talk about it in public life.

"So I think it's a misread to think that the triumphalism that the right feels in its gut, that is driving so much of the political impact that they have, is the *only* impact that religion has on American politics. Day in and day out, in all the social-service entities working in the public-interest world, religious values are being played out equally in American life and in an equally genuine, effective way."

ONE SUNDAY MORNING at Prestonwood Baptist Church in Plano, Texas, a suburb of Dallas, I watch as police officers direct traffic into a stadium-sized parking lot. The people leaving the cars stream into a vast, horizontal structure along the back of the lot. They pass under a soaring archway and through a waiting rank of glass doors. I have left the comfort of my Sunday morning routine, a worship service rooted in the nineteenth century, and entered the air-conditioned, plushly carpeted, high-tech world of twenty-first-century worship.

A pop chorus gets the crowd clapping and singing, prompted by giant screens along the walls. Six trumpets, electric guitars, and drums back the singers and an enormous choir standing on semicircular risers. The comfortable, theater-style seats at Prestonwood sweep across a vast worship space. It is comfortable. It is reassuring. It is not for me, but I can readily see why this crowd of thousands has come from near and far to be here.

After the baptism of several new members are projected on the enormous, and beautiful, projection screens, the pastor, Dr. Jack Graham, greets the huge crowd. He gets a special guest to stand for a round of applause: the senior U.S. senator from Texas, Republican Kay Bailey Hutchison. Dr. Graham delivers an interesting and affirming sermon, and sends the multitude out, fortified for the coming week. Prestonwood offers a full-service ministry, special activities to fill out the rest of Sunday afternoon for members of all ages (including lunch for a large seating, to be drawn in by signs proclaiming today's menu in the broad corridors), and I meet the pastor.

In his office are pictures of Dr. Graham with various Republican dignitaries, including the best-known Texan in American politics, George W. Bush. He knows why I have come to talk to him, and notes, "It was ironic that the senator was here today." With a silver mane and healthy tan, Dr. Jack Graham looks like much of Prestonwood's congregants: comfortable. The lampoon version of huge churches that might live in the minds of hard-core secularists or the unchurched is not on display in Plano that morning. The message was not a fiery rant about *them and us,* but an exhortation to be a better person.

Dr. Graham tells me the wider culture is catching up with something that has been happening among evangelicals for decades: "Christians who previously thought that politics was dirty and we don't want anything to do with it got more involved in the process and certainly are publicly outed now regarding that."

Like Land and Mohler, Dr. Graham says in a way this is nothing new. "So there's no question that there's more personal and political involvement by churches than in the past, but it's always been present, and I'm hopeful. The civil rights movement of the '60s came out of the churches, came out of the African American churches. The church was two-sided, unfortunately, back during slavery. The church should have done something. We've had to apologize because we did nothing. Where was the church during those years of slavery? It was silent and often accommodating."

Is it right for the church to take strong, public political stands? "Some of it depends on what your politics are. Sometimes politics on the left by the church is acceptable and politics on the right is not as acceptable. But for me—I can't speak for anyone else—but for me the balance is in maintaining your real mission. I could turn this whole church into a political-action committee. We have people constantly requesting endorsements, the signatures and petitions. We do a minimal amount of that because that's not our purpose. Our purpose is not to be a political-action committee.

"Our purpose is to fulfill the mission of Christ on earth and, when it comes time, to step up to the plate and speak out on the issue of the sanctity of life, and believe it or not, there are more evangelicals interested in social justice than imagined. More and more evangelical Christians are concerned about poverty and helping the poor and ministering to the poor. We maybe go about it in a different way than some."

I wondered whether there was a big difference, on the Sunday morning before the Tuesday of Election Day, between suggesting that people vote and suggesting who they vote for? "First of all, it's illegal to do that, so you're breaking a law of the land. If I get up and say go vote for Kay Bailey Hutchison, I have just crossed the line, legally. So absolutely. We don't, we do our very best. I want to say that we don't endorse candidates, but people know. They know who I voted for for president and what my persuasion is politically, so I don't have to stand up and say, you know, vote this way or vote that way."

They know? How do they know?

"By my preaching and my teaching. I mean, if they're politically astute at all; I mean they can add two and two and get four. So, you know, it's kind of a silly way to put it, but I'm sure there wasn't a person in the congregation that would have thought that I supported John Kerry for president, because they know what I believe and what I preach and what I stand for, and if they pay attention to what he was saying. So I'm just saying that's the example. I don't know if that's crossing the line or not. To me it isn't. To me it is talking about issues.

"And of course there is quite a bit of hypocrisy, really, because evangelical Christians get pretty well called on the carpet for stepping on the line or over the line on that, and on the other side, I was just infuriated. That's too strong a word. I was righteously ticked off that John Kerry was making appearances in churches every week during the campaign. He has every right to do it, and those parishes have every right to have him, and that's fine. George Bush didn't speak in any churches. But people knew of his faith and what he believed, and supported him based on that, not on the fact that he made appearances at churches. So anyway, I'm just kind of going off on that. John Kerry got up and quoted scripture in an Atlanta church and talked about the president—in fact, the scripture that I quoted this morning in James where 'Faith without works is dead.' And he was attacking the president on the fact that he's got this faith that's dead because he doesn't help people. So, boy, you know had George Bush stood up and used a scripture to attack his opponent, can you imagine what would have happened?"

To be a politically aware conservative Christian in the first decade of the twenty-first century is to nurse a sense of grievance. How come we get in trouble and they don't? Could you imagine how much trouble I'd get into if I did that? All we're doing is what they do; we just do it better.

For Martin Marty, a Theologian and Lutheran pastor, it is not convincing: "There is a strong spirit of score settling and vengeance. It's the politics of resentment. A lot of fundamentalists did get kicked around; then they moved to the will to power. They found power lying in the streets and they picked it up. Catholics and mainline were kind of weary; there was a void.

"The game Land is now playing is pretending to be a beleaguered minority . . . Look what they have! White House, House, Senate, Media . . . When you're selling 29 million 'Left Behind' books, you can't say you're being ignored."

Rabbi Saperstein thinks there is divisiveness embedded in the Christian conservative message: "True pluralism presumes some measure of equality. But theirs is at best the kind of tolerance that says, 'We tolerate these minorities. We're nice to them.' But as a point in fact, much of their rhetoric is exclusionary. There is a dismissal, a whole-handed dismissal of the religious authenticity of the other side.

"Liberals talk much more about God having called us to use our wisdom to understand what is, how to apply God's values into the world today. Fundamentalists believe they can extrapolate from specific biblical quotations the answers to specific political problems that we face today. Two very different approaches to religion, and therefore they're going to sound different and they're going to feel different about it, and liberals lacking that specifity, are at a disadvantage in this, in this debate and discussion in American public life."

But is it a permanent disadvantage?

Will the public continue to be swayed by the religious appeals made during this tense and unusual time, or is there a day of reckoning approaching in different regions of the country and different segments of the American people? There are places where the wall of separation has been breached. Next we will look at some of the issues that have brought religious appeals from both sides flooding into places where religion belongs, and where it is out of place.

THREE

Demolishing the Wall of Separation

I HAVE TALKED TO hundreds of people in the course of writing this book. Everyone seems to have his or her own idea of where the "line" is. America is a nation of walking, talking "reasonable-person standards." You know that reasonable person, right? He or she is an objective, but fictional standard used in the common law to figure out what normal human behavior would be when presented with a situation.

But religion appears to be so personal and so peculiar that when a legislature tries to pass laws that encompass human behavior, the reasonable-person standard does what no reasonable person can: sprouts wings and flies right out the window.

A reasonableness test might indicate that if just about all the kids in a school say they want to pray there, you allow them to pray. A reasonableness test might suggest that a scene of human figures in a stable depicting the birth of one religion's most revered figure on the steps of city hall would constitute a quiet government endorsement of that religion's tenets. Or conversely, would a reasonable person expect the government to sponsor messages it finds odious on the city hall steps?

What would a reasonable person conclude about the right of American Indians to use plants they have used since the dawn of time to alter consciousness as part of religious ceremonies? Before we give that reasonable person a headache, how would he or she advise us about religious schools tutoring particularly hard-to-teach public school students, at public expense, on church property?

The lines are hardly bright and white. They are easy to step over, stand on, and miss all together. Throughout our history we have honored the notion that religion is one thing, and it is over here. Government is another thing, and it is over there. Do not sit down and write me a nasty letter, at least not yet. The phrase "separation of church and state" appears nowhere in the Declaration of Independence, the Constitution, or the Bible, for that matter.[1] Yet is it the very notion that a majority religious belief cannot privilege that belief in a community, a county, a state, or a country that has made religion such a vibrant part of our lives in America.

The Constitution and American history make it clear that the founders of the country had no intention to form a confessional state, says the Reverend Barry Lynn, leader of Americans United for the Separation of Church and State. "People can tell you on the left, right, or center that we know exactly what the framers intended, but in fact we don't know. We know general principles only because these documents were written in what subsequent jurists have often called 'majestic generalities' because clearly the Bill of Rights was designed, unlike other provisions in the Constitution, with considerable vagueness, and deliberately so."

Thus, Lynn says, the United States is not a religious country, even with a vital religious life. He explains the paradox this way: "I think the tremendous power of the way America has done it is that we do have a vital religious atmosphere. I mean, we still have the highest church-attendance percentage, highest percentage of people who believe in God, highest percentage of people who go to a religious institution regularly, of anyplace in the world. And we do it, I think, because religion is a voluntary act. And it is also an act that in virtually every faith demands our participation in every sense. We choose to go to events, services, rituals. We choose voluntarily to support those, that faith in which we find comfort, if any faith does that for us."

Two rough rules of thumb emerged from the scores of hours of my interviews. The more religious, the more observant a person was, the less likely the person was to be bothered by public religiosity and the mingling of religious and political persuasion. The Americans most concerned about a tightening embrace between religion and the day-to-day work of running the country were members of so-called mainline Protestant denominations (Lutherans, Methodists, Presbyterians, Episcopalians, Congregationalists) and secular Americans who profess a family or cultural affinity for one faith or another but have no active congregational life.

These are "rough" rules of thumb because the landscape is pockmarked with exceptions. The exceptions illustrate how difficult it is to make any hard-and-fast rules about the American political and religious scene.

I talked to New York State assemblyman Dov Hikind during a legislative session that saw him trying to craft a compromise bill that would create some kind of benefit for families that send their children to parochial schools. Hikind's district features one of the densest concentrations of Orthodox Jewish voters anywhere in the world outside Israel. He is a Democrat, an Orthodox believer, and unworried by a more intimate relationship between church and state, a prospect that concerns many other American Jews: "I would tell them not to lose any sleep. They don't have to worry about the tyranny of the church. I haven't noticed any poll where this issue is anywhere on the list, that we're moving toward registering people by religion. There's this overheated 'Oh, my God, look where we're going' talk from some American Jews. I think there are groups out there that have an agenda. I don't think the average American is concerned that if we continue along the path we're on, the Catholic Church is going to run the country.

"I don't think it is a concern. I don't think it should be a concern. I don't think it will be a concern. We won't wake up one morning and say, 'How did this happen?' I just don't see the possibility of the tyranny of one particular religious group taking away the rights of others . . . If anything, I think there's more tolerance than ever."

Not all Jews are as sanguine as Hikind about the future of non-Christians in America. Abraham Foxman, head of the Anti-Defamation League, codified his worries in a series of speeches that got wide circulation in America in Jewish, Evangelical, and political circles. Foxman looked at the increasingly religious tone in political speech, the trends in shifting public moneys to religious institutions, the more intimate connections between Christian conservatives and Orthodox Jews, and concluded that evangelicals have as their goal nothing short of "Christianizing America."

When Foxman lowered the boom on a range of evangelical political groups in a series of news conferences in the United States and Israel, he called for Jews to organize in order to resist the political power of organizations like the Family Research Council. "Today we face a better financed, more sophisticated, coordinated, unified, energized, and organized coalition of groups in opposition to our policy positions on church-state separation than ever before. Their goal is to implement their Christian worldview. To Christianize America. To save us!"

Climb into the ring with some of the toughest political streetfighters in America, and you are likely to get your head handed to you. Even if you are no stranger to the tougher parts of the game yourself. Foxman was blasted by the very groups he warned about, such as Focus on the Family. Their spokesman, Tom Minnery, said, "If you keep bullying your friends, pretty soon you won't have any." Minnery added that what's good for all Americans is good for the country's Jews. "To the extent that America remains Christian, it remains free for non-Christian belief to flourish. You don't see that in other parts of the world."

Hikind says he just cannot see what the fuss is all about. "There isn't a single one of the so-called religious groups, from the most modern orthodox, to the most traditional, who can figure out why this is a problem. I represent a community of Holocaust survivors, and nobody here loses sleep over the things that Abe Foxman loses sleep over."

Hikind, who has traveled to Israel with evangelical Christian groups and appreciates their great love for the Jewish state, also pays no attention to the threats of conversion or worse. "Would I be offended that they believe this is a Christian country, or that they're trying to send me a message? No, I would not."

Other Jewish leaders backed away, wondering aloud whether a frontal assault on one of the most consistently pro-Israel political groups in America was a smart move for Foxman. Jeff Ballabon of the Center for Jewish Values told the *Forward,* one of the country's oldest and most respected Jewish journals, "It's repugnant from the standpoint of Jewish values and indefensible from the point of view of Jewish interests. Around the world, Islamic fundamentalism has Jews in fear for their lives and the only significant friends and allies those Jews have are American Christians. So, of course, Foxman attacks our friends using innuendo and bigotry. And what's their crime? They want religious freedoms in their own country. Let's set the record straight: The policies ADL attacks are policies embraced by non-Christian groups, including Jewish groups. Responsible Jewish leaders should repudiate Foxman's bigotry."

In all the back and forth over the strategy and the politics, Eugene Korn, director of Jewish Affairs for the American Jewish Congress, urged a closer look at the particulars of Foxman's charges. He told the *Forward,* "The question is not what the sentiment is, but to what extent are people actively trying to implement this legally and impose it on America. Jews should have no problem at all with Christians talking about God. But putting prayer back in schools? It's not clear to me that it's a threat. Creationism? The debate needs to be played out."

Rabbi David Saperstein is an old hand at the church-state debate, and what downstream effects may be waiting for religious minorities. He represents the Reform Jewish movement on Capitol Hill, and looking back over his years discussing these issues with lawmakers, he concludes, "When I came to Washington thirty-one years ago, it was in the middle of the Supreme Court's high-water mark protection of free exercise of religion, and its fundamental support for a robust separation of church and state. The court has fundamentally abandoned the free-exercise clause as a functional, effective protection of free-exercise rights in the United States after the *Oregon v. Smith case,*[2] and has chipped away significantly at the wall separating church and state without wanting to abandon it altogether. But religious symbols are more prevalent today. Government support for religion is more prevalent today, clearly where religious schools are concerned, clearly in government funding. In general, religious discourse in American public life is far more pervasive on the airwaves, far more pervasive culturally, far more pervasive in our political life."

Saperstein points out that for decades there was a strong religious voice in public life, and it was a liberal voice. Religious and political leaders of all stripes have pointed out that religious movements were heavily involved in the civil rights struggles of the 1950s and 1960s, fair-housing campaigns in the same decades, and in the mobilization against the Vietnam War. When asked to describe an ideal relationship between religion and the state under the U.S. Constitution, the rabbi said, "The wall separating church and state has functioned as a one-way wall, primarily restraining government and doing little to restrain religious individuals or religious organizations that are accorded the same rights to free speech, publication, association, a redress of grievance that other secular entities and individuals are accorded. So that has allowed religion to robustly serve as a moral code to the conscience of the country. No restriction on the ability of religion to speak to political issues, nor should there be. The limitations that are built in come the other way. The government cannot impose religious views on any person. Cannot choose up between religions, cannot choose religion over a nonreligion, can't endorse religious messages or oppose religious messages. It definitely shouldn't be funding overtly religious activity."

The Reverend Richard Land, of the Southern Baptist Convention, read me a section of their vision statement committing the denomination to strive for "an American society that affirms and practices Judeo-Christian values rooted in biblical authority." Their mission is "to awaken, inform, energize, equip, and mobilize Christians to be the catalysts for the biblically-based transformation of their families, churches, communities, and the nation."

At first blush, a statement like that could be read as a confirmation of Abraham Foxman's fears of a Christianized America and a takeover of the state. Land recounted a conversation with a reporter over that very issue: "Can you show me the word *state* in there? Can you show me the word *government* in there? It says, 'an American society that affirms and practices Judeo-Christian values rooted in biblical authority,' and 'to awaken, inform, energize, equip, and mobilize Christians to be the catalysts for the biblically-based transformation of their families, churches, communities, and the nation.' Now, if we are to convince a majority of Americans that they should be a society that affirms and practices Judeo-Christian values rooted in biblical authority, then of course we have the right to have the representative government reflect the mores of the society, don't we?" Land says minority religionists and Christians of other creeds have nothing to worry about. If his organization's view of the best America for the most people wins, it will be through the ballot box, not through forced conversion.

For every reasonable forecast of the American future from an evangelical leader—forecasts that might leave you thinking, "What's all the fuss about?"—there are others that are not nearly as reassuring about the country's secular future.

John Danforth, a retired U.S. senator, does not remember exactly when the shift to the new politics happened, but remembers seeing small signs all along the way. I asked him how he made his decisions about when to talk or not talk about religion in his campaigns. He was, after all, an Episcopal priest. "It was just the way it was. I don't remember just one day sitting down at a table with a piece of paper and saying I'm making a conscious decision. The whole time I was in politics, I never tried to use religion in that way. I mean, I did religious stuff. I mean, I was always affiliated with a parish church and I would do funerals. When I was in the Senate, for example, I presided at John Heinz's funeral. But it wasn't a program; it was who I was. I think it's a recent development for the Republican Party to be so identified with a particular political movement."

This is a movement former ambassador Danforth has no hesitation in naming as bad for the country. Perhaps counterintuitively, in the face of all the current Republican success, he has declared that change bad for the party as well: "How do traditional Republicans put up with this? They put up with this because it's a winning combination, for now. It won't last.

"It won't stand the light of day," Danforth said in 2006. "The more people think about it, the more people will resist it. People do not want a sectarian political party, including a lot of people who are traditional Republicans."[3]

Albert Mohler, of the Southern Baptists, widely heard on Christian radio nationwide and a denominational leader in educating clergy, told me he does not worry about the political implications of a closer relationship between churches and government. It is not a problem, Mohler said, because such relationships are transitory and respond to current events. "I would have to say there's a false assumption in this debate. I arrived at my graduate study twenty-five years ago. When I came to seminary, the Southern Baptist Convention had a more moderate liberal leadership. What was then the Christian Life Commission of the SBC, an important policy-setting body for the church, was just as aligned to the Democratic Party as it is to the Republicans today.

"What happened is, evangelicals were awakened to the fact that some of our dearest concerns were not safe in the hands of politicians. When you're looking at the layout of the different parties, you have to pay close attention to the candidates. If you think human life is to be protected from conception to natural death, go down the list of who's running with each party. You really don't have that hard a choice to make."

If Mohler does have a worry, it is that getting cozy with the powerful could lead to compromises injurious to the faith and the mission of the church. When I asked him if politicians have let Baptists down, and whether they have to be called on it, he replied, "Yes, and even more emphatically, yes. The fact is evangelicals are continually learning a more sober-minded lesson in political engagement. What you think is safely 'in' can end up being negotiated away. A law can be passed only to be shot down in court. The way politics works in that regard can be anathema to those who operate out of deep moral principle."

It might come as a shock to those secular Americans, Democrats, and outsiders who see no daylight between Republicans and conservative Christians and the party-church pair as daily getting their way in Washington that some evangelical supporters of the GOP think the electoral muscle they supply has not been sufficiently rewarded. Mohler said there's "a lot of anxiety among evangelicals that so little progress has been made on so many fronts." While the Bush administration has responded with conservative-Christian-friendly appointments and policies in areas such as family planning, education funding, and religious freedom, the big societal changes that groups like the SBC were hoping for have not materialized.

At the same time, Mohler worries, power has its temptations: "I think there is a danger of political seduction. I worry about some of my evangelical colleagues liking politics too much, finding it all too seductive. I believe the real problems faced by humanity are spiritual, not political. We are not politicians. We preach the gospel of Jesus Christ.

"I do not allow my schedule or commitments to get co-opted by the political. I do have a radio program, a large Internet site dealing with cultural engagement. My first and foremost identity is not as a political entity; it's as a Christian minister. I'm not sure there's any one answer for all individuals or for all times. We tend to be more engaged when events erupt, but politics is also about an ongoing structure—formal events and ceremonies, receptions, meetings and briefings. You have to be very careful that the trappings of power do not seduce."

To this, Welton Gaddy, a fellow Baptist minister but 180 degrees away from Mohler when it comes to Christian political involvement, might say, "Amen." Gaddy takes great pains to explain the subtleties of his stand, and what he believes is the historic Baptist position. He does not insist that Christians stay away from politics. He is not saying they should not organize and vote. "Christians have a commission to be involved in every phase of life including politics and to be there as followers of Christ and as advocates for the moral values that you find in the New Testament.

"As citizens of a democracy, we had to recognize a form of compromise. If we insisted that our nation become Christian, we would not only harm the integrity of Christianity by entangling it with a particular government, we would jeopardize and probably lose the kind of freedom that had given evangelical Christians in the United States an opportunity to establish themselves and espouse their evangelistic policies and so forth. I still think there's great credibility in that point of view.

"Now, I realize the problems of that for some people, and I have said I have real questions about whether an absolute Christian fundamentalist could enthusiastically support the kind of no establishment of religion that is viewed in the United States Constitution. The same could be said about a fundamentalist Muslim or a fundamentalist Jew. But I think it is a part of the wisdom of religious believers in the United States to not infringe upon those religious-liberty phrases in the Constitution, because they have been the friends that have allowed various religions to thrive in the United States and to do so without becoming involved in conflict with each other."

This is tough for people all along the religious spectrum. When we spoke, Gaddy put great stock in the fact that one of the only times the Constitution mentions religion is to affirm that there is no religious test for public service. Just a few minutes later he wondered aloud whether a fundamentalist could be a good steward of the establishment clause of the First Amendment.

No one I spoke with over the years of interviews thought a publicly identified atheist could be elected president of the United States. Almost all spoke of the reassurance people of all religions derive from knowing major politicians have some religious commitment.

Should that be a big part of the choice we make? Should a voter project spiritual competence onto the issues that challenge the country? Does regularly going to mass signal any ability to rein in the federal budget deficit? Does seeing a candidate leaving church with a Bible in hand give you any reassurance that a politician will be a skillful diplomat or a tough negotiator?

During a trip through South Carolina, I was reminded of just how much faith identification matters to voters. Across race, class, party affiliation, and denomination, Carolinians talked about how important it was that a candidate be religious. After Sunday morning worship at Shandon Presbyterian Church in Columbia, Caroline Puckett said, "I think it's important for a lot of Southerners to have a candidate that has a strong faith. I think the question would be what their intentions are, what their motives are in professing their faith. Is it to get the Southern vote, or is it to project their image as being, you know, a Southerner? But I think it definitely is important, as long as people perceive it as being sincere."

On the outskirts of Columbia, the massive Bible Way Baptist Church is as uniformly black as Shandon Presbyterian was white. After a morning of inspired singing, high-energy, and overtly political preaching, Charles Dickerson agreed with his fellow Christian across town: "I think that we live in a country of morals, and unless we have a moral leader, then we can't expect for the right thing to be done when, in fact, the nation is tested."

That time of testing was often cited as the very moment when the religious faith of an elected leader would be most reassuring. President Bush skillfully wove religious themes through his talks to the nation in the days and weeks after the September 11, 2001, terrorist attacks. It was not surprising that the people of the country responded to the president in those same weeks with the highest approval ratings of his entire tenure.

The difference between "God talk" and other policy discussion is that religiously tinged speech almost entirely releases a politician from accountability. The assertions are not checkable. There is no "other side" that can be put forward without calling into question the politician's sincerity and religious faith. A promise to reduce the budget deficit in three years can be analyzed and checked. A declaration that God has given the gift of freedom to humanity cannot.

"Checkability" is not some pedantic objection. When an elected official uses "God talk" as "policy talk," the intermingling of the two creates a kind of unassailability that is harmful to America, for people of all religions. When George W. Bush was in Canada for a meeting of the G-8, he got word that in the latest Pledge of Allegiance case the court had found for the petitioner, California atheist Michael Newdow. The president pronounced the decision "ridiculous." Later in the summit, during a news conference with Russian president Vladimir Putin (in some countries atheists can be elected president), President Bush responded to a question about the nomination of Harriet Miers to the Supreme Court: "We need common-sense judges who understand that our rights were derived from God, and those are the kind of judges I intend to put on the bench."

What?

Common sense. I am with the president there. Definitely a plus.

However, understanding "that our rights were derived from God" may not be a credential that can be assessed under the advise-and-consent clause of the Constitution. For a president who has declared there should be no litmus tests, that is certainly a religious test for public office that violates the Constitution. Wonder how the vetting process establishes these qualifications? I shudder to think of White House examinations of legal writings, educational background, and professional temperment also including questions regarding the nominee's belief that the laws laid down in Jewish and Christian Scripture trump the manmade laws of the Constitution.

A frequently asserted idea in these conversations is that the law made by legislators, reviewed by courts, and enforced by courts around America is fully consistent with the values of Scripture. People who say that must have their fingers crossed that the other discussant will not check or will simply take the allegation with a grain of salt. The Hebrew Bible and its Christian successors are full of notions that are simply noxious to the ideas put forward in American law. Some of the examples are trivial, some surprising. A vast document like the Bible, full of notions about daily life twenty to thirty centuries ago, cannot help but strain from the pressure of examination under the light of contemporary life.

For example, as we debate the wisdom of state-run boot camps instead of jail for incorrigible boys, and when to try teens as adults rather than children, we might consider this advice on juvenile justice from Scripture: "If a man have a stubborn and rebellious son, which will not obey the voice of his father, or the voice of his mother, and that, when they have chastened him, will not hearken unto them: Then shall his father and his mother lay hold on him, and bring him out unto the elders of his city, and unto the gate of his place; And they shall say unto the elders of his city, This our son is stubborn and rebellious, he will not obey our voice; he is a glutton, and a drunkard. And all the men of his city shall stone him with stones, that he die: so shalt thou put evil away from among you; and all Israel shall hear, and fear."[4]

It is interesting to contemplate where in this country a state representative or senator might propose the death penalty for disobedience. The disobedience of a son is, after all, a violation of the fifth commandment, one of the Ten Commandments, which, we have been told again and again in political debate, is the basis for Western and American law. How long would the debate last? Would the Death for Disobedience bill make it out of the committee because legislators would be too scared to vote against it?

Or would it, like so many proposals of its kind, simply expose the chasm between what Americans really want from the Bible and what they say they want. The same Americans who throng school board meetings demanding religious instruction cannot, by a vast majority, even recite the Ten Commandments.

A lot of the "God talk" in American politics is feel-good filler, unaccountable. Ringing phrases about what God wants, about his abundant blessings on America and her people, and assertions about this being a nation "under God" demand nothing of us as a people. Citing the Bible gets bellowing approval from audiences, but takes those same cheering throngs nowhere uncomfortable, nowhere challenging, down to no difficult debates about how we as a people divide our bounty.

The Reverend Welton Gaddy told a story that points out the problem with the political embrace of religion: "In the state in which my church is located, in Louisiana, President Bush made a speech recently. He went to an African American church in Baton Rouge, Louisiana, on Martin Luther King's birthday. In the course of his speech—which turned out to be a lot about the faith-based initiative—he turned to the pastor, who was sitting behind him, and took the Bible from his hand. He held up the Bible, and he said, 'This is the guidebook for the faith-based initiative. This is what we're trying to do, because we're trying to change people's lives.'"

Gaddy's voice rises. "The Bible, a guidebook for a public policy? . . . Now, President Bush is the chief executive officer of this nation, pledged to defend the Constitution. He was speaking as a religious leader, not worried about the constitutional implications of that rhetoric. No president in contemporary America has the luxury of being insensitive to religious pluralism. It will divide religions in a destructive manner, and it will project ultimately a reaction to religion that will prove negative. The nation will be hurt and religion will be hurt."

In these years of political debate over religion, much of the skirmishing has gone on in Washington, D.C., where saying things is often mistaken for doing them. Like flu viruses trading genes, religious talk has become infected with the lazy habit of mistaking being religious with sprinkling religious references around like confetti. Religion ends up being like a state of matter in science, a thing you are as a status, rather than a set of propositions that lead you to believe and actually modifies your actions.

Look at all the attention given to Harriet Miers's membership in an evangelical church. James Dobson, head of Focus on the Family, might have let it slip a little early that he was getting back-channel reassurance from Karl Rove on Miers's "fitness." Rove, he said, assured him "that Harriet Miers is an evangelical Christian, and that she is from a very conservative church, which is almost universally pro-life."

Perhaps this was merely the president being consistent with his own publicly stated litmus test for federal judges, that they believe in God. It does illuminate the difference between the rigorous faith preached by Jesus and spread by Paul, and the fairly easy tossing off of religious-themed code lines in speeches and membership in key churches as sufficient in and of themselves.

The judiciary has been a particularly difficult arena for the marriage of religion and politics. It has tempted religious leaders to sign on to political goals they may not fully understand, and exposed our politicians to opportunities to pander that they may later regret pursuing.

The first came in April, 2005, followed by Justice Sundays in August, 2005 and January, 2006. There have been, at this writing, three Justice Sundays. These events demonstrate a very intimate connection between elected officials and religious organizations, in seeking to mobilize church-related voters to rise up against the perceived evils of our current judicial system.

The Justice Sunday rules would appear to include the idea that no statement of government perfidy can be too outrageous, no exaggeration of the role of religion in making day-to-day law is too over-the-top, and no disappointment, no slight, is too small to be construed as abuse and discrimination against Christians and other people of faith.

An interesting theoretical journey gets you from the constitutional provisions spelling out how judges are selected and confirmed to the idea that too many contemporary judges are oppressors, and their aspiring successors victims. Start with the idea that in the United States Senate, members who are asked to pass judgment on judicial nominees may decide that judges likely to overturn judicial precedents in key areas might not earn their vote. If, as in the case of *Roe v. Wade,* there is also a religious component to the issue under debate, a new wrinkle enters an essentially political spat.

It turns out, or so goes the stated rationale of Justice Sundays I, II, and III, that if you vote against judges favored by Christian conservatives, you are not merely someone they disagree with on a matter of politics. In the final analysis, you are anti-Christian. The Justice Sunday logo shows a young fellow looking down at the tools in his hands: in one, a gavel; in the other, a Bible. Over one shoulder was the question "Public Service?" and over the other, "Faith in Christ?" Floating above this set of options was the legend, "He should not have to choose." In fact he does not have to choose. The list of the most powerful people in the country in the early years of this century is chock-full of believers, all the way from the famously born-again president of the United States through the leadership of the chambers of the national legislature through the most recently confirmed members of the Supreme Court.

Given what we found out about Chief Justice John Roberts's strong Roman Catholic upbringing and serious adult commitment to the church, and the very similar story for Justice Samuel Alito, Jr., that befuddled teen in the Justice Sunday poster would appear to have only one possible choice if he wants a high-level career: both.

Some straw men are impossible to do without. Tony Perkins, one of the leaders of the powerful and well-organized Christian conservative organization the Family Research Council (FRC), said at the time of the first Justice Sunday, "We think everyone has a right to express a point of view, but these men and women waiting on confirmation, several of them for years, have the right to be told if they are going to be hired or not. More importantly, the American people have the right to know what their elected officials are doing in Washington. I respect those who disagree. They have every right to disagree, but we have every right to discuss this and every issue affecting our communities and our families.

"This simulcast would not be necessary if the Senate's most liberal members would distance themselves from the interest groups that hold them in thrall. It's time to bring some transparency to the process and it is time to give these nominees an up or down vote," Perkins added.

Perkins is a strong and effective leader who has helped build the FRC into an institutional powerhouse. I wonder how much thought he spared the Clinton-era judges who never even got a hearing, much less an up-or-down vote. My purpose in bringing them up is not simply to make the "Oh, everybody does it" point as much as to wonder at how different the experience can be for jurists who get bottled up in the nomination process with the muscle of conservative American Christendom behind them. Many Clinton-era nominations withered in obscurity, with no one to shed a tear at their passing. But now, when Senate Democrats threatened to use the body's own rules to gum up the process, it can be construed not just as politics, but as religious bigotry.

That charge of oppression is ruefully noted on the other side of the debate. It is hard for Americans who voted for John Kerry in the last election, tried to block the confirmation of Justice Alito to succeed Sandra Day O'Connor, or try to elect a Democratic Senate in 2006 to imagine how often-invoked and deeply felt that narrative of oppression is on the other side.

"It is getting comical," said Scott Appleby, director of the Kroc Institute Institute for International Peace Studies and professor of History at the University of Notre Dame. "They're bad winners. The thing is that they've won by that kind of rhetoric, as the outsider who's being discriminated against. It's like Nazi Germany or whatever. But at a certain point it becomes just ludicrous because they're running the country or they're having a big say in running the country. So whenever they can, they slam the *New York Times* or the liberal media or whatever. And they're going to have to come up with a better strategy than that."

In Justice Sunday II—God Bless This Honorable Court!, speakers ran the ideological gamut from A to B, and included the aforementioned Tony Perkins, Dr. James Dobson of Focus on the Family, former senator Zell Miller (D-GA), Supreme Court nominee Robert Bork, then House majority leader Tom Delay (R-TX), Eagle Forum president Phyllis Schlafly, Prison Fellowship Ministries leader Chuck Colson, and Bishop Harry

Jackson, senior pastor of Hope Christian Church in suburban Washington, D.C., a strong supporter of the Bush reelection campaign and the only black speaker. Bishop Jackson told the crowd that judges of faith would be a boon to Americans of color: "If justice matters to anybody in America, it matters to minorities and to people who have historically been at the bottom of the barrel."

Jackson promised a new political coalition with the power to dictate the course of American politics: "I believe that what God is doing today is calling the black church to team with the white evangelical church and the Catholic Church and people of moral conscience, and in this season we need to begin to tell both parties, 'Listen, it's our way or the highway.'

"You and I can bring the rule and reign of the Cross to America, and we can change America on our watch together." While a lot of pastors promise "transformational leadership," rarely do they promise to change the whole political dispensation of the country.

The Justice Sundays may not have, on their own, changed the political character of the federal bench. They may not have smoothed the way for Justices Roberts and Alito (and because of growing conservative animus toward her nomination, they certainly did not help Harriet Miers). What they may have accomplished is substantial all the same: the creation of a network of politically motivated conservative Christians, reachable through the various outreach arms of national conservative groups—cable TV, e-mail, Internet, direct mail—and by proxy through clergy on Sunday. A people who are well-organized, motivated, angry, and constantly being told they are oppressed is a new audience for the political argument about the makeup of the federal judiciary. A new weapon is now in the conservative Christian armory, sheathed at the moment, but ready to be drawn at a moment's notice in service of one party's aims. Anyone who is really interested, rather than feigning interest, in the independence of the federal judiciary should watch the coalition created by Justice Sundays in the coming years. The argument that judges had better do what "we" want or else (evidenced by Congressman Tom DeLay in his reaction to the Terri Schiavo court decisions) mocks the belief that judges owe their first fidelity to the law and not the political passions of the public.

The Christian conservative movement has been on a pretty steady win streak in recent years, and one they earned fair and square. They closely read the regulations governing relationships between churches and campaigns, creating sluice gates of money from politically organized Christian conservatives channeled to campaigns and issue crusades. They outhustled, outthought, and outorganized their political opponents in the secular world.

But the internal contradictions of their movement become harder to hide when you win so much and wield so much influence. It is harder to escape the spotlight that inevitably shines on any set of political actors who find themselves in the catbird seat. It is difficult to juggle the message of overthrowing your secular tormentors with the message that people have nothing to fear from your victories. It is hard to tell people, and have them believe you, that the Christian conservative movement is out to return America to the Lord, and that secularists and minority religionists will not notice the change.

It is impossible to both pay tribute to the genius of the founders' conception of a secular state and continue to pound away at the notion that church-state separation is "a lie of the left." The contradictions inside the movement are real, and as some like Albert Mohler caution about being used by a political system that is interested only in victory, others insist that the reconstruction of American politics to reflect America's religious roots is just getting started. Because they have worked hard and turned out votes and beaten their adversaries over and over, the result will be an America where a married woman who thinks she has too many kids will find it much harder to get an abortion, where fewer American children will get sex education that is actually about sex, and where more public money will be made available to primarily religious organizations that also do social service work.

Some of the fear and trembling among less religious Americans is overwrought. Dark mutterings about criminalizing sex, Christianity as an official religion, and husbands dominating wives come from cherry-picking religious TV programs and adding a pinch of melodrama. But it is hard to totally discount their misgivings when Richard Land tells the story

of meeting then-governor George W. Bush, who in response to speculation about a presidential run said, "I believe God wants me to be president,
but if that doesn't happen, it's OK." The Southern Baptist leader took
some comfort in and some pains to point out that the future president did
not say, "God wants me to be president," only that he believed it was true.
To many conservative Christians, drawing a line between certainty and
mere belief is reassuring. For millions of other Americans, that is a distinction without much of a difference.

One important difference between the way God is invoked by the
president today versus how it was done in other eras in American history is
that then "God talk" provided a rhetorical flourish, a flourish of trumpets
at the close of an address. In the Bush era, "God" also provides a lot of the
thrust of the argument. While defenders may point out all the times *God*
appears in the words of Lincoln, Wilson, both Roosevelts, Eisenhower,
Carter, and others, the Almighty has now moved from the wings to the
center of the speech, and this is something new in presidential rhetoric.

In his 2003 State of the Union address, the same address in which he
ran down Saddam Hussein's fearsome inventory of the most dangerous
weapons in the world and his well-advanced plans to make more, the
president closed this way: "We Americans have faith in ourselves, but not
in ourselves alone. We do not know—we do not claim to know all the
ways of Providence, yet we can trust in them, placing our confidence in the
loving God behind all of life, and all of history.

"May he guide us now. And may God continue to bless the United
States of America."

Unpack that statement with me. First point: Americans believe in
themselves. Truer words have rarely been spoken, and in few other places
in the world will people revel in the notion that they are "Number One."
Point two: While Americans believe in themselves, they also believe God
has a role in their destiny. So far, so good.

Point three: We don't know what's going to happen in the future, and
cannot claim that we do. Yes and no. In January, 2003, the president could
never have guessed that his case for war in that speech would unravel so
utterly and entirely, or that American troops would still be fighting and

dying in Iraq three years later. One thing we today know he did know was going to happen, based on years of interviews with military and diplomatic people now out of government and able to speak freely: The president knew he was going to war against Iraq. And by the time he gave the next State of the Union address, he had.

Point four: While we do not know what is going to happen, we can put our trust in God's provision and place our confidence in it. This God guides our activities now, just as he has guided all of history. I pray that he continues to bless our country now.

Now we have a problem.

It is at the core of the problem with having your only constitutional chief executive officer, elected by all the people, become your theologian-in-chief in addition to the constitutionally provided function of commander-in-chief. In that State of the Union address, the president laid out a case for war. He spoke of massive stockpiles of sarin gas, botulinum toxin, anthrax, mobile biological laboratories, and the means to enrich uranium.

Did the same God who guides all of history guide the policy makers and speech writers behind those words? Did a providential God move Iraqi defectors to spin fanciful tales of fearsome technical prowess on the part of a decadent regime that could not even generate enough electricity?

Did God get the United States into the Iraq War?

The slippery genius of the rhetoric in the speech simply leaves that hanging out there for us. If Governor George W. Bush of Texas believed in 1999 that God wanted him to be president, as Richard Land recounts, then how many steps does it take from there to the case for war, and the observation that God directs human actions in history.

What I believe in all of this is not relevant, except insofar as I am a citizen. I am just asking the questions. What you believe is very relevant because of the important work of being a citizen that you have to do. Where is the line that should not be crossed? When does the comforting notion of a religious faith that might aid someone doing one of the world's toughest jobs cross over into a problematic melding of "my will," and "God's will?"

God is eternal. Presidents serve four-year terms, with one shot at contract extension. If the choice of government leaders boiled down to a superior ability to trust in God, I could propose a slate of excellent preachers and first-rate theologians to run our government. Your garbage would not necessarily get picked up or free-trade disputes get settled, but we would have leaders who trust God.

Americans should remember, not just during the Bush administration but for the rest of our future together, that God cannot be impeached, cross-examined, or recalled. There are no checks and balances to constrain God, or the chance to fire a shot across God's bow in the midterm elections.

The reason we have all those restraining instruments in our hands for presidents is that they are fallible and frail, as humans tend to be. They can give voice to our noblest dreams as a people, as well as incorporate our all-too-real talents for mendacity, cowardice, stubbornness, and vanity.

As the links between religious and political movements have become more common and more powerful over the last quarter century, people who know I am religious and cover politics for a living ask me what I think is happening. They ask because they want to check on a conclusion they, in many cases, have already reached.

"Do you believe (*fill in the name*) really means it? Or is he, or she, just using religion for effect, to get religious people to vote for them?" It is a cynical and dreary view of human nature. I am a reporter, and not a psychic. I cannot look into people's hearts and intellects and tell you what is there. I could never doubt the stated faith of another person without rock-solid evidence to the contrary. In many cases it is the interrogator's own lack of faith, in God or in human nature, that makes him willing to reduce leaders to cunning liars and those who follow them to witless dupes.

You may wonder sometimes just who is using whom. The Reverend Joe Wright got a lot of attention with his invocation in the Kansas House of Representatives. In it, he included the "Joe Wright List of What's Wrong With America." Invocations are often anodyne affairs, usually harmless. There may have been some nervous toe-tapping in the House of Representatives as the day's work was supposed to begin. Was the pastor talking to God, with some state representatives coincidentally overhearing, or talking to the people he disagrees with and using God as a prop?

63

Heavenly Father, we come before you to ask your forgiveness. We seek your direction and your guidance. We know your word says, "Woe to those who call evil good." But that's what we've done.

We've lost our spiritual equilibrium. We have inverted our values. We have ridiculed the absolute truth of your word in the name of moral pluralism. We have worshiped other gods and called it multiculturalism.

We have endorsed perversion and called it an alternative lifestyle.

We've exploited the poor and called it a lottery. We've neglected the needy and called it self-preservation. We have rewarded laziness and called it welfare. In the name of choice, we have killed our unborn. In the name of right to life, we have killed abortionists.

We have neglected to discipline our children and called it building self-esteem. We have abused power and called it political savvy. We have coveted our neighbor's possessions and called it taxes. We have polluted the air with profanity and pornography and called it freedom of expression. We have ridiculed the time-honored values of our forefathers and called it enlightenment.

Search us, Oh God, and know our hearts today. Try us. Show us any wickedness within us. Cleanse us from every sin and set us free. Guide and bless these men and women who have been sent here by the people of the State of Kansas, and that they have been ordained by you to govern this great state.

Grant them your wisdom to rule. May their decisions direct us to the center of your will. And, as we continue our prayer and as we come in out of the fog, give us clear minds to accomplish our goals as we begin this legislature. For we pray in Jesus' name, Amen.

Joe Wright wants the legislature of the state of Kansas to come in out of the fog. Hearing his invocation probably got their attention. Is taxation really a violation of the Tenth Commandment? Of course the good men and women of the Kansas house would erupt in red-faced fury if anyone suggested they begin their day with private devotions, in which God's grace might be requested for the state of Kansas as a whole, or the gift of wise decision-making for the state reps. Though no one likes to admit it, saying grace to open the legislative session is political and religious theater, meant for elected officials to demonstrate their piety to one another and to their constituents.

Oh, sure, there are a couple of swipes made at the prayerful evenhandedness one might require in a bipartisan body. The unborn and the abortionists are mourned. Abuse of power and the lottery come in for a shot. But gay Kansans (and rest assured, there are gay Kansans) should know that a preacher has been invited to use their statehouse as a pulpit and denounce them as perverts. Non-Christian Kansans should know we made a mistake in allowing them to worship other gods, all in the name of multiculturalism.

Those representatives who might be indulgent parents might think twice about the wrath of an invoked God for those who push self-esteem too hard. Again, the one unspoken problem with public religiosity is that it is not really meant to do any particular thing. Take Wright's suggestion that the state has rewarded laziness and called it welfare. We might all reread the New Testament and wonder whether Jesus himself would include that particular riff in an opening prayer in Wichita. Will Kansas state representatives take the bit between their teeth and vote to end aid to families with infirm or minor dependants? Would they quickly introduce a bill to revoke the First Amendment in Kansas so that swearing might be made illegal?

That particular invocation got a lot of ink, and a lot of reaction in Kansas, but ended up, as a lot of public religion does, being meaningless.

FOUR

Onward, Christian Soldiers

THE SAVIOR REVERED by more than two billion Christians around the world is often called the Prince of Peace. But that same master told his followers, "Think not that I am come to send peace on earth: I came not to send peace, but a sword."[1] Since the Emperor Constantine told his subjects he had seen a vision of the cross blazing in the sky with the words *"in hoc signo vinces" (by this sign you will conquer)* in the year 312, Christianity has had a constantly shifting relationship with war and warriors.[2]

One of the most disturbing aspects of the disappearing borders between American politics and Christianity in recent decades has been the melding of religion, war support, and the military services. Among conservative Christians the near-unanimous and uncritical support for the Iraq War has been only the latest iteration of a religion that sees its own needs and desires so deeply enmeshed with that of the state that it is willing to abandon or ignore its most sacred principles to keep the relationship alive.

Please understand me: what you read here is not an attempt to undermine the case for the Iraq War or to insist that Christianity would regard that conflict as illicit. What I mourn is the loss of independence of the church in the wider marketplace of ideas and the willingness of conservative Christians to embrace the first part of that label to the detriment of the second.

Christian just-war theory has been a central concern of the church for 1,600 years, and appropriately so, since the countries where most Christians lived were in near-constant warfare for much of that time. The concerns in framing the test for a just war were twofold: when a cause for hostilities is justified; and once a state has decided to go to war, how that conflict is prosecuted in a just way.

In the centuries since Augustine of Hippo wrote about what constitutes a just war and just warfare, theologians and leaders have critiqued and amended, embraced and affirmed, what a Christian should consider before killing to further the interest of the state. Just-war theory asks the citizen to consider whether the cause sought by the conflict is just, whether the destruction brought to the enemy is proportional to the wrong to be righted by state violence, and whether all other options have been exhausted before war was unleashed. In this reputedly most Christian of all Western nations, this central concern of the historic church was pushed to the margins of the national debate over the Iraq War. Discussion of just-war theory in 2002–2003 became the province and property of liberal churches, antiwar organizations, and Roman Catholic scholars and clerics.

Christian leaders have made war for purposes of the state since the existence of Christian leaders. As in the case of the Crusades, many of these leaders have tried to take their own wills or the wills of various popes and temporal allies, and make them those of the whole state, and God. But the Christian religion is something else altogether. The religion, no matter how you slice it, is not predisposed to war. War may be necessary. War may be unavoidable. Whatever the circumstances, in *religious* terms, it is not approached with relish or happy anticipation, but as a dreaded task.

President George W. Bush may end his speeches with the civic prayer "May God bless you, and may God bless the United States of America" and assert that God is "not neutral" in the wars between freedom and fear, and justice and cruelty, but he was less comfortable talking to his countrymen and countrywomen about the moral and ethical boundaries of warmaking.[3] Leaving those boundaries undiscussed and undefined illustrates the difficulties and real challenges of invoking religion in such a volatile part of national policy making. This and many other uses of the political appeal of faith as a campaign tool and persuasive motif should also demand a matching obligation to ask the hard questions of policy makers and ourselves about what that religion actually requires.

In other words, those of you who want a closer relationship between religion and policy making in this country should not presume that desire can be ordered à la carte. The uses of Christianity in American politics do not extend only to whether or not teenage girls need help in avoiding getting pregnant and what form that should take. Jesus, mum in the Gospels on the subject of birth control, had plenty to say about loving your enemies, praying for those who despise you, and blessing those who curse you.[4]

America has failed in this requirement, preferring to showily shout "Under God" during the Pledge of Allegiance rather than engage the challenge of using the moral imagination to understand what that same God really wants in Iraq. The very real security needs of the United States were mixed with the desire for revenge after 9/11, along with the elevation of the needs and desires of Americans above those of people elsewhere in the world (very American, but not very Christian), to create the conditions that have made possible sinful and damaging excesses on the battlefield, in the prisons, and on the streets of Iraq.

As a kid standing for the recessional hymn, I dutifully sang this lovely, century-old hymn by English novelist and poet John Oxenham:

> *In Christ there is no East or West,*
> *in him no South or North,*
> *but one great fellowship of love*
> *throughout the whole wide earth.*
>
> *In him shall true hearts everywhere*
> *their high communion find,*
> *his service is the golden cord*
> *close-binding all mankind.*
>
> *Join hands, disciples of the faith,*
> *whate'er your race may be!*
> *Who serves my Father as a son*
> *is surely kin to me.*

In Christ now meet both East and West,
in him meet South and North,
all Christly souls are one in him,
throughout the whole wide earth.

Postwar American Christianity taught middle-class, middle-brow, middle-American social and cultural values, but also a universality in the faith. It was a time of scratchy black-and-white films in elementary school about our "foreign friends"; Disney's "Small World," stressing the globe-straddling solidarity of kids around the world; and the notion taught on Sunday morning in denominations across the spectrum that Christians praying in a sub-Saharan hut, a thatch-roofed shelter under the blazing Indian sun, or an ornate sanctuary in northern Europe were all my brothers and sisters.

What I was *not* taught, even in those intensely patriotic Cold War decades, was that God had chosen America as the instrument for His Will in the world. In the church I was taught, in ways explicit and implicit—in textbook illustrations of Jesus talking with smiling children clad in the folk dress of the world, in exhortations to support foreign missions, or in the heroic death of seminarian Jonathan Daniels, shot during the civil rights struggles in Alabama—that Christianity was not an American religion, and the American state was not necessarily Christian.

America's purposes, as was hotly debated during the Vietnam War, were not necessarily God's. It was to the country's credit when they were, but there was certainly no guarantee they would be. Yet here we are, 140 years after Lincoln's famous warnings to the contrary, easily conflating God's desires, purposes, and will with those of the American people and their leaders.[5]

The Reverend Barry Lynn, of Americans United for the Separation of Church and State, told me the appropriation of American symbols by conservative Christians is one of the most significant trends in American religion in the last thirty years. It is a trend that creates problems in and outside the United States: "One is that civil religion, this kind of use of imagery from both the political and the religious sphere, does tend to cheapen the expression of religion. But then also it sends an interesting and dangerously interesting message to the rest of the world, and that is that when the president or the vice president talk about democratization, for example, in the Middle East, to a lot of the Arab and Muslim world that word *democratization* means Christianization, and we don't help any in this country when we do things like send General Boykin from the army out in his army uniform to give speeches in churches announcing that we're going to win against the Muslims because our god is real and theirs isn't, which gets a day of play on NBC here, but gets weeks if not months of attention in Arab news outlets."

Lieutenant General Boykin was promoted, not punished, after his declarations, in uniform from the pulpits of conservative churches, that he would get the better of his nemesis, Somali warlord Mohammed Farah Aideed, because "I knew my God was bigger than his. I knew that my God was a real God and his was an idol."

Again in uniform, he told another conservative Christian audience that America would prevail "because we're a Christian nation, because our foundation and our roots are Judeo-Christian . . . and the enemy is a guy named Satan." To another audience General Boykin proclaimed, "We in the army of God, in the house of God, kingdom of God, have been raised for such a time as this." The reporting of these sermons from the general has reflected just the kind of secular outrage that evangelicals lampoon in their scathing critiques of the media and the unchurched.

If you think there is a problem with the general's behavior, you ought to try to tease out what that problem is. Contrary to some of both the secular outrage and the conservative Christian backlash, the problem is not that the general is an evangelical Christian. The problem is not that he goes to church and appears to be deeply committed to his beliefs.

The problems, such as they are, are rooted in why we have a military, what the uniform represents—not only to the wider American society, but to the world at large—and what it is advisable for an American general in uniform to say in a public gathering. When a citizen puts on the uniform, especially one festooned with the symbols of flag rank, he or she is no longer simply speaking for himself or herself. At the risk of sounding simplistic, that is part of why uniforms are, well . . . *uniform*. They attach the wearer to a larger institution and, in the case of General Boykin, one that belongs to every American and represents every American. For the same reason that President Bush does not generally deliver Sunday sermons on his understanding of the divinity of Jesus or the consecration of bread at Holy Communion or the inerrancy of Scripture, it is questionable whether the general's musings on Islam, divine will, or indeed, politics, are necessary or desirable. As an American citizen, I am far more interested in General Boykin's ability to defend this country against its enemies than I am in his belief that the outcome of the 2000 presidential race was divinely ordained. That did not stop General Boykin from sharing with an audience in Sandy, Oregon, that George W. Bush became president because the Creator trumped the ballot box, making the Texas governor chief executive even though the citizens of the United States picked Al Gore for the job. Said Boykin, "He's in the White House because God put him there."

The deeply problematic vision of a general in uniform telling an audience that God overruled the voters in choosing our current president may creep you out, but it did not bother the secretary of defense, Donald Rumsfeld, too terribly much. The secretary declined to censure the general in any public way for his remarks to church audiences. When asked by reporters to comment on the Boykin remarks, Rumsfeld first said he did not know the "full context" of the Boykin speeches, then added, "There are a lot of things that are said by people that are their views, and that's the way we live. We are free people and that's the wonderful thing about our country, and I think for anyone to run around and think that can be managed or controlled is probably wrong."

The then-chairman of the Joint Chiefs of Staff, General Richard Myers, backed up his boss and said, "There is a very wide gray area on what the rules permit. At first blush, it doesn't look like any rules were broken."

Let us, for the moment, accept the bland contention that a senior general making it sound like a Muslim warlord's supreme deity is "an idol" while we are in the midst of a globe-straddling struggle against Islamic radicals is *just fine.* Just move on folks, nothing to see here, no rules have been broken.

Let us move the question from the realm of the law, marching in endless columns of tiny type through hundreds of pages of books, to common sense. Is there a difference between the constitutionally affirmed rights of Private Citizen Boykin, and the way public comments of generals in uniform are heard, read, and understood? In other places in the world where there is no difference between the pronouncements of uniformed generals and the policy of the state, how long would it take you to explain that the general's remarks do not reflect the policies of the United States?

Perhaps you have noticed in the intervening years since those remarks were made that you have not seen any juicy quotes from any particularly pious generals about God choosing presidents, combat against Satan, or similar topics. The weakness of the conservative Christian arguments against secular government becomes manifest when high-ranking evangelicals make remarks injurious to our national objectives around the world and then take refuge behind the skirts of the secular U.S. Constitution to save their hides. It is up to the individual believer to decide whether General Boykin is a good theologian. It is up to every American to decide whether it makes good sense for the general to present his personal worldview dressed as a representative of the United States.

THE CORE TENSION BETWEEN what is a personal profession of faith and its intersection with one's duty as a citizen is at the core of conflicts currently tearing up the Air Force Academy and the chaplain corps of the armed forces as a whole.

The United States Air Force Academy in Colorado Springs, Colorado, is the youngest of the service academies for the youngest of the services. It has been graduating officers in the U.S. Air Force for almost fifty years, and women into the officer corps for almost thirty years. Located amid the Rockies at more than seven thousand feet above sea level, the academy qualifies as a bona fide tourist attraction, bringing more than a million visitors onto the grounds each year.

Attorney Mikey Weinstein, class of 1977, is among thirty-five thousand graduates, and an unlikely rebel. An officer in the Judge Advocate General's Corps (JAG), registered Republican, attorney in the Reagan White House, son of a Naval Academy graduate, and father of two Air Force Academy grads, Weinstein has little fear of attempts "to paint me as a tree-hugging you know, Northeastern, Chardonnay-sipping liberal Democrat." He is proud of his family's multigenerational commitment to military service, and of what an exceptional profile that is for a Jew.

So it is with a mixture of sadness, regret, and amazement that Weinstein has sued the government he has served for much of his adult life and, in particular, the Air Force Academy for its treatment of cadets who are not self-identified evangelical Christians. Weinstein said, "We are creating a caste of people who are children of a lesser God."

The Air Force Academy alumnus echoes recent Supreme Court decisions when he insists, "We must ensure governmental neutrality between religion and religion and between religion and no religion." He has said since the beginning of his battle with the academy that he had no idea how bad things had gotten in recent years for members of religious minorities until his son was home on leave. Curtis Weinstein told his father of being called "a fucking Jew," of being marched back to barracks from dining hall with other cadets as part of "a Heathen Flight" of those who did not choose to take part in evangelical Protestant worship. He was asked by a fellow cadet, "How do you feel that you killed Jesus?"

Some of this is little more than the same old nonsense that American Jews who are part of majority Christian organizations have had to put up with for centuries. Mikey Weinstein recognized his son's problem from his own time as a cadet. "Was I made fun of for being Jewish? Yeah, but it was done in the way that any eighteen- to twenty-two-year-old would deal with it. You've got to have thick skin. It was never done in a malicious way. Except for one time when one of my close friends called me 'Jew Boy' one too many times and I jacked him up against the wall. I was choking him. In fact I have my ring on right now; he's the guy that designed our ring. The guy's name was Dave Mason, and when I put him down—I guess I don't know how long I had him jacked up against the wall—he said he was sorry and he didn't realize it pissed me off so much." Weinstein said he never did it again.

He maintains there is now something very different going on at the school, the kinds of things that cannot be solved by a quick shove against the wall or a word from a senior cadet: "My kids were constantly called 'fucking Jews'; they were constantly told, with smiles on the faces of the people telling them, that 'you are, you and your people are, complicit in the execution of Jesus Christ. Your ancestors are lost. There's still a chance for you and your descendants if you will simply accept the Lamb and be washed in the blood of the Lamb.' I don't know how else I can tell you that. When I found out about that, for a guy like me who was born without a temper, I pretty much went through nuclear. And I began to realize what had happened, and the more I peeled the onion back, the more I began to see that this has been going on for a very, very long time."

The problem, as Weinstein sees it, is different from those that might be presented at most other institutions of higher learning in the United States. What makes it different is similar to what makes military life different from civilian life. Cadets at the U.S. Air Force Academy are more than students; they are already members of the nation's military. They live highly structured, controlled lives, with their movements and their behavior under constant scrutiny, with deference to ranking authority not just advised, but required. When they gather for assemblies and meals, and on the parade grounds, cadets are not where they want to be, but where they must be, which makes the introduction of religious messages by senior officers less like advice, in Weinstein's view, and more like coercion that has no place in a federal institution.

"When you have a senior person, no matter whether you're a four-star general or a four-star sergeant, and you're talking to someone junior to you and they're talking to you, your superior's talking to you about a particular religious faith, in this case evangelical Christianity, 'Get out of my face!' is not an option. And listen, if you're a twenty-one-year-old male prison guard, and you have completely consensual sex with a forty-five-year-old female prison inmate, that is still statutory rape. It can never be consensual. It can never be noncoercive."

That coercion, Weinstein said, took many forms, from aggressive promotion of the Mel Gibson movie *The Passion of the Christ* on campus, to encouraging evangelical cadets to witness to brother and sister cadets, to the air force football coach proclaiming that his players were in fact members of "Team Jesus Christ" and should be as present and accounted for at Sunday morning services as they were on the football field on Saturday.

In April 2003, the academy commandant, Brigadier General Johnny Weida, sent an e-mail to the cadet corps recommending their participation in that year's National Day of Prayer, to "ask the Lord to give us the wisdom to discover the right." The commandant told his cadets, "The Lord is in control. He has a plan for every one of us." In another e-mail General Weida admonished the cadets to remember that their first responsibility is to God.

For ten years an advertisement ran in the cadet newspaper, signed by one hundred officers and supervisors from the academy, that included a reference to verse from the New Testament's Acts of the Apostles: "We believe that Jesus Christ is the only real hope for the World."[6] Official academy events at which attendance for cadets was mandatory were opened by Christian prayer invoking the aid of Jesus Christ. At a basic training exercise a conservative Christian chaplain exhorted his cadet congregation to pray for the souls of those fellow students who chose not to attend.

These blatantly religious messages sent to cadets throughout the school year left air force critics with the strong impression that improper pressure was applied to cadets, something that should be the last thing they should have to worry about at a government installation. In response to Weinstein's sleuthing and a steady chorus of complaints, the air force launched its own investigation into religious practice at the academy.

The service's one-hundred-page report conceded some lines had been crossed and some unwise decisions made. The report's ultimate conclusion regretted those acts, but rejected the allegations concerning a pervasive atmosphere of preference for conservative Christian denominations by the senior staff of the academy and an unwelcoming environment for cadets who were not evangelical Christians. The air force report commended the leaders of the academy who had put various tolerance and diversity programs into place, concluding these programs responded in an appropriate and timely manner to the problems in Colorado Springs.

One person who was not satisfied was Mikey Weinstein: "They're saying, 'Look, if we accommodate everybody, no one has a right to bitch.' My response is, 'No, that's not it at all.' If you let all 5,600 of the recognized religions on this planet have total access to the machinery of the state, you haven't created any unconstitutional equanimity. What you've created are 5,600 violations of the Constitution. I don't care if you give separate rooms in Fairchild Hall at the academy to the Jews, the Buddhists, the Hindus, the Jains, the Shintos, the Wiccans, the atheists, and the agnostics. That's not what the point is." The point, Weinstein insists, is a military that does not include or exclude, promote or discourage, a cadet's personal religious decisions. "And the disgrace and the embarrassment is that I had to go before a federal judge to get the air force to agree to that, and of course they haven't agreed to it and we're in a lawsuit now.

"I don't know what little else I can ask of the air force. I'm asking the court to force the air force to never again require an air force member to involuntarily, against their will, be proselytized or evangelized or pressured about changing their religious status on duty. It's astonishing that I had to sue about that." Since that suit was filed, Weinstein has become a story magnet, getting phone calls and faxes, e-mails and handwritten notes, from current cadets and academy grads detailing what he sees as a pervasive pattern of practice that includes matters large and small, from merely annoying slights to seriously flawed practice, starting with the commandant and heading all the way down to the barracks floor.

The deluge of negative press—including the heavy coverage in the *Washington Post*, the *New York Times*, and the Colorado Springs area's main hometown paper, the *Gazette*, with steady coverage of the story by reporter Pam Zubeck—goaded conservative Christians into action to defend the academy and the chaplains now under fire. Colorado Springs is often called the Evangelical Vatican, because it is home to large and influential national organizations such as Dr. James Dobson's Focus on the Family, influential and well-attended megachurches, and the National

Association of Evangelicals' leader, Ted Haggard, senior pastor of New Life Church.

Tom Minnery, of Focus on the Family, is just one of the conservative Christian leaders seeking to turn the tables on Weinstein: "Christianity is deeply felt and very important to people . . . and to suggest that it should be bottled up is nonsense. I think a witch hunt is under way to root out Christian beliefs. To root out what is pervasive in 90 percent of the group is ridiculous." Though not one of the critics of the Air Force Academy suggested that cadets from conservative Christian denominations not be allowed to practice their faith, for Minnery and others that became the core of the defense: "If 90 percent of cadets identify themselves as Christian, it is common sense that Christianity will be in evidence on the campus." Focus on the Family's own publication quoted one academy graduate, Tom Clemmons, as saying evangelicals were something like an oppressed minority. According to him, "The secular humanists kind of run the show, by and large. Now, while we do have Christians at the Academy and in the air force, it's definitely a minority."

Focus on the Family did not let on that there is a tension in the overall message. The Air Force Academy can not be the 90-percent Christian institution Tom Minnery describes *and* the secular-humanist-driven school observed by Tom Clemmons. The two narratives traffic in two frequently employed motifs in modern conservative Christian circles: a majority that should not be expected to water down or compromise on public professions of faith to satisfy the demands of a secular minority, and an oppressed church hunkering down under the cultural weight of a godless, elite establishment.

Then, in 2006, the National Association of Evangelicals (NAE), the nation's largest grouping of conservative Christian churches, moved to intervene in Weinstein's case against the academy, in order to defend evangelical chaplains. The air force had no public comment, but Kyle Fisk of the NAE told the Colorado Springs *Gazette,* "We have been in collaboration with the Air Force attorneys working on this case. It is the policy of the Air Force to remain neutral when it comes to intervention, but we believe we are doing the Air Force a service." Fisk noted that the air force had not encouraged or collaborated with the NAE's filings: "We simply are defending all people's faith and their right to free expression with their faith." The preferred tool used by religious groups in lawsuits like this is the *amicus curiae,* or friend of the court, brief, laying out its legal theories and point of view on the side of the aggrieved religious party. It is a sign of the seriousness of the case to the NAE, or their expectation of victory, that it is intervening directly in the case.

Meanwhile, the air force continues to wrestle with the problem. A study by Americans United for the Separation of Church and State concluded this is not an armed-services-wide problem, but one particularly afflicting the air force, which accounted on its own for almost all of the fifty-five complaints involving religious practices and the services in the years leading up to the Weinstein suit.

At the invitation of the Air Force Academy, a delegation of observers from the Yale Divinity School spent time watching chaplains and cadets at work on the Colorado Springs campus. In its report, the Yale team said that what is called the General Protestant Service on the Air Force campus might better be called the General Evangelical Service or Protestant Praise Service, to indicate that Protestant cadets from the mainline denominations might find a very different style of worship provided by the school.

The leader of the Yale task force, Professor Kristen Leslie, told a hearing of the House Armed Services Committee's Subcommittee on Military Personnel that many of the chaplains and officers she observed were unable to make what she saw as a crucial distinction: "It was clear in my mind that in that environment there was not a clarity with some of the leadership, both chaplains and other leaders, on the difference between good pastoral or spiritual care and evangelism." Leslie, an ordained United Methodist minister and pastoral-care teacher, told the committee she also saw plenty that was right about the relationship between chaplains and students, especially in the challenging environment of cadet basic training for first year students.

In her testimony, Leslie noted that the air force's own report gave the academy a largely clean bill of health. It is a diagnosis the academy does not yet deserve. For one thing, she said, "with . . . the apparent exoneration of some of the chaplains' actions, it says that there is not a clear understanding between what is good spiritual or pastoral care and how that bumps up against, as we're saying, religious freedom. Secondly, what we saw was not consistent with good order and discipline, in fact, more likely, as these basics and as the cadre are working to become leaders in the nation's air force, we didn't see how this was helping them to negotiate the variety of religious expressions that certainly are out in the air force." It took long enough for a grown-up to get there. While so many were looking at the air force controversy through the lens of religious freedom and what that freedom means in the context of a hierarchical armed force, Leslie was asking what was, in effect, the toughest question of all: Did it make sense to take young men and women who were being trained at great expense to become the future leaders of the air force and emphasize what made them different from each other? Would it contribute to the discipline, cohesion, and solidarity of a fighting force to declare to impressionable young people that while some of their comrades may be capable officers, they were in permanent spiritual deficit?

The professor told the subcommittee members, "We were left with the impression that in that environment, these eighteen- to twenty-two-year-olds were left trying to negotiate how to be in the environment with different religious traditions sitting side-by-side, because we were seeing examples where the leadership was not giving good guidance." That leadership includes a commandant who thinks it is appropriate to tell his cadets "the Lord is in control," a football coach who thinks his players are members not only of the academy's famed Eagles but also something called "Team Jesus Christ," and a head chaplain, Brigadier General Cecil Richardson, who in the face of pushback from the academy's leadership and the brass in Washington, declares, "We will not proselytize, but we reserve the right to evangelize the unchurched." As a group they are probably not the best team to lead young cadets to wisdom about service in a diverse modern force.

While several of the congressional representatives focused their questioning on the academy representatives and plans for reform, several Republican members implied the academy's critics want to stifle the voice of evangelical Christians. Congressman Mike Conaway of Texas said, "I'm a Christian, and Jesus Christ is my personal savior." Conaway added, "I hope that doesn't offend you." Later Conaway reflected, "Through this whole discussion, I felt attacked because of my Christian beliefs." Congressman Walter Jones of North Carolina read out a constituent's letter rewriting the words of the Marines' hymn: "From the halls of Montezuma to the halls of political correctness."

Congressman Trent Franks of Arizona looked to President Bush to come to the cadets' aid: "I truly believe that the president of the United States, if he fully understood the realities that are present in this circumstance, would respond in an effective and decisive manner."

When the House of Representatives took up a debate on the ongoing situation at the academy during 2005, Congressman John Hostettler upped the ante, inflaming an already emotional debate. Hostettler said legislation condemning proselytizing at the Air Force Academy was part of a "long war on Christianity" waged by "the usual suspects, Democrats." The Indiana Republican did not see a debate over the right way to run a pluralistic, taxpayer-funded service academy, but part of a compulsive antireligious struggle for near-term political advantage. "Like a moth to a flame, Democrats can't help themselves when it comes to denigrating and demonizing Christians," Hostettler said.

Democrats jumped to their feet and demanded that Hostettler's remarks be "taken down," that is, stricken from the House record, while silencing the congressman for the rest of the day. Hostettler stuck to his statement as scowling Democrats approached his desk to challenge him and more conciliatory Republicans jumped into the breach and tried to head off a vote on Hostettler's remarks.

Finally, the Indiana Republican stood and asked that his final sentence, about "demonizing Christians," be stricken from the record. Meanwhile, a compromise piece of legislation passed in the House asked for monitoring of progress at the Air Force Academy through regular reports to Congress. It went nowhere in the Senate.

While Capitol Hill might have been split on the question, the academy's superintendant, Lieutenant General John W. Rosa, Jr., appears to understand he has a problem on his hands. In a speech to the Anti-Defamation League in the spring of 2005, General Rosa said, "The first thing we did—the first thing I did when I got to the Academy, I acknowledged we have a sexual assault issue, we have cultural problems, we have a religious-respect issue at the United States Air Force Academy. You have to tackle it head on. You have to figure out what is the problem, and not treat symptoms and move on. You have to tackle it. But really you have to cultivate respect. Because this is a respect issue. It really is when you come down to it. It is an education issue and a respect issue. We have to cultivate that with respect for one another, through education, training, and accountability. And once you set that bar, and you say this is what we expect from you, you hold people accountable."

The superintendent promised the Jewish civil rights group he would institute the needed reforms, as he did when he was called in to take over at the academy after a wave of sexual assaults shook the school to its foundations, and he closed by saying, "This is a tough issue. I don't have to tell this group that. We have been fighting and working this issue for two hundred years in this nation. It is a very, very emotionally charged issue. We want to make sure that cooler heads prevail, teams come together, and let's solve, and work, and let's get better. That is my charge to you."

Supporters of the military culture and veterans have thrown down their experience in uniformed service like a winning hand at cards, trumping every other player at the table in political debates for years. People who have not served, the story goes, cannot possibly understand the bonds between service people and how different life in the chain of command is from the loose, "anything goes" norms of civilian life. Yet again and again—in the navy's Tailhook scandal, in the Air Force Academy's rash of sexual assaults—it often turns out military life is more like the rest of American life than its most devoted admirers would care to admit. Problems that in other contexts are supposed to be handled by orders, discipline, and clear guidance from above can get messy right at the firing line.

Ask Lieutenant Gordon Klingenschmitt.

The air force major decided to make a move to the chaplain's service mid-career, and after his training, changed services and lost rank in order to do it. Now a naval lieutenant and a chaplain, Lieutenant Klingenschmitt finds himself embroiled in conflict with his superiors aboard his ship and the Department of the Navy. In the meantime, he has become a cause cele-bre for right wing Web sites, conservative Christian congregations, members of Congress, and evangelical chaplains across the services.

I talked to Klingenschmitt days after he ended fourteen days of hunger strike over the right to proclaim the name of Jesus Christ in corporate prayer aboard ship or when acting in official capacity as a chaplain. He had been stripped of his uniform, forbidden from functioning as a chaplain, and threatened with discharge from the service before the hunger strike.

Having broken his fast with a communion wafer while celebrating the Eucharist in front of the White House, Klingenschmitt, a priest in the Evangelical Episcopal Church, spoke with a measured jubilation in the winter of 2005. He had made progress, he said, but was far from his goal: "I knew that the law gave me a right to pray in Jesus' name. But I was shocked and dismayed to discover that in 1998 the chief of navy chaplains had signed a policy memo enforcing religious discrimination and telling me I had to exclude myself if I prayed in Jesus' name.

"I filed a complaint this year against the chief of navy chaplains, complaining that his 1998 policy memo was an illegal attempt to abrogate U.S. Code. And he wrote back to me in August of this year, 2005, and he said in writing that if I pray in Jesus' name, that I'm denigrating other faiths. So he refused to revoke his policy memo. That memo still stands today in contradiction to public law and we need the president of the United States to enforce the law since 1860 that allows us to pray according to our bishop's faith instead of the commanding officer's government civic religion."

The current law and practice in the navy allows chaplains to perform rites according to the norms of his denomination: "An officer in the chaplain corps may conduct public worship according to the manner and forms of the church of which he is a member."[7] The rules change for mandatory-attendance gatherings of sailors of different faiths, like grace before meals or a benediction before dismissal. In those cases, inclusive prayers are recommended, and Lieutenant Klingenschmitt sort of complied: "My prayers have always been inclusive, because I say the following phrase at the end of my prayers. I say, 'We pray to you Almighty God, and I pray in Jesus' name. Amen." So anyone who feels free to pray to Almighty God can say amen, and I'm the only one who says, 'in Jesus' name.' "

That threading of the devotional needle did not pass the commanding officer's test. "When the chief of navy chaplains in 1998 signed an illegal policy memo which says if I pray in Jesus' name that I ought to exclude myself from participation in public events as the prayer giver, he is attempting, with the stroke of one admiral's pen, to abrogate U.S. Code and the United States Constitution. He violates the Constitution which he swore to uphold by censoring my prayers."

Rear Admiral Louis Iasiello, the navy chief of chaplains and a Roman Catholic priest, made his policy clear in a statement on the Klingenschmitt matter in the summer of 2005: "Chaplains can pray however they like in sectarian worship services, but that in public ceremonies where attendance is mandatory for sailors and officers of many faiths, they are encouraged to use inclusive wording. If a chaplain is uncomfortable with that, he should decline to give the benediction."

Klingenschmitt called it "censoring his prayers" and a "constitutional violation," but Rear Admiral Iasiello saw it differently: "We train our people to be sensitive to the needs of all of God's people. We don't direct how a person's going to pray. Because everyone's own denomination or faith group has certain directives or certain ways of doing things, and we would never—it's that whole separation-of-church-and-state thing—we would never want to direct institutionally that a person could or couldn't do something."

To bolster his point, Klingenschmitt pointed to the Supreme Court's decision in *Lee v. Weisman,* a school-prayer case in which a chaplain was ordered by a school principal to offer nonsectarian prayers: "And the Supreme Court ruled that when the government tried to control the content of someone's prayers, they were enforcing a civic religion on the entire audience. And it violated the establishment clause. And it violated the First Amendment. So there's already a ruling out there that the government cannot control the content of our prayers nor even attempt to do so."

I put it to the navy chaplain that it appeared from the regulations that chaplains were a bit of a different animal from, let's say, a pastor or a parish priest. They were meant to represent their specific denomination in certain worship, but at the same time offer a more generic spiritual guidance and comfort to sailors of any and all faiths. I asked if his duties might, on a given day, include "being with people when they're under tremendous stress—in danger of their life, taking the lives of others, faced with accidental death and loss of people they value and love—where you might be called upon to sit with a Jewish soldier who's having a really rough week because of the loss of a comrade or a Roman Catholic soldier, or sailor, who is in the midst of a spiritual crisis, where they might not want services from you that are directly tied to your denominational background, but more general visitation and pastoral care from just someone who's a member of the chaplain corps?"

He agreed. Sort of. "The chaplain's job is to provide for members of our own faith, to facilitate for members of other faiths, and to care for everybody. And as a Christian chaplain, my job is not to say Jewish prayers or Muslim prayers, but to facilitate for the free exercise of a Jewish or Muslim sailor to practice their own faith. And I do that by advocating for their right to express their faith freely, just as I would have the right."

Then Klingenschmitt told me a story that illustrates the clash between the very American tradition of struggle for complete religious freedom and the more restricted world of the armed services. "We have a tradition at sea that at ten PM somebody comes on the ship's microphone and says the short traditional prayer. Well, I asked my commanding officer to share the prayer and take turns with a diversity of faiths instead of one civic religion. I said, let my Muslim sailors pray to Allah on the ship's microphone. Let my Jewish sailor pray in Hebrew to Adonai. Let my Roman Catholic in the name of the Father, Son, and Holy Spirit. And I will take turns with them and I'll just pray in Jesus' name on every fourth night. But my commanding officer disapproved my request. He said, no, chaps, I'm not comfortable with that. You keep saying the prayers, but from now on I want you to pray Jewish prayers. And so I obeyed him. For eight months I only prayed based on the Psalms."

Is Gordon Klingenschmitt a lone man striking a blow for religious liberty? Or is he being insubordinate and sowing the seeds for the destruction of his own career? "Since I continued to end my prayers in Jesus' name, and the chaplain school director had defamed me by telling my commanding officer I was an immature chaplain for claiming an academic right to pray in Jesus' name, my commanding officer told the Navy board to end my career, in writing, saying that Chaplain Klingenschmitt over-emphasized his own faith system, and he was talking about my sermons and prayers."

It turns out the rules have not changed recently. For Lieutenant Klingenschmitt, this was a struggle that began when he was still a trainee as a chaplain, one who said of his military career, "I had already served my country, I wanted to serve God." He told me, "When I attended chaplain school, they gave mandatory lectures to all junior chaplains, and they had senior chaplains with clipboards who evaluated our prayers for their content. And they praised us if we prayed only to God. But if we prayed in Jesus' name, they gave us counseling. And they told Muslim chaplains, don't pray to Allah in public. You should only do that in private. And they told Jewish chaplains don't pray to Adonai. Roman Catholics, don't pray in the name of the Trinity. Evangelicals, don't pray in Jesus' name in public. And I challenged that."

Doesn't *Allah* simply mean "the God" in Arabic, and *Adonai* mean "Lord"? Was Klingenschmitt making a problem where there was not really that big a difference in the first place? When sailors heard their ten P.M. prayers over the ship's public address system, could they simply hear through their own ears a version of "God" that made sense to them?

No. The chaplain said that the "God" a Catholic, Evangelical, Jewish, and Muslim sailor might mention in their prayers are, in fact, different beings. So, in Klingenschmitt's view, there was no way to pray an honest consensus prayer. "I pray to the God of Abraham, Isaac, and Jacob. And his name is Jesus Christ. Muslims do not pray to Jesus Christ. Jews do not pray to Jesus Christ. Abraham, Isaac, and Jacob did not pray to Jesus Christ as I do."

The navy chaplain's struggle against the service goes on, as he hopes for a presidential order to clarify his situation and endorse his reading of the U.S. Constitution. In the meantime, seventy members of the U.S. House of Representatives have crowded into his corner, lobbying the White House, and the Pentagon. Republican congressman Walter Jones of North Carolina has written legislation to protect the chaplain's right to pray "in Jesus' name." Jones told PBS, "Our men and women in uniform are in Iraq and Afghanistan to defend freedom. And yet in this country we're having our chaplains being denied their freedom to pray in the name of their faith."

If Lieutenant Klingenschmitt thought his commanding officer was an incompetent fool, he would not have a First Amendment right to tell me that. It is widely understood that members of the military do not enjoy unencumbered rights to free speech. Had Klingenschmitt's commanding officer ordered him not to talk to me, our interview would have been a violation of military rules and landed him in a kind of trouble unique for an American citizen who decides to talk to a reporter. For better or worse, the taxpayers of the United States do not employ clergy who then go ahead and practice their vocation in any way they see fit while collecting the public dime. There might have been significantly less tolerance for Lieutenant Klingenschmitt in another time in the military's history, despite his insistence that his free-exercise rights go back further than the U.S. Constitution to the very first days of the Continental Navy.

There has already been a kind of vindication for Klingenschmitt, whatever the navy eventually decides: "All the admirals in the Navy appear to be against me right now. And yet over seventy congressmen have written to the president advocating my position. Over two hundred thousand Americans have petitioned the president on my behalf and other evangelical chaplains or other chaplains who want to pray in Jesus' name. Over thirty pro-family organizations representing 80 million Christian believers in America have written to the president. And the White House spokesman last week came out and said the president is committed to policies that allow religious diversity of expression for their chaplains. America is on my side."

The new communications tools that connect churches and believers and national religious organizations can create virtual crowds and big pressure almost overnight. Many of the same constituent pieces of support now writing letters on behalf of Lieutenant Klingenschmitt pulled together in the mid-1990s, when an army medic named Michael New became a right-wing rock star while remaining almost unknown in the wider America.

Specialist New had been ordered to report for duty with the rest of his unit as part of the United Nations peacekeeping deployment in Macedonia. This meant adding a United Nations patch to his sleeve, and a blue baseball cap with the UN symbol in place of his beret. New refused to appear in formation with the specified UN modifications to his otherwise unchanged U.S. Army uniform. Today's "Army of One" commercials do not promise aspiring enlisted men and women they will be able to make their own rules and wear what they want to do their work.

Michael New was dishonorably discharged, and the army stuck by its rules through repeated appeals to the original decision. He told the crowd that came to welcome him home after his discharge, "The UN Charter is based upon very subjective man-made regulations and its 'human rights' are given by the men of the United Nations. These rights are not like those we have been endowed with by our Creator, but rather can be modified or taken away by the UN. I saw from my own study that the UN's authority and founding principles are diametrically opposed to the founding documents of America, my own country, and its government."[8] Long before thousands flocked to his tiny Texas hometown to hear his speech, Pat Buchanan, right-wing radio, and thousands of conservative Christians rallied to his cause. There were dark mutterings about a New World Order and the Book of Revelations' connections with the United Nations' future One World Government. Michael New's refusal to obey a lawful order was mixed in a potent stew with end-times theology and a conservative Christian hatred and distrust for the United Nations (not to mention an abiding distaste for President Bill Clinton, who dispatched Americans to Macedonia).

That neat, linear portrayal of the armed services as places of discipline, deference, and cohesion has taken a lot of hits in recent decades. While elected officials play an endless game of "Can You Top This?," seeking a

form of political inoculation against accusations of being insufficiently patriotic, the military has managed to break the spell all on its own.

Just as religion has done politics no particular favors in their intimate
and tightening embrace, one part of our national life that has recently enjoyed a resurgence of public esteem may be working to declare itself the
sole property of just one group of Americans: evangelical Christians.

Take a look at a book by Bobby Welch, a soldier and evangelist, called
*You, the Warrior Leader: Applying Military Strategy for Victorious Spiritual
Warfare.* Drenched in symbolic and heavily freighted language, it offers
lots of advice to military officers on using Christian principles for winning
objectives and souls. In one excerpt, Welch quotes a fellow member of the
Officers' Christian Fellowship and an Iraq War vet, who reflects on the
Christian profession of arms: "Thankfully, a Christian officer can have accountability. There are bound to be other Christian officers, such as a men-
tor at the same installation or a peer in your organization who desires
exactly what you do—accountability in pursuit of Christ's call. If confident
and competent junior officers pursue the Christian disciplines and bear
fruit, then their true boss is glorified." [9]

When meditating on loyalty and its meanings, Welch writes, "The
Warrior Leader is given loyalty as a gift when he deserves it—when he
trains and equips his people well and cares for and treats them as colabor-
ers and examples of the Warrior Leader Christ Life he talks about. No
loyalty is more true and long-lasting than that of fellow soldiers who trust
their leader to take them through the risks and dangers of spiritual combat." Though Welch returns to the general and the vague over and over
again, so that *combat* and *warfare* could plausibly read as metaphor, virtually every example, anecdote, and quote is drawn from the Bible, or from
military men and their work as leaders in the armed services. "Brigadier
General Samuel L.A. Marshall said, 'Loyalty is the big thing, the greatest
battle asset of all. But no man ever wins loyalty of troops by preaching loyalty. It is given to him as he proves his possession of other virtues.'" [10]

With generals recommending religious beliefs and encouraging young
men and women in uniform to witness to comrades of different faiths or
no faith . . . with chaplains questioning the spiritual fitness of other unit

members not at prayer . . . and confinement in the rigorous and structured atmosphere of a military academy used as an opportunity to encourage one particular form of religious expression at taxpayer expense, a dangerous new line has been crossed.

Real-life soldiers' reminiscences and shelves full of movies from World War II give us one vision of the intersection of religion and the soldier—of the American in uniform as an only lightly theologically inclined fellow who, when in peril and the stress of warfare, finds a general yearning for prayer and comfort that could be met in any number of ways. What mattered was the bond with all comrades in blue, in khaki, or camouflage. Chaplains held the hands of the dying of all faiths, calmed the fears of men preparing for battle, no matter what their religious background, in a way useful to that serviceman at that very moment.

We now live in an age of something new. As our country is home to more and more people of non-Christian faiths or no faith at all, one particular stripe of American religious experience has surged into the chaplain's ranks. The language of war, patriotism, and religion are commonly fused into a new alloy. This metal may be strong for some. But anyone who cherishes the notion that the uniformed services should be a living and visible expression of who we are as a people might find a cause for concern in the religious wars now being fought by our warfighters.

Next we look at a battle now under way at home that is shaping our religious debates, and our political ones, in surprising ways.

FIVE

To Have and to Hold . . . Over My Dead Body

LIKE ANY GOOD CHESS PLAYER, a reporter checks on his or her skills by looking four or five moves ahead. Though it is most important to excel in the "Here's What Happened" business, the "What Does It Mean" business is also a vital component of making a living. I tell you this as a way of explaining a blown call in 2003, when *Time* put two sets of smiling, attractive, "normal-looking" gay couples, one male, one female, on two alternating covers under the headline "Is Gay Marriage Next?"

My answer was "No!" followed quickly by "Next question!" The Supreme Court had just released its opinion in the case called *Lawrence and Garner v. Texas,* striking down laws against sex between two people of the same sex (and other forms of, shall we say, nonprocreative sexual congress between men and women) in Texas and around the country. The ruling was, predictably, hailed as a milestone by gay people and as another step toward the Fall of Rome by conservative Christian organizations, denominations, and commentators.

I found myself strangely unmoved by the entire spectacle, because strictly symbolic laws end up being rarely enforced and unjustly enforced when they are dusted off for application. The *Lawrence* case began with just such a case of selective prosecution. John Lawrence and Tyron Garner were spending the evening in Lawrence's Houston apartment. A neighbor called the police to report a "weapons disturbance," and officers responded. When they entered the apartment, they found Lawrence and Garner having sex.

The responding officers, instead of meekly apologizing and heading back to the squad car to laugh, high-five, and report what they had just seen on the radio, arrested the two men and held them overnight in jail.

The pair were charged with violating Texas's Homosexual Conduct law and fined $200. In another day and age, John Lawrence might have quickly packed up the contents of his apartment and moved far away to escape the disgrace and community judgment expected to rain down on his head. In the twenty-first century Lawrence did something quite different: he sued, and brought down centuries of legal tradition in America. States have always sought to regulate the private conduct of their citizens. Over time, laws against various sexual practices have been used less and less, have narrowed in many states to apply to gay couples only, and have simply lost out to the need to prosecute murderers, robbers, and drug offenders.

The state of Texas fought to maintain a state interest in Lawrence and Garner's behavior, to retain the ability to prosecute gay sex, and to pull out the statute from time to time to punish men and women they caught. When I read the decision, it did not strike me as a disaster that Houston police would no longer be able to arrest two men they found in bed together as a result of a false report. Laws banning gay sex in thirty-five states would crumble, and the states could get back to educating kids, maintaining highways, and naming state birds and flowers.

So those nice-looking gay fellows and lesbians on the cover of *Time* pulled me up short. What was *Time* doing? Trying to start a fight. Trying to stir the pot? I knew marriage-equality battles were making their slow and steady way up the judicial ladder in states around the country. I knew efforts to give gay couples a set of relational rights routinely and unquestioningly found in marriage were heading to courts and polling stations. Would the simple act of removing state interest in policing sex lead to the altar and the county registrar's office? Yes, it would. But it is more a case of correlation than causation. There is no denying that eleven months after the *Lawrence* decision had sparked a mainstream, middlebrow newsweekly into asking the provocative question about gay marriage, television cameras thronged courthouses across Massachusetts to see happy men and women of all ages, decked out in a range of finery from the traditional to the eclectic, say, "I do."

Marriage is an issue ready-made for a religious and political national screaming match. Like barnacles encrusting a massive tanker, this big institution has been covered over time in a thick coating of emotional, legal, religious, and cultural layers. Marriage is the focus for long-honored and emotionally freighted cultural practice that centers on places of worship (so that even the least religious couples among us long for the swirl of the organ and the long march up the aisle offered by a church wedding). At the same time, marriage is an institution regulated by government.

In an interesting way, church and state both keep their hand in. Wedding licenses may be signed by a cleric serving as an officiant, but it is still the county that issues the document. Many religious bodies have required preparation for marriage within their sanctuaries, but it is the state that steps in to play an enormous part when so many marriages come to their sad end in divorce. The ancient church may have played a great role in regulating the behavior between couples when the ceremony was done, but throughout history the state has also played a great and growing role in defining what marriage is, who may choose it, and what bonds of obligation and responsibility will be enforced over the life of the marriage and even when it is over.

Early in the presidential election year, President Bush put down his marker, proposing an amendment to the U.S. Constitution to make it impossible to legalize gay marriage at the state level: "Marriage cannot be severed from its cultural, religious and natural roots without weakening the good influence of society. Government, by recognizing and protecting marriage, serves the interests of all.

"Today I call upon the Congress to promptly pass, and to send to the states for ratification, an amendment to our Constitution defining and protecting marriage as a union of man and woman as husband and wife. The amendment should fully protect marriage, while leaving the state legislatures free to make their own choices in defining legal arrangements other than marriage."[1]

IT IS NOT HARD to imagine that when the Supreme Judicial Court of Massachusetts, the state's highest court of appeals, cleared the way for gay people to marry each other, there was flying confetti, high fives, and cham-

pagne toasts in the offices of gay legal advocacy groups, and at the offices of
the Republican National Committee (RNC), the Bush-Cheney 2004 reelection headquarters, and the Christian Coalition.

It was almost too good to be true. Here was an issue guaranteed to energize and enflame older, more rural, more religious, and more conservative voters. It must have been near-impossible for President Bush and
RNC chairman Ken Mehlman to believe that this gift, wrapped in a laven-
der bow, had also been sent from the home state of the man who was increasingly likely to be the Democrats' nominee for president, whose
Beacon Hill mansion sat a short stroll from the state capitol in Boston.
How is this for a chronology? May 2004, gay men and lesbians share joyous smooches on the sidewalks outside courthouses and county buildings,
and just a few weeks later in July, Senator John Kerry has to carefully
thread his way through women in white wedding dresses and veils to accept his party's nomination for president.

Of course the public never saw that Republican joy. All that was rolled
out for the cameras was a grim, mournful determination to save one of
society's most cherished institutions from the destruction sure to be
wreaked, not only on marriage but on American life, by this new right.
Once the president made "the defense of marriage" a central plank of his
2004 campaign, he knew he could rely on the votes of millions of mobilized
conservative Christians. The party organizers and their church allies knew
they could put up a ferocious battle with no need for restraint or worry
about giving offense.

And they knew they had John Kerry in a box. The senator said, every
time he was asked, that he, like President Bill Clinton, supported the notion that marriage was between a man and a woman. That didn't matter.
Republicans and their conservative Christian allies understood that as a
matter of tactics, if not of law, they could hang gay marriage around John
Kerry's neck and tie the Massachusetts court decision around his ankles
like a ball and chain.

Defense of Marriage Act laws took on local coloration—some banning even the possibility of civil unions, some just training their fire on
marriage alone—and were included in the menu of choices for 2004 vot-

ers. The federal-level Defense of Marriage Act (DOMA), passed in 1996, allowed each state to deny recognition to any same-sex relationship legally recognized in another state. In the following years, states passed their own DOMA laws. The conventional wisdom was that gay marriage initiatives on state ballots in 2004 helped only George W. Bush. John Kerry's electoral alliance was so fragile and perilous he could not afford to campaign against these ballot questions without alienating possibly capturable voters in battleground states, and he couldn't support them without turning the stomachs of liberal voters and gay Democrats, who were a small but important part of the coalition. This made Kerry a punching bag by default. The president could insist to rapturous applause that he was defending the sanctity of marriage, while his challenger could hope the subject did not come up.

While the Massachusetts court decision created a political bludgeon with which to pummel Democrats in 2004, the opposition also realized that this one sizable state's decision could "normalize" what for them is an unthinkable outcome. The ripples that went out from a courtroom in Boston have shuddered through churches and caucus rooms and legislative chambers ever since.

Victoria Cobb is a young mother in her twenties, and an anti-gay-marriage activist. Cobb is one of the organizers behind Virginia's efforts to head gay marriage off at the pass, by blocking the possibility through legislative action and constitutional amendment. Talk to Cobb and you get a full tour through the strategic and social thinking of conservative Christians who have made marriage the line in the sand for their movement.

As we talked, Cobb repeatedly insisted that opening marriage to gay people represented a redefinition of an institution that had changed little over millennia. I wondered aloud whether even recent centuries, during which married women were treated as legal children and as their husbands' property, might not show that marriage had been under constant change. She replied, "I just don't see what relevance any of that has to this issue. Sure, there have been changes in the law over time. But this is one change marriage can't stand as an institution.

"If you can define marriage in any other way you want, then marriage has no definition. We often ask the other side, how then would you define marriage? As a union between any two people that love each other? Why is it limited to just two? They can't answer that question.

"For a bisexual individual it won't be illegal to marry a man and a woman." The specter of polygamy has become one of the core threats of gay marriage for its opponents. I asked Cobb whether, if polygamy was a real worry, it would not be possible to craft a law that would limit marriage to two legally competent and consenting adults?

"Again, why just two? And ultimately, why just adults?" Cobb then opened up a Pandora's box full of threats to marriage and every other social norm. She said, "We have already significantly redefined childhood. We have made it possible for children to become independent of their parents, given them the right to sue their parents. Who knows, will we now lower the age of adulthood?"

"There are even papers and reports"—she drops her voice, to threaten and dismiss in the very same moment—"They've been strongly rejected—but there are studies that allege the right to consensual sex between young children and adults. As I say, fortunately they have been denounced.

"Redefining marriage opens up many possibilities. There are polygamists petitioning courts right now, knowing that this is happening right now." Slippery slopes are everywhere in Cobb's view of the social landscape. Make one thing legal, and everything is suddenly open for renegotiation. Let a man marry a man, then groups of men will be able to marry. Let a woman marry a woman, and the marriage of children is up for consideration.

Victoria Cobb is consistent in her approach. There are no subtleties in her political program as executive director of the Family Foundation of Virginia. There can be no opening of the door to gay civil rights, not even a crack. So civil unions, or any form of recognition of gay couples short of marriage, can be considered.[2] Cobb said, "Anything that purports to be marriage, no matter what you call it: civil unions, domestic partnerships, registries, all undermines marriage. And we have already undermined the institution enough as it is."

Cobb is also against clubs begun at the high-school level to combat gay-bashing and exclusion, often called "gay-straight alliances." She has worked from school board to school board to try to have them banned: "They don't have anything to do with academics or athletics. Let's find out what's in those clubs and let's have parents consent to their kids being involved."

She was backed in her efforts in the Virginia House of Delegates by Delegate Matthew Lohr, who introduced a bill that would allow schools to shut down any student group that encouraged promiscuity. "This bill is not aimed at one particular group," the delegate told the house. "The intent is to give local school boards more control over the types of groups which use the buildings."

Cobb believes that any form of social, cultural, or legal tolerance of same-sex relationships, indeed, of homosexuality itself, opens the door for its wider embrace. "That is what it will be, the cultural norm that will be taught to their child. When they talk about the choices that face them as an adult, it will be Option A, Option B, All of the Above, None of the Above."

If normalization is the threat, then Lee Swislow may be Victoria Cobb's worst nightmare. She is executive director of Gay and Lesbian Advocates and Defenders, GLAD, a legal group that provided much of the intellectual and organizational muscle that made gay marriage a reality in Massachusetts. She thinks she knows why the opposition kicked up into a new gear when the Supreme Judicial Court made its decision: "One aspect of same sex couples getting married for these last few years is, we are winning the framing war. In debates in Massachusetts, the criteria has become the sky hasn't fallen. Nothing has really happened. During the debate on the constitutional amendment [a debate in the state legislature that followed the court action], it was pointed out that people had been getting married for months and the sky hasn't fallen, the world hasn't ended. That's the metaphor people are using, and that just tickled me. If you go looking for other harms, you just don't see it."

As for the idea that acceptance for gay marriage and polygamy are linked, Swislow said, "Those of us fighting for marriage equality have always been very clear about what we're fighting for, and about what our justification is. The interesting thing is, people who are fighting for polygamy think we're immoral and have no interest in working with us. And we don't see them as having anything to do with us either.

"Society makes its decision. The ability to marry the person of your desire is a fundamental right. When two people make a commitment they should be able to have that recognized. The state argued that there's a rational basis for not having same sex couples marry. The Supreme Judicial Court found there was no basis to deny gay couples marriage licenses. If polygamists want to do the same, the court will hear their arguments, and make a decision."

Swislow married her longtime partner a month after the law changed, one of thousands able to marry during the required gap between the court decision and any legislative attempt to ban gay marriage. She said that gap made a huge difference in public opinion. "Gay and lesbian people getting married has been a joyous and moving event. It's just a nice thing. And the delay gives people an opportunity to see that it's a nice thing.

"We got married outside in our yard. People that I've been saying 'Hi' to for years and don't really know came up and said hello. A construction worker came over from across the street, where he was doing his job, and struck up a conversation about his own next-door neighbor's wedding. I think people are just delighted in seeing other people be happy." The shifting tides of public opinion have not been dramatic or decisive. They have been more incremental, but their aggregate effect over the last ten years has been to give more support for gay marriage and more support for civil unions. Swislow maintains that even people who are not actively or passionately pro or con in this debate will be put off by any attempt long after the fact to tell people who have been married for years that this was all a big mistake and they are just two single people.

Meanwhile Cobb is working hard to make sure there will be no recognition in Virginia of Massachusetts marriages and no legal recognition for any gay relationship in her state. To that end, she has traveled the state to visit churches. "Our coalition, VA for Marriage.org, is often asked to come into a church during a service, asked to present the issue, asked to do a seminar, on this particular ballot measure that's coming up."

I asked Cobb how she felt about stumping for a ballot measure in the sanctuary during a worship service. Was it appropriate? "It is wholly appropriate that those with deeply held religious views are encouraged and instructed on how to let those views apply in the society. This is a wonderful opportunity to be able to inform citizens that they have a unique chance in a democracy to be able to make their voice heard."

Did this particular issue belong in church more than, let's say, a road tax or a school-construction bond? "Absolutely, simply because marriage is something everyone has experienced in one way or another. Maybe you grew up with two parents in a long-term marriage. Perhaps you've experienced life without a married family. Maybe you've been a child of divorce, or raised children as a single parent yourself. Because of that, people are extremely motivated. The family unit is central to everyone's life experience."

I was trying to find out if there were any lines you should not cross, anything inappropriate to such a campaign. Was it all right for a pastor to step into the pulpit and say, "Here's how I think you should vote?"

Cobb had no problem with it. "Many pastors are educating the people themselves, and it's wholly appropriate for them to be preaching on the issue of marriage." The political question is merely an extension of the preaching and teaching of the church, therefore, Cobb said, "it's only logical to let folks know that their church has a teaching on marriage, and what that teaching is.

"For instance, at the Church of the Cross of Virginia, there's a massive petition drive we've been doing. Hundreds of churches have wanted to make that petition to save marriage available to their congregations. Marriage is a pulpit issue. Preachers preach on adultery, divorce, marriage. It's a question of encouraging your church not to be in a bubble, not to be removed from important battles going on around them in society."

Swislow, too, has seen the church hard at work in the marriage debate. "There was a statewide signature drive, led by a coalition of churches, with the Roman Catholic churches taking a leadership role. Bishops sent letters to priests telling them they had to have petitions read out in their churches. Again, the Roman Catholic church was the lead church, but many other churches were involved in lobbying legislators to vote for the constitutional amendment to overturn the court. Now we're seeing increasing opposition coming from the churches. On the other hand there is the Religious Coalition for Freedom to Marry, clergy and congregations supporting freedom to marry, but of course that is much, much smaller."

Now a veteran of the struggle for what she calls "marriage equality," Swislow said fighting the churches on public policy is more complicated and more difficult than debates over garden variety differences of political opinion: "I think there's a downside that there isn't with other political advocacy. It's already hard enough to get a nuanced message through in this society." For example, one threat heard repeatedly from churches in the fight over gay marriage is that churches will end up being forced to marry people they do not want to marry. Once the implication is out there, and repeated enough, Swislow said, it has to be addressed. "We've had to say again and again on this matter we respect every religion's right to do whatever it wants when it comes to marriage. That is an absolute. But it also has to be said that we are also opposed to any religion trying to make law for everyone else."

The status of marriage in America as a religious and civil institution makes it hard for people to tease apart what is essentially civil, and what is essentially religious about getting married. Swislow said that creates an opening for the other side. "The right plays on that. When Bush says in his speeches, 'We must protect the sacred right of marriage,' it's sacred in their world of religion, but it's not sacred in the civil realm. He's done a good job conflating the two. It's easy because most people get married in church, even if they're not particularly religious. We're talking about a civil, secular institution, that the secular world can have complete say in defining."

Here is where it gets tricky. Gay marriage advocates like Swislow are strict separationists, trying to keep the debate neater by locating the struggle for marriage rights entirely in the county registrar's office. At the same time, many gay people hanker for what their straight brothers and sisters, mothers and fathers, had with few questions or qualifications: a religious wedding. A picture in the newspaper may not dig deep into the complexities of denominational rules, of the difference between a wedding and the blessing of a civil union, between a mainline denomination or the gay-founded Metropolitan Community Church. The image is powerful: two men, or two women, standing at an altar in front of a cleric clad in vestments. Swislow's vision of a church reassured by no attempt to compel gay weddings is hard to square with the open warfare now under way inside many denominations over the status and recognition of gay people and gay unions.

It will not surprise you to learn that Swislow's assurances of strict separation between county clerk and state hold no comfort for Cobb: "You're also seeing some churches and pastors engage in this more than others, because they are able to see the potential threat to religion. By that I mean they are watching, as in Canada, where same sex marriage is acceptable. They fear that if gay marriage is legalized, and they don't go along with it, they will be accused of fomenting hatred," and liable for arrest and prosecution. Her suggestion seemed a little far-fetched, but in the tightly interconnected world of threats perceived by conservative Christian churches and advocacy groups, it makes perfect sense. Cobb explained, "If hate crime laws are acceptable, then pastors in this country can see that and say, 'I won't be able to preach that homosexuality is wrong, I won't be able to preach that gay marriage is wrong, according to my convictions and tenets of faith.' "

I asked Cobb if there was a serious threat of anti-gay-marriage pastors dragged from their pulpits under hate crime laws. How serious, she would not say: "That is a consequence connected to societies that have normalized gay marriage. Would it happen? Could it happen? We oppose hate crime legislation, as applied to a lifestyle behavior choice, specifically because of the threats it poses to churches."

Despite polls in motion, Richard Land, of the Southern Baptist Convention, told me he was convinced heterosexuals-only is one social convention that simply will not change. If the other side happens to win some victories, that won't be the end of it either: "We'll just come back and try to convince them that they're wrong. But we're going to abide by the law, particularly when it's law enacted by the people's representatives. But I wouldn't hold my breath. I don't know how old you are, but I wouldn't see it in your lifetime."

Swislow said, in response, that the change is already happening. "What was interesting and incredibly moving is that when the prior amendment was defeated in September 2005, many, many people changed their votes. Members of the legislature who a year earlier voted against marriage and for civil unions, this time voted for marriage.

"Some of them stood up in the chamber and said, 'My religion, not the church, said this is the right thing to do.' Many Roman Catholic legislators voted against the constitutional amendment saying, 'This is the right thing to do.' There's a split between hierarchy and the laity on this one."

Years after her wedding, and legally closer to defeating efforts to turn back the clock, Swislow still does not think the battle is over. Catholic Charities informed Massachusetts the social service agency would no longer handle adoptions under the terms of its state contract because of the legally established adoption rights for gay couples. Governor Mitt Romney, a Republican, spent years trying to convince party members nationally that he might have been governor, but did not approve of what was going on in his own state. He has tried to pass a bill allowing Catholic Charities to continue adoption placements without doing business with gay couples. Said Swislow, "It's not a surprise that he's pandering to the religious right. They're giving up their contract to do adoptions, and legislative leaders are saying there's no chance that Romney's bill is going to pass."

In 2006, the New Hampshire legislature voted against an amendment to the state's Bill of Rights that would have defined marriage as the union between a man and a woman. After a lopsided 207–125 House vote, the measure's cosponsor in the upper house, Senator Jack Barnes, decided not to pursue the amendment further: " 'The people' is the third rail in politics, and obviously the people that voted against it didn't want to hit the third rail."

The House sponsor, Congressman Michael Balboni, asked lawmakers to pass the amendment "if you believe as I believe that no governmental body should redefine what has been mankind's definition of the marital union for thousands of years. That four unelected individuals in the state of Massachusetts usurped legislative authority and took it upon themselves to unilaterally redefine marriage for the millions living in that state." Balboni was using an increasingly central weapon in the anti-gay-marriage arsenal: resentment of the courts and for judicial review.

In this argument, it is only legislative action and voter initiative that constitute legitimate lawmaking authority. After she questioned the legality of judges ruling in favor of gay plaintiffs on equal-protection grounds, for the third time in our conversation, I asked Cobb, "Do you think *Brown v. Board of Education of Topeka* would have been endorsed by Virginia voters?"

Some Virginia counties closed their public schools entirely rather than integrate. The state fought a rearguard action against integration that lasted into the 1960s, all resulting from Supreme Court action rather than that of the Virginia legislature. Cobb's reply was the answer to a different question: "I will say this, there are many African Americans who find it appalling that gay rights is framed as a civil rights issue. There's never been a day when homosexuals have been denied the kind of rights black people were denied in this country. There have never been separate water fountains, separate schools. There is no comparison between the struggle for civil rights and the homosexual agenda."

She continued, "Everyone has a right to marriage. Everyone has that right. And we all have restrictions as to whom we can marry. I can't marry a child. I can't marry someone who is already married." I pointed out that along with age restrictions and laws against bigamy, until the Supreme Court's ruling in *Loving v. Virginia,* a black person could not marry a white person in the state of Virginia. Again, it took a court to clear the way for something voters would not have approved. "You're right," said Cobb. "But in that case we were still talking about marriage between a man and a woman."

Just as Swislow and gay legal advocates believe the opposition will not give up or give in, Cobb believes the same of her opponents. "There's no question that they have lost in every legislature, and continue to go to court. It's a long battle. Here in Virginia we have already put into a law a ban on same sex marriage. We have already done those things. But because those that oppose marriage have lost in the legislature, they have gone to court."

Should constitutionally guaranteed rights be put to a vote? Swislow said, "Voters always want to vote on everything, but one of the things I love about America is the Constitution. I wish it was more clear from civics classes—if people even take civics classes—that we have a constitution that protects minority rights. The courts system protects minorities through guarantees in state and federal constitutions. There are certain things that shouldn't be voted on by the country, and that's one of them.

"If our constitution guarantees that right, then it shouldn't be voted on. Sure, I would like public opinion to move so I think we should win that vote. Certain things shouldn't get put to a vote . . . I don't think we want to go down that road. I would like to see things change so that a majority would approve if it were put to a vote.

"Still, I don't think fundamental rights should ever be put up to a vote."

The fear and resentment of having gay marriage injected into society's bloodstream by the courts alone should not be dismissed as some dark obsession of conspiracy theorists or the fundamentalist fringe. For all the lampooning from left of center of conservative America (and yes, that is a two-way street), the people who believe the America they knew and understood has been slipping away from them have a rational and well-earned distrust of judges. The millions of Americans who believe the country is in the midst of a long walk to decadence see the road we are on paved by court cases.

How were the Lord's Prayer and the Bible kicked out of school? *Abington v. Schempp*. How were states prohibited from banning abortion? *Roe v. Wade*. How could judges decide that we couldn't make gay sex a crime anymore? *Lawrence and Garner v. Texas*. Did judges decide we couldn't have the Ten Commandments posted in our schools in Kentucky? Just read *McCreary County v. American Civil Liberties Union of Kentucky*. The feeling social conservatives have of standing on unstable ground, heaving and cracking and ready to bust apart, is real. They need reassurance—and soon—that the courts are not enemies of their liberty and peace, but guarantors of both.

The conservative argument for gay marriage, articulated by the closely reasoned and heartfelt books by writers like Jonathan Rauch, Andrew Sullivan, and Bruce Bawer,[3] does not want to bash down the barriers of separate treatment and exclusion purely out of an equal rights–equal protection motivation, though those are not entirely absent. Marriage, they suggest, is good for gay people for the same reasons it is good for straight people. These authors reassure conservatives through their insistence that the subset of gay people who want to be married (by no means do all want marriage) desire all the stability, mutual care, and security that their opponents say heterosexuals find in marriage.

The very "two-ness" of marriage, its status as a civil and contractual relationship, along with its deep parallel traditions as a religious rite, creates an entrée into the battle for conservative Christians who seek to control the terms of debate by excluding the mechanistic and legal from their emotional appeals, training their fire almost exclusively on the rights and status of children and the inherent sinfulness of homosexuality.

As has been noted in earlier chapters, injecting religion into public policy making in a diverse society ends up pitting contestants against one another who speak to the issue in mutually incomprehensible languages and bring mutually exclusive worldviews to the battlefield. In their campaigns against gay marriages, conservative Christians always return to the refrain that it has long been established that the ideal home in which to raise children is an intact one featuring a married mother and father. In their ripostes, pro-gay-marriage activists contend that many gay households already feature children, biological and adopted, so the point is a moot one. In addition, many more gay households will remain permanently childless, rendering the social science on intact families irrelevant and, at the very least, a rebuke to the millions of straight couples who already enjoy full marriage rights and end up fighting over their children in court. The result is stasis. That the ideal family in economic and social terms features married parents never contends with the internal contradiction that thousands of gay parents would be married, if only they were allowed.

You should not be sure that blocking the right to marriage with a cornerstone argument about children for a heavily childless interest group is a contradiction, Victoria Cobb warned. "If marriage rights were extended to homosexuals, government could not deny them the right to raise children. And children are not some private matter. The reason the government has a vested interest is simple. Governments end up having to pay for, and tend to, the consequences of fatherlessness. Those include children born out of wedlock, children who fail at school, and abusive parents." Is Cobb asking gays who want to be married to pay the freight for the failures of countless heterosexual couples?

Cobb answers by likening opening marriage to gays to other tinkering with "traditional" social forms over the last fifty years. "I'll give you an example: no-fault divorce. In the sixties, all the cultural trends, all the pseudo-science, was saying children would fare better if their parents were able to split more easily, lower the level of conflict in the home, and seek personal happiness. Forty years later that is a completely failed social experiment." Her point is that twenty-first-century America should be more risk averse and not repeat with gays new approaches to marriage that have weakened the institution.

Paul Rimassa is an Episcopal priest who runs the Center for Sexuality and Religion in Wayne, Pennsylvania. As he watches the Roman Catholic Church, in which he was raised, wrestle with sexuality and celibacy among clergy and his adopted church in a destructive family feud over homosexuality and ordination, he wishes all the combatants would get back to basics: "God looks upon homosexuals and heterosexuals equally. The bottom line is not so much how we procreate biologically. That's proven down through the centuries to be very easy to do. It's been done many times to produce children, and not produced loving relationships either for the parents or for the children. What God wants us to do is procreate, but just as importantly, to nurture our offspring and nurture one another, and that's being done by straight and homosexual couples."

Embedded in Rimassa's call for tolerance is a deep truth that is not often acknowledged by either side in the debate: the profound effect of decoupling the sex act from pregnancy and child-rearing. The refinement of mechanical and pharmacological approaches to birth control, the biological impossibility of conception during homosexual activity, the continuation of sexual relations long after menopause, and the postponement of child-rearing by many couples until later and later in life have all moved in tandem with biological and legal structures in creating new and challenging ways of being a parent.

You can have children and not raise them, raise children and not have them, raise children born on the other side of the planet, and raise children begun with your own biological material but nurtured until the day of labor and delivery in the body of a total stranger. One reason that the infertility of gay unions is no longer so commonly thrown in their faces as a rebuke and "proof" of God's disfavor has to be that a number of straight people are also coming to parenthood in ways never imagined by the prophets, apostles, and martyrs of old. Our ethical and legal systems are playing catch-up in a world where long postmenopausal women can deliver children, and an unrelated person can carry a married couple's child.

It is often asserted in these debates that marriage is an institution shaped for the human family by unchanging truths, not open to change, challenge, or renegotiation. American women who fill the ranks of activists working against gay marriage by saying marriage has not been fundamentally changed over time would be horrified to be sold by their own families to their new husband. The idea that their husbands would have to speak for them in public, that they could be ordered to make room for another wife in the home or excluded from raising their children after weaning on the insistence of their husbands, would not sit well in these first decades of the twenty-first century. These women may be on much firmer ground proclaiming, not that marriage is an unchanged institution, but that after years of battering and devaluation, this is one change it will not be able to sustain.

Those who work against gay marriage from a religious point of view are deeply burrowed into America's churches but every bit as deeply invested in America's politics, and understand that the opportunity to present gay marriage as a threat to straight marriage slips a tiny bit more from their grasp with every subsequent marriage of two men or two women. If politics is the art of creating electoral or issue-based coalitions out of great masses of people, religion can also be a way of creating identity and solidarity out of the vast millions.

For Christian churches to create a social "other" out of gay Americans is becoming a bigger challenge than it might appear at first glance. Gay people do not live in some unknown city on the opposite side of the planet. They did not land here in small numbers from a place that we do not know or understand. So while their sexual "otherness" can be waved in your face like a bright pink flag, gay Americans were and are our brothers and sisters, aunts and uncles, sons and daughters, and mothers and fathers. The mantle of "otherness" fits badly on the shoulders of people you know as well as your own two hands.

The tectonic shift under the feet of Massachusetts citizens described by Lee Swislow since gay marriage became legal there is well understood by her opponents. That is the reason for the frantic organization and the fevered description of threat as lobbyists head to state legislatures around the country. That gradual shift toward acceptance also makes me wonder whether Richard Land is right about never seeing widespread recognition of gay unions in America in my lifetime.

The conservative Christians who form the foundation of the Bush electoral coalition know this fight is a long one and take heart from the fact that they have won far more often than they have lost. Meanwhile Swislow has seen the gradual drop in strong opposition reflected in public opinion research as being more significant than the much slower rise in support. "Generally, people don't want any one religion or group of religions imposing their morality on the rest of us. A lot of the religious opposition to marriage equality is based on a morality that sees homosexuals as fundamentally immoral, and sinful, and wrong. If you hammer home that message enough, people get desensitized. I'm not surprised to see opposition dropping. After a while, if you don't share that strong revulsion for gay people, you say, well actually, why not?"

The Reverend Rimassa does not see gay marriage on the horizon, but thinks a form of legal recognition for gay unions is inevitable . . . eventually: "I think it's going to be a long time from now. I've learned never to say never, but I think it's going to be a while. What we end up with in this country may not be called marriage. I'm going to use the word marriage, but it may work itself out differently down the line." What gay people win will be more in the civil realm than the religious, even if people continue to change their minds, Rimassa said. "Those legalized unions, as opposed to, say, marriage as a religious document, come to the heart and soul of where people live anyway. It does not eliminate them from being married in the eyes of God."

Marriage was a strictly civil affair until the church took it over, Rimassa said. At the heart of the commitment are the partners, not the church or the state. "Two people marry one another in their exchange of vows. They are just as married in their promises to each other as if they made them in front of a priest or rabbi."

The campaign against further civil rights for homosexuals in all spheres of daily life—employment, housing, property, marriage and so on—cannot be removed from the overall approach toward sex held by conservative Christian churches and their activist allies. Conservative Protestants and Roman Catholics, together with a majority of American Christians, have become more sex-positive in recent decades, affirming the part in the natural order and the role in the mutual joy of a couple that sex provides.[4] However, that aspect of human life can be located only inside marriage. It is illicit everywhere else.

Many gay people want to find a way to live their lives with the fidelity, dignity, and mutual affection expected and celebrated in heterosexual marriage, and have their union protected by law. That means, by definition, that a legal architecture for their lives together must be built without the approval of many of the largest and most influential religious groups in the United States. These groups will not drop their opposition unless their purely religious prerogatives are protected in any new legal approach to gay marriage in the civil realm. Without that protection, the pros and the antis may just have fought their way to a draw, and a long stalemate.

Republicans have been watching the currents in American religion and American integration very closely and have worked very hard to woo a new and unexpected set of tiebreakers into their camp. Blacks and Latinos are creating new churches and enlivening old ones. How their religious lives intersect with politics may be a critical issue in a rapidly browning America. We'll explore that in chapter eleven.

Our next stop is another one of the hottest of the hot buttons, the Ten Commandments.

SIX

Take Two Tablets ...
And Call Me When the Fighting Starts

YOU REMEMBER THE SCENE: Amid thunder and smoke, God tells Charlton Heston what the children of Israel must, and must not, do. Fingers of flame rip through rough-hewn stone, and Aramaic characters appear, even as God himself speaks English to Chuck Heston. And there you have it. Law. Right from an actor's lips, to Cecil B. DeMille's microphones, to the lawn of the Texas State Capitol.

I am not making fun of the prophet Moses, the Children of Israel, or the Creator, YHWH. I have roughly sketched out the path of the great law of the Decalogue from Mount Sinai, to a "theater near you," to the home of the Texas legislature. That is because, boys and girls, the monument that became the subject of the Supreme Court's 2005 ruling on display of the Ten Commandments in public places was not sparked by a religious artist seeking to display his devotional work in a public place or a zealous legislator seeking to force his personal code of ethics onto a public park. Nope, the Texas Ten Commandments lawsuit begins with the cinematic Ten Commandments.

The monument that graces the outside of the Texas Capitol was part of the publicity for the DeMille masterpiece, and monuments just like it are outside courthouses and government buildings around the country through the good offices of Paramount Pictures and the Fraternal Order of Eagles. Eagles from aeries (lodges) across America sold tickets, did advance publicity, held bake sales and car washes, to raise money for the monoliths, and a portion of all the ticket sales in a given area went to underwrite the costs of the biblical code.

Volunteerism enthusiastically met commerce, and then dragged government into the proceedings. As a result of court cases around the country various counties and municipalities moved their monoliths to privately owned land to avoid the lawsuits and the hassle. Texas never had. So it happened that a homeless attorney named Thomas van Orden sued the governor of Texas, Rick Perry, to get the Ten Commandments monument removed from the grounds of the state capitol.

Van Orden alleged that having the stone carving on the lawn of a state building violated the establishment clause of the First Amendment, that is, "congress shall make no law respecting an establishment of religion." The question is as simple as that: Does having a monument depicting the core moral teachings of Texas's majority religion on the lawn of the home of the state legislature imply that Christianity is, in fact, the state religion?

Different arguments have swirled around this and similar questions for years. The answers have at times been evasive, at times disingenuous. Some local officials have answered that the Ten Commandments depiction was merely meant as historical representation and not as a religious installation at all. It has been argued that because the Decalogue forms the basis for our legal code, this is a foundational historical text, and therefore any assessment of its public display should look beyond its religious content.

It is impossible to peer into the hearts of the lawyers who make these assertions to establish whether they believe these statements are true, or are merely tactical or casual pieces of sophistry meant to fudge a difficult argument. Honest or not, these assertions do contain testable propositions.

Are the Ten Commandments the basis for American law, as is so often alleged during political debates? The basis for most of the national legal code and that of the various other jurisdictions around the country is English common law. Sure enough, theft, adultery, murder, and perjury are all against the law, and those laws have deep roots in common law.

However, God handed down far more than prohibitions against murder, theft, and adultery when he came to Moses and the Children of Israel at Sinai. The very first thing he did was forbid them to worship any other gods but himself. Though that is the first of all the commands, laws that in return for compliance with God promised long and happy lives, not believing in the Creator of Hebrew scripture is not against the law anywhere in the United States.

In both of the encounters with God in which the commands are transmitted to the people, Yahweh also mentions that you should not make any object to represent him or any object to be worshipped. Again, this is not against the law anywhere in America. Taking the name of the Lord in vain might not be in good taste and certainly is a good way to offend others, but is not against the law nationally or, as the Constitution sometimes says, "in the several states."

The Decalogue continues with reminders to keep the seventh day of the week holy, set apart from the other six days in which you go to work and pursue your normal activities. If anything, the legal momentum of the last half-century has been strongly against the enforcement of so-called blue laws that restrict the kinds of commerce conducted on Sunday, the Christian Sabbath.

While honoring your father and mother might be (a) good manners, (b) decent behavior, (c) advisable for a peaceful and happy family, reverence toward one's parents is not the law of the land or of any jurisdiction in America. After the already agreed-upon proscriptions against theft, murder, adultery, and bearing false witness, we arrive at thought crime.

Envying the possessions of the people you know is forbidden by God. It is understandable that a creator would not want his people to be consumed by desire for the things that others have. It is corrosive to the human spirit, an exhausting emotion, to want the things that others have in a way that leaves you unable to be thankful for the things that you have.

That's the idealists' version, anyway.

We are reminded twenty-four hours a day in our culture that desire for things is one of the most powerful forces in human life. Of our two main national parties, it is the one that has tried to carve out the greatest space in the public sphere for religion that also believes that human desire for things is a powerful and motivating emotion.

I don't tell you all this to belabor a pedantic riff on the irrelevance of the Ten Commandments. They are a constant call to a more decent life for all who believe in God's call to humanity to love neighbor as self and God above all. But what if you don't believe that?

Or what if you believe in many of the constituent parts of the Ten Commandments, but not all of them? What if you believe that murder and theft are wrong, but do not believe a god ever had to tell humanity that to make it true?

There are now tens of millions of Americans who tell public opinion researchers they have no religion. We should all hope that they are willing to obey the laws, too. What gets you to follow the law may be different from what motivates your next-door neighbor, the woman in the next cubicle at work, or the driver in the car in front of you.

In countries where the God of Abraham, Isaac, and Jacob, of Sarah and Ruth, is not revered, not believed in, not cited as the source of law, are bad things still illegal? Let's check.

Thailand is a kingdom of 64 million people, 95 percent of them Theravada Buddhists. The first monarch, King Rama Thibodi, established the legal code and the Buddhist faith, basing Thai law on Hindu and traditional beliefs. Murder, theft, and lying under oath are all illegal, though the Ten Commandments handed down in Hebrew scripture have little relevance to Thai daily life and virtually no relationship to the country's history.

In India a national court system sits above a complex network of local courts following tribal and local customs. In some areas there are also Islamic courts. Over a billion Indians live in a country a third the size of the United States. Though the overwhelming majority of Indians are Hindu, the country's modern history has kept a strong tradition of nonsectarian civil service and judiciary. For centuries in India, theft, murder, and adultery have been illegal, but this was most recently reiterated in the 1973 Code of Criminal Procedures. Despite a long sojourn in India by the British Empire, with an established church headed by the monarch, Christian customs took little root in Indian life.

In Russia, ruled by an avowedly atheist government for most of the last century, the 1993 constitution reiterates the secular nature of the state.[1] In article 20, the constitution codifies the right to life.

The fight over the Ten Commandments often appears to have nothing to do with God's commands themselves and everything to do with contemporary politics. Once again, the politics of self-representation and the politics of stake-pounding are at work on the walls of Kentucky public buildings and on the lawn of a Texas government building. The idea is to pound a marker into the ground or on a wall and say, "This thing is mine. It is for you to decide whether we share it or not. By pounding this stake in the ground, I force you to react. But I get to make the first play. You may be a relative newcomer to our country. You may be a Christian or a Jew, or not. But this thing . . . this courthouse, this school, this government building, represents the power to represent that is controlled by my group. You decide. Either you're in or you're out."

The implied exclusion perceived by religious outsiders in Christian-majority America is not conceded to be an issue by those searching for more opportunities to display religious texts in public places. They may fully understand it. They may not. Either way, no careful warrior in this fight will say into a microphone or to a waiting reporter with a notepad, "Do I realize that Muslims/Hindus/atheists/Jews do not subscribe to or believe in the ideas expressed in that document? I sure do! That's the whole point!"

The Reverend Martin Marty, as a theologian and Lutheran pastor, reveres the Ten Commandments. He also laughs when he reflects on the efforts to place them, or take them off, public places of display. "If this was about the Ten Commandments, you would see them on front lawns all over America. You don't. The whole point is to send a message by putting it in a prominent public place."

In the recent Ten Commandments court cases, it became important for the justices to understand motive in order to pass judgment on the message itself. Both the strict separationists and the religious-display supporters used previous legal opinions, public statements of those involved in placing the Commandments in the first place, and religious statements of this country's founders.

In the briefs, pleadings, and marshaling of history, the Ten Commandments were given multiple and contradictory historical roles to play: the Decalogue was understood to be holy writ, posted for a religious purpose, posted for a merely historic purpose, meant to communicate a message to modern Americans, not meant to send that same message, and hilariously edited in their effect. Is the meaning of "I am the Lord thy God. Thou shalt have no other Gods before me," anything *but* religious?

It has repeatedly been pointed out by all sides in this tug-of-war that Moses the lawgiver holds two tablets in displays carved into the walls of the Supreme Court itself. Okay. Swell. Hammurabi, Napoleon, and Confucius are up there, too, but no one is trying to plant the Code of Hammurabi on the lawns of state supreme courts around the country, post the Code Napoleon on schoolhouse walls, or install a two-ton granite sculpture depicting Draco's Athenian law code in the lobby of the Alabama Supreme Court. The combatants on both sides of the question fully understand why. Though Western law has many inspirations and influences, as acknowledged by the Supreme Court Building's architects, contemporary debates all seem to boil those influences down to the Ten Commandments.

Splitting the baby, if you will excuse the Old Testament reference, becomes the order of the day. In his opinion in the Texas Capitol case, Chief Justice Rehnquist wrote, "Of course, the Ten Commandments are religious—they were so viewed at their inception and so remain. The monument, therefore, has religious significance. According to Judeo-Christian belief, the Ten Commandments were given to Moses by God on Mt. Sinai. But Moses was a lawgiver as well as a religious leader. And the Ten Commandments have an undeniable historical meaning, as the foregoing examples demonstrate. Simply having religious content or promoting a message consistent with a religious doctrine does not run afoul of the Establishment Clause." Consistent with a religious doctrine? Or a religious doctrine in and of itself?

Justice Clarence Thomas concurred with the chief and set a very high bar for violating the constitutional prohibition of an established American faith: "In no sense does Texas compel petitioner Van Orden to do anything.

The only injury to him is that he takes offense at seeing the monument as he passes it on his way to the Texas Supreme Court Library. He need not stop to read it or even to look at it, let alone to express support for it or adopt the Commandments as guides for his life. The mere presence of the monument along his path involves no coercion and thus does not violate the Establishment Clause."

When I walk the attractive and interesting grounds of the Texas Capitol in Austin, I find little that is erected there to have no effect, communicate no larger message, or reinforce no larger truth. The monuments all seem to have a point. If the Commandments installation had as little communicative power as Justice Thomas would indicate, you would have to wonder why its defenders worked so hard to keep it there.

Shortly thereafter in his opinion, Justice Thomas, an adult convert to Roman Catholicism, punctures a hole in the disingenuous attempts to relocate God's law, given to his people on Mount Sinai, in some location other than religion. By so rigorously defining the establishment clause, making it almost inviolable short of President Bush appointing bishops and performing exorcisms, he is free to openly allow more religious display. His concurrence has little sympathy for pussyfooting around the core question, so he criticizes "the Court's precedent attempts to avoid declaring all religious symbols and words of longstanding tradition unconstitutional, by counterfactually declaring them of little religious significance. Even when the Court's cases recognize that such symbols have religious meaning, they adopt an unhappy compromise that fails fully to account for either the adherent's or the non-adherent's beliefs, and provides no principled way to choose between them. Even worse, the incoherence of the Court's decisions in this area renders the Establishment Clause impenetrable and incapable of consistent application."

Justice Thomas sees clearly how long years of attempts to split the difference have left no one happy, and concludes what is needed is a clearer message that will leave only strict separationists unhappy. Do not try to keep the monument on the lawn by saying it does not mean anything, advises Justice Thomas. Go for broke. Admit it means plenty, keep it there, and declare that it, though it has a clear meaning and message, is incapable of implying that the state of Texas endorses the Ten Commandments for the inward digestion of its citizens or recommends following those ten laws.

In his bracing dissent, Justice John Paul Stevens shows he, too, wants words to mean what they mean and comes to the opposite conclusion from his colleague Justice Thomas. "The sole function of the monument on the grounds of Texas' State Capitol is to display the full text of one version of the Ten Commandments."

The opinion then runs through, for those who might have forgotten, what the Commandments actually command, one through ten. Then Justice Stevens makes a series of simple and unremarkable declarations:

> Viewed on its face, Texas' display has no purported connection to God's role in the formation of Texas or the founding of our Nation; nor does it provide the reasonable observer with any basis to guess that it was erected to honor any individual or organization. The message transmitted by Texas' chosen display is quite plain: This State endorses the divine code of the "Judeo-Christian" God.
>
> For those of us who learned to recite the King James version of the text long before we understood the meaning of some of its words, God's Commandments may seem like wise counsel. The question before this Court, however, is whether it is counsel that the State of Texas may proclaim without violating the Establishment Clause of the Constitution. If any fragment of Jefferson's metaphorical "wall of separation between church and State" is to be preserved—if there remains any meaning to the "wholesome neutrality" of which this Court's Establishment Clause cases speak—a negative answer to that question is mandatory.

To his credit, Justice Stevens takes the Commandments out of the abstract realm and plants his reasoning as firmly in the soil of the state grounds as the monument erected by the Fraternal Order of Eagles in the first place. Riffing off the briefs and oral arguments, he moves from the purely speculative realm to a stone carving of Moses' law, put up by real people in a real place at a particular time with very specific stated reasons:

> *The desire to combat juvenile delinquency by providing guidance to youths is both admirable and unquestionably secular. But achieving that goal through biblical teachings injects a religious purpose into an otherwise secular endeavor. By spreading the word of God and converting heathens to Christianity, missionaries expect to enlighten their converts, enhance their satisfaction with life, and improve their behavior. Similarly, by disseminating the "law of God"—directing fidelity to God and proscribing murder, theft, and adultery—the Eagles hope that this divine guidance will help wayward youths conform their behavior and improve their lives.*

For Justice Stevens, there is just no getting around it. The Commandments are a religious text, they appear in a prominent public location for a religious reason, and they imply by their very installation that the state of Texas endorses the source and the message itself. Though the opinion in *Van Orden v. Perry* did not stray there, it would be difficult, if not impossible, to find a member of the Texas house or senate who would declare publicly that the Ten Commandments outside their offices on the lawn are not meant to communicate a moral truth to the people of Texas. Indeed, dissent draws a contrast between the whole of the people of Texas and the legislators who work inside: "I do not doubt that some Texans, including those elected to the Texas Legislature, may believe that the statues displayed on the Texas Capitol grounds, including the Ten Commandments monument, reflect the 'ideals . . . that compose Texan identity.' "[2] But Texas, like our entire country, is now a much more diversified community than it was when it became a part of the United States or even when the monument was erected.

Today there are many Texans who do not believe in the God whose commandments are displayed at their seat of government. Many of them worship a different god or no god at all. Some may believe that the account of creation in the Book of Genesis is less reliable than the views of men such as Darwin and Einstein. The monument is no more an expression of the views of every true Texan than was the "Live Free or Die" motto, which the state of New Hampshire placed on its license plates in 1969, an accurate expression of the views of every citizen of New Hampshire. Though "Live Free or Die" might seem a narrow choice to Granite Staters, it has no religious content. But Justice Stevens did not prevail. A five-vote majority led by the chief justice won the day. The Fraternal Order of Eagles' message of Torah truth remains on the capitol grounds in Austin.

But the Ten Commandments on the walls of Kentucky schools did not survive that day's court opinions. You might say Moses went one-for-two on that day in 2005. The case had some similarities to the Texas case, but some differences that ended up carrying the day.

In the case called *McCreary County v. the American Civil Liberties Union of Kentucky,* the state was forced to defend its decision to post the Ten Commandments, what it called their "precedent legal code," on the walls of every courthouse in two counties. Under pressure, the state had added other documents over the years to dilute the presence of an excerpt of Scripture, but it was demonstrated in briefs and argument that the state authorities' original intent in making the installation was to transmit a religious message to Kentuckians.[3] That sealed the Commandments' doom on the walls of Kentucky public buildings.

Again the vote was 5–4. Justice Antonin Scalia, on the winning side in Texas, was now writing in furious dissent. He assembled a long list of historic quotes from Framers and Founders, including Washington, Jefferson, and Madison. The acknowledgments of a Supreme Being were found in private letters and public proclamations. Certainly if the matter under dispute had been whether many of the founders of the United States believed in God, Justice Scalia would stand on solid bedrock. However, what he was trying to demonstrate was that the founders' understandings of who was being invoked by references to God could be extended to what was on their minds when they wrote, debated, and ratified the Constitution of the United States. Justice Scalia argues against Justice Stevens's dissent in the Texas case in which Stevens warns against a Christian understanding of sacred texts in public displays:

> *All of the actions of Washington and the First Congress upon which I have relied, virtually all Thanksgiving Proclamations throughout our history, and all the other examples of our Government's favoring religion that I have cited, have invoked God, but not Jesus Christ. Rather than relying upon Justice Stevens' assurance that "the original understanding of the type of 'religion' that qualified for constitutional protection under the First Amendment certainly did not include . . . followers of Judaism and Islam," I would prefer to take the word of George Washington, who, in his famous Letter to the Hebrew Congregation of Newport, Rhode Island, wrote that, "All possess alike liberty of conscience and immunities of citizenship. It is now no more that toleration is spoken of, as if it was by the indulgence of one class of people, that another enjoyed the exercise of their inherent natural rights."* [4]

He goes on to quote more of President Washington's famous letter to the Jewish congregation of Newport, Rhode Island. That is an interesting view into the sentiments of the first president, perhaps, but hardly a pillar of constitutional law.

Justice David Souter was not buying what his colleague down the bench was selling. Washington may very well have sent cordial greetings to a Jewish congregation in New England, but that does not change history, he writes.

> *While the dissent fails to show a consistent original understanding from which to argue that the neutrality principle should be rejected, it does manage to deliver a surprise. As*

mentioned, the dissent says that the deity the Framers had in mind was the God of monotheism, with the consequence that government may espouse a tenet of traditional monotheism. This is truly a remarkable view.

Other members of the Court have dissented on the ground that the Establishment Clause bars nothing more than governmental preference for one religion over another, but at least religion has previously been treated inclusively. Today's dissent, however, apparently means that government should be free to approve the core beliefs of a favored religion over the tenets of others, a view that should trouble anyone who prizes religious liberty. Certainly history cannot justify it; on the contrary, history shows that the religion of concern to the Framers was not that of the monotheistic faiths generally, but Christianity in particular, a fact that no member of this Court takes as a premise for construing the Religion Clauses. Justice Story probably reflected the thinking of the framing generation when he wrote in his Commentaries that the purpose of the Clause was "not to countenance, much less to advance, Mahometanism[5] or Judaism, or infidelity[6] by prostrating Christianity; but to exclude all rivalry among Christian sects."

The restrained and genteel reasoning, the judicial jujitsu of Supreme Court opinions, made useful journeys into the country's intellectual and legal history. Outside the stately confines of the court, the message contained in *Van Orden* and *McCreary* reverberated around the airwaves, in print and in electrons. The split decision allowed citizens on both ends of the continuum of church-state arguments to declare victory and cry foul.

Also well away from counting secular angels dancing atop separationist pins are the public antics of Judge Roy Moore of Alabama, the so-called "Ten Commandments Judge," who fought to keep a monument to the Mosaic law in his courthouse. The monument, Moore's crusade, and eventual removal are all covered in chapter eleven.

What is a constant source of fascination to me is the degree to which people express the need to find validation of their own personal beliefs in the action of the government. Culturally, they would appear to be working at cross-purposes with themselves. In recent decades, Christian conservatives have consistently spoken to their publics in a strong antigovernment tone. Government, in their narrative, is not the distilled will of all the people. It is not an institution in which we all share ownership, pride in its successes, and shame in its failures. Instead, government is an appliqué, slapped onto the outside of the essential core of American life, remote, alien, self-ratifying, and often hostile to the dearly held beliefs and desires of ordinary Americans.

Sitting atop the pile of alien forces, imposed upon good Christian folk by outside powers, is the court system. Christian conservatives regularly castigate the very concept of judicial review, that is, the idea that individual citizens can challenge the constitutionality of legislative statute through the courts. As we have noted elsewhere, one of the most inflaming aspects of current battles over social issues like gay marriage is the role of the courts, as much as the core conflict itself.

Jesus and the Gospels, Moses and the prophets, Paul and the disciples, are all silent about judicial review. The secular demigods of America's history, the founders (or at least the avowedly Christian ones), were not silent on judicial review. What's more, the early generations of the American national government and the judicial branch came to some accomodation on this idea, not recently, but two hundred years ago. *Marbury v. Madison,* the case widely credited with establishing judicial review beyond legal assault, was decided in 1803, when the Supreme Court under John Marshall (also up there in the Supreme Court friezes with Moses and Napoleon) ruled that the court can invalidate any law that is repugnant to the Constitution.

Back then, the November presidential elections were not finalized until February, and the new president not sworn until March. In the few weeks between the ratification of his defeat and the inaugural of his successor and rival, Thomas Jefferson, President John Adams appointed forty-two Federalist partisans to judgeships. The jurists were ratified by a

123

Federalist-dominated lame-duck Congress the day before the new president took office.

In a bizarre complicating factor, Chief Justice John Marshall had to judge the handiwork of Secretary of State John Marshall. The chief justice had taken office the same day as Jefferson, after serving as Adams's secretary of state. The new president had treated twenty-five of the forty-two new appointments as void as of his first day on the job, and one of the spurned jurists, William Marbury, a newly appointed justice of the peace in the District of Columbia, sued to keep his job.

The Marshall court, then just six judges strong, decided against Marbury and the out-of-work judges.

Treasured symbolic signs, like "under God" in the Pledge of Allegiance, "In God We Trust" on national currency, and posted religious messages in public places have more and more become the *casi belli,* the "occasions for war," in the struggle over separationism, and the courts the battlefield.

I asked former U.S. senator and Episcopal priest John Danforth about the battles over the Ten Commandments in public places. "I have seen this as just being not a big issue. There are some true-believing church-state separatists, you know, to the point where they don't want 'In God We Trust' to be on the currency, for example. I mean there are people who are just really into that. On the other hand, there are people who believe that, make this point—I think there's a case on this—that the 'One Nation Under God' in the Pledge of Allegiance is the establishment of religion. And so they file lawsuits about it. So it's a kind of a hypersensitivity to the issue, which is not me.

"I mean I certainly support the separation of church and state. But there are people who are . . . the true-blue separatists, like the no-currency people, on one hand. But on the other hand, there are people who believe that we must put God back in our schools. Or we must put God back on our lawns or whatever, as though the future of faith depends on the public, on these, what I would say, kind of minor issues.

"They gather on the steps of a building and pray and so on, and hold up signs all related to whether the Ten Commandments is in the courthouse in Alabama or wherever it is; they're very invested in it. So they think that they're fighting a bigger battle on a very little field."

I then asked the senator if he could imagine walking into a courthouse in Alabama, not a believer of any sort, or a Muslim, a Hindu, or a Ba'hai. Greeting you in the rotunda are 5,200 pounds of Ten Commandments. Would you walk into that courtroom convinced that you, a member of a minority religion, are going to get a fair shake? He answered without hesitation, "I would be more worried about the case I had than about that."

He then followed up with a wider point. "I don't think that the future of the faith or the future of the country depends on a Ten Commandments monument being in a courthouse. On the other hand I don't think that the fact that a Ten Commandments monument is in the courthouse means that the walls of separation have come crumbling down and we've somehow developed a theocracy."

So, as befits his long career in politics, the Reverend Danforth ends up between two hotly conflicted camps in a current controversy. The Reverend Rick Scarborough, a Baptist pastor and influential evangelical leader, told his followers he sees very important things at stake after the twin 5–4 decisions on the Commandments: "We will continue to work for the right to display that document, which is the moral foundation of America, and for the right of all Americans to publicly affirm the sovereignty of the Creator, just as the Founding Fathers did in the Declaration of Independence."

Scarborough knows any American can hang the Ten Commandments anywhere and in any form on his or her property. He or she can post them in any language, as a scroll, on stone tablets, or painted as a fresco on the façade of their home. The question is, does it belong on public property, owned by all of us, paid for and maintained by all of us? He dismissed the arguments of the majority in *McCreary v. the ACLU of Kentucky,* criticizing the "liberals' " reasoning that an avowedly religious display was a "violation of their fictitious doctrine of church-state separation (words which appear nowhere in the Constitution)."

His and other conservative Christians' desire to proclaim religion from a public platform has come in for rough treatment in the nation's highest courts (though that might change with the elevation of Chief Justice John Roberts and Justice Samuel Alito, neither of whom were on the bench for the Texas or Kentucky cases). The Reverend Scarborough is trying to rouse his troops to battle on behalf of former Judge Roy Moore: "The case of former Alabama Chief Justice Roy Moore was much clearer. Here, there were no sanitizing secular documents. Moore's monument stood alone in the Alabama Judicial Building. The Chief proudly proclaimed that it was there to remind the public of America's Christian roots. In other words, Moore's case was clearly about the First Amendment right of the American people to publicly acknowledge God, and that is why the Court refused to consider it."

Again, I have no doubt that Scarborough understands that Americans still have the right to "publicly acknowledge God," as they do more regularly than the citizens of any other industrialized nation on the planet. Judge Moore did raise his own money for the monument, rather than forcing the Alabama taxpayers to chip in, but even as chief judge, the courthouse is not "his." Nowhere in the judge's job description did it say that the job included "reminding people of America's Christian roots."

The Alabamans and people who thronged into Montgomery from across America to pray for Judge Moore and the Commandments unquestionably saw the removal of the judge and the monument as another sign of American decadence. The judge said his problems had made him an instrument of another power: "God has chosen this time and this place so we can save our country and save our courts for our children."

Appointed judges removed Moore from office and backed up Alabama's decision to remove the monument from the court. In the face of Moore's refusal to remove the monument, his eight colleagues on the state supreme court finally overruled him.

In the years since the 2003 decision, Alabama has not fared particularly well, or particularly badly. The state's fortunes progressed in the same way they would have were the 2.6-ton granite monument still in the court rotunda. The people who lay prostrate on the court steps mourning the monument's removal generally credit God with tremendous power and influence in people's daily lives.

Why didn't God intervene to keep the monument in the courthouse? Why didn't God move the Alabama supreme court judges to back their colleague Roy Moore? Why didn't God shift the heart of U.S. District Court judge Myron Thompson away from his opinion that the monument constituted an unconstitutional endorsement of religion? Why didn't God stop the Southern Poverty Law Center, one of the lead plaintiffs seeking the monument's removal, from filing its briefs? Doesn't God care?

In our next chapter, we look at how the American commanders in the Culture War increasingly look to child soldiers to enter the battle.

SEVEN

Child Soldiers in the Culture War

WHEN GROWNUPS FIGHT TO a draw these days, they send in their kids as reinforcements. The never-ending fights over curriculum, conditions, funding, testing, teaching methods, and the moral components of education set up a junior-varsity version of the adult division of culture war: do we do what works or what matches our moral convictions?

It is a fundamental question. Education is at its core an aspirational thing. We do not want poor kids to stay poor or to have their poverty block opportunity. We do not want kids with difficulties learning things to end up not learning them. We do not want rich kids to do better simply because they are rich. In theory, we want to do the best we can for the greatest number of kids. We never, as a public policy decision, announce that we have found these kids over here uneducable and now want to put resources in the places where they will have the greatest payback. What we do in practice is another matter, but I am talking about aspiration here.

In that way, education is like religion. Those who are religious see at the end of some journey a saner, more complete, more functional, more decent human being. Add "smarter" and the brief for education is similar. As much as "running government like a business" has become a motif of modern political debate, education is one government service we most definitely do not want to run like a business.

Education does not simply pull up stakes when a territory becomes too expensive a place to do business. Education cannot cream the best customers and leave others to fend for themselves. Education often responds to negative returns by spending more money per customer rather than less. We don't want education to run like a business.

So education—unlike road maintenance, sanitation, and parks

departments—becomes the societal institution where a potent mix of our dreams, desires, and social fantasies collide with the more hard-headed need to make sure public money is spent effectively and well. The resurfacing of an arterial street tells you something about a community's priorities. The way that same community educates its children tells you much, much more.

It is therefore no surprise that the struggles over education are more ferocious, more personal, more abstract, and more concrete than those on most other fronts in the Culture War. When you look at our schools, you can see what kind of society we are, what we value, and what we think is important. The fights over sex education, intelligent design, bilingual education, school prayer, inclusive curricula, and whether or not the Ten Commandments hang in the hallways are a natural outgrowth of that communal projection of all our anxieties onto the schools.

However, the playing out of those anxieties and conflicts on the stage of the local public schools has had some blind spots, even in a nation as avowedly religious as our own. Until the blink of an eye ago in historical terms, school systems spent much less on the education of black and Mexican children than they did on white children, and sent them to separate schools. In the decades since *Brown v. Board of Education of Topeka,* school systems have shown little reluctance to send the children with the greatest educational needs to the schools with the poorest funding streams and most degraded physical plants. Jesus might have counseled special help for the poor and commanded a special concern for "the least" among us, but that did not push local authorities best acquainted with the paradoxes of educational funding to change very much.

In the years after *Brown,* school systems throughout the South embarked on resistance and resegregation, and white flight and busing battles tore apart the big urban centers of the North. We still found plenty of time to fight about school prayer. The four decades since the big prayer decisions have not cooled the ardor of many Americans for school-based devotions. In the meantime, the nostalgia for the effects of prayer has only magnified its dwindling memory.

A 1959 Pennsylvania law attempted to preserve morning devotions by requiring them this way: "At least ten verses from the Holy Bible shall be read, without comment, at the opening of each public school on each school day. Any child shall be excused from such Bible reading, or attending such Bible reading, upon the written request of his parent or guardian." In drafting the law this way, legislators created an interesting challenge for school systems, parents, and eventually the courts.

Substituting Bible verses for a traditional prayer avoided the problem of secretarian conflict over what was in the prayer. The requirement that the verses be read "without comment" was an attempt to put a roadblock in front of theological instruction from preachy instructors. The legislators anticipated complaints from individual students or families by exempting anyone who did not want to participate. In the abstract classroom of the imagination debated in the Pennsylvania legislature, no children feel excluded, ostracized, pressured, or defensive. In that abstract classroom, the lone believer in a minority religion is not pointed out to the class by a mean or heedless teacher, or hassled by fellow students who repeat invective heard around the family dinner table. In that abstract classroom, and doubtless many other real ones between Pittsburgh in the west and Philadelphia in the east, the law worked beautifully.

That did not stop *Abington v. Schempp* from inexorably making its way to the Supreme Court of the United States. The court ruled against the mandated Bible verses. Writing for the majority, Justice Tom Clark endorses unbridled religious freedom and complete secularism in government institutions: "The place of religion in our society is an exalted one, achieved through a long tradition of reliance on the home, the church and the inviolable citadel of the individual heart and mind. We have come to recognize through bitter experience that it is not within the power of government to invade that citadel, whether its purpose or effect be to aid or oppose, to advance or retard. In the relationship between man and religion, the State is firmly committed to a position of neutrality."

"*. . . the inviolable citadel of the individual heart and mind.*" It is a beautiful phrase. Taken with the reliance on the home and church, it strongly challenges the idea that an institutionally backed form of religious instruction is not necessary to the moral education of children. But if the citadel of the heart and mind is "inviolable," and it is not within the power of the government to invade, how come children are potentially harmed by Bible verses at the opening of the day? This is part of the eternal tension over these questions. We have long accepted in law that children are different from adults and face the implied coercion of adults in a different way. People of goodwill and otherwise who have seen the inclusion of sacred text into the instructional day have long asserted that its benefit would outweigh the potential harm to the unchurched or members of minority religions.

The late 1950s and early 1960s were the last time the nation's school-children constituted a nearly homogeneous faith profile as they walked through the doors of the nation's schools. A small but constant Jewish minority was limited in geographical scope. A much larger Catholic minority was heavily concentrated, but shared the basic Christian worldview likely to be presented in a prayer written in the legislature or a Bible reading.

In the 1960s, the U.S. Congress changed the formulas under which immigrants were allowed into the United States. The old national quotas that welcomed nearly nonexistent French immigrants in greater numbers than the far more numerous Chinese were scrapped, with little comment at the time. That mid-1960s change released the forces that created twenty-first-century America, a far more diverse place linguistically, racially, religiously, and culturally than could have been imagined by the nine men who sat in judgment on *Abington v. Schempp.*

The Ellis Island generations of American immigrants had been absorbed and assimilated. After reaching astounding peaks both in percentages and in raw numbers in the first three decades of the twentieth century, immigration slowed to a trickle during the Great Depression and World War II. Americans—who read *Life, Look,* and the *Saturday Evening Post,* got 90 percent of their television from three broadcast networks, and got their news from papers that ranged in the main from slightly right of center to slightly left of center—had created a consensus culture between the end of the world war and the escalation of the war in Vietnam.

The Supreme Court decisions of the era anticipated a different American classroom from the one for which local boards and state legislators tried to create "neutral" prayers and Scripture readings. In New York State, the Board of Regents wanted public school children to augment the Pledge of Allegiance and a patriotic song with the following prayer, read aloud in the presence of a teacher: "Almighty God, we acknowledge our dependence upon Thee, and we beg Thy blessings upon us, our parents, our teachers, and our Country."

Who could object? No Jesus. No Mary. No Trinity. No specific Bible citation. No denominational fingerprints at all, in fact. The board of education in the small upstate community of Hyde Park was sued by parents objecting to the morning devotions. The prayer was composed by civil servants and recommended in a "Statement on Moral and Spiritual Training in the Schools."[1]

The state authorities seemed not to anticipate that anyone would be offended by the mandated prayer. The parents of ten students sued, challenging the constitutionality of a Board of Regents prayer, no matter how generally crafted it might be. The state's highest appeals court sided with the Regents, seeing no constitutional problem as long as no children were compelled to participate in the prayer.

Justice Hugo Black, writing for the majority in the 1962 Supreme Court Case *Engel v. Vitale,* found that a state-written prayer by definition violated the establishment clause of the First Amendment, since it was on its face an endorsement of a religious practice. Anticipating the arguments decades later about public displays of the Ten Commandments, Justice Black would not accept the idea that these devotions were not religious:

> *There can, of course, be no doubt that New York's program of daily classroom invocation of God's blessings as prescribed in the Regents' prayer is a religious activity. It is a solemn avowal of divine faith and supplication for the blessings of the Almighty. The nature of such a prayer has always been religious, none of the respondents has denied this and the trial court expressly so found. . . .*
>
> *The petitioners contend among other things that the state laws requiring or permitting use of the Regents' prayer must*

*be struck down as a violation of the Establishment Clause be-
cause that prayer was composed by governmental officials as a
part of a governmental program to further religious beliefs.
For this reason, petitioners argue, the State's use of the Regents' prayer in its public school system breaches the constitutional wall of separation between Church and State.*

*Under [the First] Amendment's prohibition against gov-
ernmental establishment of religion, as reinforced by the provisions of the Fourteenth Amendment, government in this
country, be it state or federal, is without power to prescribe by
law any particular form of prayer which is to be used as an
official prayer in carrying on any program of governmentally
sponsored religious activity.[2]*

Justice Black and the majority rejected the idea that a truly neutral
government under the First Amendment could not reject a prayer without
signaling an unconstitutional hostility toward religion. The opinion countered that "nothing could be more wrong."

In tune with opinions and dissents on these subjects that flamboyantly
embrace religion while rejecting government-sponsored religious practice, Justice Black talks at length about the inseparability of religion and
American history, while also conceding "an awareness that governments
of the past had shackled men's tongues to make them speak only the religious thoughts that government wanted them to speak and to pray only to
the God that government wanted them to pray to. It is neither sacrilegious
nor antireligious to say that each separate government in this country
should stay out of the business of writing or sanctioning official prayers
and leave that purely religious function to the people themselves and to
those the people choose to look to for religious guidance."

Again and again the attempts to thread the needle with just the right
words or just the right intent failed. Slamming the door on the historical
argument made by Justices Clarence Thomas and Antonin Scalia, that the
establishment clause had only the modest ambition of ending the pre-
Revolutionary practice of supporting state churches by association and

with taxpayer support, Justice John Rutledge wrote in *Everson v. The Board of Education of Ewing Township, New Jersey (1947):*

> *The [First] Amendment's purpose was not to strike merely at the official establishment of a single sect, creed or religion, outlawing only a formal relation such as had prevailed in England and some of the colonies. Necessarily it was to uproot all such relationships. But the object was broader than separating church and state in this narrow sense. It was to create a complete and permanent separation of the spheres of religious activity and civil authority by comprehensively forbidding every form of public aid or support for religion.*

To those who would cite American history as a justification for an intimate relationship between religion and the state, and religion and public schools, opinion after opinion threw history back in their faces. The Pilgrims and others who escaped church establishment, government-written and -mandated prayers, back in England established the same once they were in charge and beyond the reach of the king. Escaping religious oppression, it was recalled in several opinions, created little tolerance in the theocracies of the early American colonies, where religion was a tool of social control.

Just as the majority decisions in *Abington v. Schempp, Engel v. Vitale,* and other school prayer cases were cited by secularists and strict separationists for decades to come, so has the dissent of Justice Potter Stewart given ammunition to the other side. At 8–1, *Abington* was not a closely decided case. But Justice Potter's reasoning has offered encouragement to those fighting back against a careful exclusion of religion from the schools ever since. He wrote, "It is, I think, a fallacious oversimplification to regard the [religion clauses] as establishing a single constitutional standard of 'separation of church and state,' which can be applied in every case to delineate the required boundaries between government and religion. . . . As a matter of history, the First Amendment was adopted solely as a limitation upon the newly created National Government. The events leading to its adoption strongly suggest that the Establishment Clause was primarily an attempt to insure that Congress not only would be powerless to establish a national church, but would also be unable to interfere with existing state establishments."

Here, Justice Stewart lays the foundation for every religious advocate who has ever drawn the distinction between the First Amendment's protection of freedom *of* religion rather than freedom *from* religion:

> *If religious exercises are held to be an impermissible activity in schools, religion is placed in an artificial and state-created disadvantage. . . . And a refusal to permit religious exercises thus is seen, not as the realization of state neutrality, but rather as the establishment of a religion of secularism, or at least, as governmental support of the beliefs of those who think that religious exercises should be conducted only in private.*

Just as conservative Christians betray little interest in the rights of minorities when it comes to keeping worship out of public schools, strict separationists are vague when it comes to the artificiality of a "high wall" when millions of children march into schools carrying a vessel already full of religion: their heads. The socially desirable and court-endorsed values of nonexclusion and secularity of daily instruction does run into very real problems when a teacher, who may or may not be religious, stands in front of twenty-five seats filled with walking, talking, thinking variables.

An increasing number of American children come from homes with no religious practice or instruction at home. At the same time, there are millions whose young minds are on fire with what they are taught about heroic virtue, compassion, and miraculous adventure contained in sacred texts. Following what they think are the dictates of central administration standards, teachers sadly squelch the presentation of religiously themed compositions, show-and-tells, and book reports from religious children, helping to fill the anecdote arsenal of Christian conservatives trying to illustrate government's overreach and compelled conformity.

Common-sense standards keeping religion out of the government-presented curriculum are extended to what children write, feel, draw, talk about, and express to the class. It also sends rearguard actions in the Culture Wars spinning off into irrelevant battles that do not apply to government neutrality. A teacher asking an elementary school student not to profile a religious figure to fulfill a class assignment has picked a fight with no winners and has likely engaged and enraged parents who might otherwise have been allies.

One aspect of these debates I find bewildering is the discussion of schools by adults who opine as if they have never been to school themselves. The theory "Children should be able to pray when they are at school" seems to trump the real question, "But how?" Those who talked of God and religion as being "all but driven out of the public schools"[3] would not, could not, acknowledge the fact that the court decisions did not make prayer in school illegal. The decisions did, however, make school-sponsored prayer unconstitutional. Keep that in mind.

While religious Americans, and notably Christian conservatives, cherish their ability to talk to the government, they discount the way the government speaks for and to us all when the sort of speech the conservatives desire is excluded. Government and government institutions such as schools are owned and sustained by us all, so when they speak, their messages carry a unique weight in the wider society. Conversely, secularists hardly notice when the messages they cherish are the ones chosen as a matter of course by government, offending by their very content the religious co-owners with whom they share the state. Hence the emotional and sometimes panicky reaction to religious songs at holidays, and the equally powerful reaction to their exclusion.

That one-way-street tendency leaves secularists feeling aggrieved when local boards try to undermine the teaching of evolution and unmoved by others' outrage when schools exclude even individual student expression of religious faith. We all own the schools, so they cannot reflect the views of one group.

The latest manifestation of the "Sez who?" problem of the public schools is the teaching of biology. One of the great giants of modern science, Charles Darwin, is under renewed attack. Or, perhaps more to the point, what is new about the latest frontal assault is its relative success in being taken seriously at the local and state level across the country.

As with the debates over climate science, the debates over evolutionary theory are one-sided: maybe one in a hundred scientists has serious enough doubts about evolutionary biology to try to force changes in the curriculum. Conservative Christians have realized that to have tiny religious schools and home-schooling networks leading tours through natural history museums and describing the coexistence of humans and dinosaurs would never amount to a culture-changing victory. It would not be enough to go your own way and nurture an American Christian counterculture and remain marginalized and ignored.

The Christian Coalition playbook of the 1980s and 1990s presented a plan for gradually winning power in the wider society, and it began with running in school board races across the country. These elections, often run in a separate cycle from more prominent up-ticket races, can easily both serve as a laboratory for training Christian candidates for office and put real hands on real levels of power at relatively little cost. Conservative school boards have had a lot to say in recent years about sex education, school health clinic policies regarding reproductive health, approved texts in English classes, and approved plays and musicals in drama classes.

These boards have made the most waves and gotten the most ink nationwide for their assault on Darwin. Across the country, most recently in Pennsylvania, Kansas, Ohio, and Arkansas, science standards have been modified to suit the interests of organized Christian groups casting doubt on evolution. Repeated public opinion polls show large majorities of Americans believe God made the world as is, that modern humankind is not the result of gradual evolution over a long period of time, and that the world is younger than conventional science curricula teach their children.

That is interesting, I suppose. If a majority of Americans decided there was no gravity, that two plus two was not four, or that Columbus sailed in

1592 instead of 1492, we would probably not rush headlong into debates heading for the Supreme Court.

After local elections produced a Christian conservative majority on the Dover, Pennsylvania, school board, the board passed a resolution requiring a statement to be read before any lesson in which evolution was taught. It read:

> *The Pennsylvania Academic Standards require students to learn about Darwin's theory of evolution and eventually to take a standardized test of which evolution is a part.*
>
> *Because Darwin's Theory is a theory, it is still being tested as new evidence is discovered. The Theory is not a fact. Gaps in the Theory exist for which there is no evidence. A theory is defined as a well-tested explanation that unifies a broad range of observations.*
>
> *Intelligent design is an explanation of the origin of life that differs from Darwin's view. The reference book* Of Pandas and People *is available for students to see if they would like to explore this view in an effort to gain an understanding of what intelligent design actually involves.*
>
> *As is true with any theory, students are encouraged to keep an open mind. The school leaves the discussion of the origins of life to individual students and their families. As a standards-driven district, class instruction focuses upon preparing students to achieve proficiency on standards-based assessments.*

It was, by any standard, a strange disclaimer to read to students. What it boiled down to was this: "We have to teach you evolution, and you have to learn it well enough to be tested on it. We would like you to consider other evidence, because we don't necessarily believe that what we're teaching you is true."

Bryan Rehm was working as a science teacher in the district's high school. He remembers rumors started flying around the science faculties in the district about the board's unhappiness with the curriculum. At a meeting with the board, Rehm remembers one member in particular, Alan Bonsell, had plenty of objections. "He kept saying over and over, 'Monkey to man, you're not going to tell my kid that we came from monkeys. You know there are holes so big and dark in evolution I can drive a truck through them.' These are things he kept saying over and over.

"We started explaining to him, we don't teach monkey to man because the developments in evolutionary theory are so much at the cellular and molecular level. That's where the progression is happening and that's what's applicable to those things they're going to need to know when they go to college if they choose to pursue biology, and really that's where employment is leading. Look at biomedical research, those areas that are emerging in the future job market. They don't need to know about monkey to man; they need to know about microevolution and about the changes in DNA. So we try to explain to them that's where the lesson is focused."

Rehm said that through his department chair, the board started pushing for revisions in the science curriculum. "They'd say, 'We need to see these revisions you're making.' And we'd say, 'We're not making revisions, because we're not going to teach it.' " Around the same time, the district reached a renewal period for all the science textbooks. Physics, chemistry, anatomy, and physiology, all arrived. No biology. The board informed the faculty, Rehm said, that it would not approve an order for the new biology text "unless the teachers also looked at *Of Pandas to People,* which it felt was a much better biology book and it took care of this evolution problem."

Board member Bonsell took a particular interest in the intelligent-design text, Rehm said: "At one point in time he went so far as to suggest that that book should be ordered instead of the high school teachers' selection. Later, he wanted it to be ordered with the high school teachers' selection. And in the end he ended up taking a collection at his church to have between fifty and sixty copies of the book donated. At that point in time, the expectation was that those books would be in all the biology classrooms, on the shelf as they referenced alternative books in the classroom." Like the reading of the disclaimer at the beginning of an evolution lesson, a Gresham's law of pedagogy would be placed in front of the students.[4] Here is our "real" textbook. And by the way, we have another text that asserts the first textbook is wrong, if you would like to look at it.

The school board in Dover was not going to make the mistakes of previous school authorities. Tennessee's Butler Act, in 1925, straight out prohibited the teaching of anything other than the account of the creation of the world set forth in Genesis: "That it shall be unlawful for any teacher in any of the Universities, Normals[5] and all other public schools of the State which are supported in whole or in part by the public school funds of the State, to teach any theory that denies the story of the Divine Creation of man as taught in the Bible, and to teach instead that man has descended from a lower order of animals."

More than forty years after the Butler Act, Arkansas tried to pass an openly confessional standard for the teaching of biology, like Tennessee's. In *Epperson v. Arkansas,* in 1968, the Supreme Court delivered a sharp and unequivocal slap:

> *No suggestion has been made that Arkansas' law may be justified by considerations of state policy other than the religious views of some of its citizens. It is clear that fundamentalist sectarian conviction was and is the law's reason for existence. Its antecedent, Tennessee's "monkey law," candidly stated its purpose: to make it unlawful "to teach any theory that denies the story of the Divine Creation of man as taught in the Bible, and to teach instead that man has descended from a lower order of animals."*

Perhaps the sensational publicity attendant upon the Scopes trial induced Arkansas to adopt less explicit language. It eliminated Tennessee's reference to "the story of the Divine Creation of man as taught in the Bible," but there is no doubt that the motivation for the law was the same:

to suppress the teaching of a theory that, it was thought, "denied" the divine creation of man. The Supreme Court went on to say:

> Arkansas' law cannot be defended as an act of religious neutrality. Arkansas did not seek to excise from the curricula of its schools and universities all discussion of the origin of man. The law's effort was confined to an attempt to blot out a particular theory because of its supposed conflict with the Biblical account, literally read. Plainly, the law is contrary to the mandate of the First, and in violation of the Fourteenth, Amendment to the Constitution.

With controlling law precedents like these, subtlety is now the order of the day. The Dover board was hemmed in by the science standards for the state of Pennsylvania. It could not order the local schools to drop evolution altogether, but could open a slight crack in the impenetrable façade of Darwin. Tell students you are teaching them the science they need for the test and that the real info is available in the closet.

Of Pandas and People has a problem in common with many of the intelligent-design texts. It spends a lot of time calling into question various parts of the Darwinian story of the differentiation of species. It is an interesting critique, for the nonscientist, of evolutionary theory. The one thing it does not do is turn the corner and say, "Here's what we think happened instead of what the other guys think happened. We've just spent a long time telling you what's wrong with evolutionary theory, now here's our version."

The Dover board used intelligent design as its standard-bearer rather than advocating a creationist curriculum, in order to more easily install an antievolutionist "scientific" theory as a fully fledged alternative to the approach that has dominated biology for a century. Most scientists are scathing in their dismissal of *Of Pandas and People*. Rehm, for example, is ferocious: "It's a total mischaracterization of scientific research, a misstatement of evolutionary theory, and an intentional disregard of real data, putting fake data in its place. There are statements in the book that are totally nonsensical. You know, expecting to find a half bird and a half fish. That's not what evolution is saying at all, and then using that as an argument to say, 'Well, see, evolution's totally false because you'll never find a half bird, half fish.' Duh. The evolutionary scientists aren't saying that anyway. Charles Darwin never said that."

Of Pandas and People, to be fair, does not say that either. Or at least, not in so many words. In a section on genetic mutation, it posits that shifts in the genomes of animals that are precursors to other branches on the evolutionary tree should reflect that genetically, and do not. It is meant as a "gotcha!" moment in the book, but seeks to disprove a point that many evolutionists do not even try to make.[6]

The modest proposal of the text *Of Pandas and People* is that what Darwin and other evolutionists did say should come under scrutiny, be tested, and if not proved, then cast into doubt. In public debates over the teaching of evolution, skeptics fall back on a handy defense: in its canonization Darwin's work has been given an unassailable place, not to be challenged in the rough and tumble of scientific discourse and research. Yes, every scientific theory has to be open to challenge and reexamination. Yes, Darwin's theory should be no different in this regard.

And as far as one federal court is concerned, intelligent design does not rise to the level of a serious challenge to a century of scientific inquiry. Intelligent-design proponents often infer a creator from nature's complexity. Finding "John Loves Mary" written on a deserted beach does allow someone on a morning walk to infer the existence of an intelligence behind the message. Inferring that someone wrote "John Loves Mary" is not sufficient to take down Darwin, especially when so much of the material now produced for schools is repurposed creationism rather than original scientific research.

The questions unleashed by anti-Darwin fights in so many states did not, as some had hopefully speculated, end with the 2005 defeat in court for the Dover school board. Though the stinging decision by the judge, John E. Jones III, rejected the reasoning of the school board in making even a modest opening to other ways of looking at natural origins, the last century has shown that all the ruling will do is serve as a temporary setback, as legal theorists try to design religion-friendly approaches to school curricula that will not fall afoul of current legal precedent. Judge Jones noted that the school board had made an inane decision, one that dragged the district into "this legal maelstrom with its resulting utter waste of monetary and personal resources."

"To be sure, Darwin's theory of evolution is imperfect," the judge conceded. "However, the fact that a scientific theory cannot yet render an explanation on every point should not be used as a pretext to thrust an untestable alternative hypothesis grounded in religion into the science classroom or to misrepresent well-established scientific propositions."

The landscape is littered with excuses. David Napierski is a member of the board that adopted *Of Pandas and People* and came up with the disclaimer to be read in the Pennsylvania district's science classrooms. To this day members of the board are angry that a literal federal case was made out of the disclaimer: "We just hope people open up their eyes in this nation and see what's going on right now. We were on trial preventing from merely mentioning a statement. We're not even teaching it,"[7] said Napierski.

That was the challenge to the science establishment. What are you so afraid of? If Darwin's and other evolutionists' theories are so sound, can't they withstand a short disclaimer and an optional reading assignment? The American Civil Liberties Union helped the Dover families who sued the school board, and their lawyer, Victor Walczak, made a Trojan-horse argument: "The Intelligent Design movement is built on the mission to bring supernatural creation into the science classroom. And Dover is the thin edge of wedge. This is the first place they're trying to get a foothold. So mark my words, if intelligent design is not stopped here, it's going to be all over the place."

But intelligent design was stopped in Dover. And the fight is not over. It is not over because of some emotional and demographic realities of the United States. Polling in 2005 showed that a majority of Americans believe God created the world in six days and made human beings on the last day before resting, as it says in the biblical account in Genesis.[8] Two thirds of people with no high school diploma told researchers they believe the six-day creation story, while only a third of people with a four-year college degree said they believe the biblical account. Among those who describe themselves as "very conservative," 74 percent said they believe in a six-day creation, while only 22 percent of those who describe themselves as very liberal said the same.[9] In another poll around the same time, 51 percent said God created human beings in their present form, but 67 percent said it was possible to believe in both God and evolution.[10]

John Morris, director of the Institute for Creation Research, sums up the problem neatly from his point of view: "Probably 90 percent of all Americans believe in intelligent-design-slash-creation. Only a very small percentage believe in strict naturalistic evolution. This is just a small slice, a minority of folks. Unfortunately that slice populates our universities; our professors are all in that minor slice, very much out of touch with mainstream America, promoting something that the rest of America gags over."

It is not clear how much popular sentiment should guide what we teach children in science class. We do not hold plebiscites on curriculum or send out a shopping list with the real estate tax bill that pays for public school in so many places in the country. Americans show a greater and greater tendency to concentrate residentially in places where like-minded people live. How will school authorities respond to challenges to evolution instruction from increasingly uniformly hostile political bases on which they depend for support?

In a West Virginia Pledge of Allegiance case, Justice Robert Jackson rejected the notion of majority rule over the intellectual and spiritual fates of others: "Finally, we cannot accept that the concept of neutrality, which does not permit a State to require a religious exercise even with the consent of the majority of those affected, collides with the majority's right to free exercise of religion. While the Free Exercise Clause clearly prohibits the use of state action to deny the rights of free exercise to anyone, it has never meant that a majority could use the machinery of the State to practice its beliefs."[11] So much for the people who want their overwhelming view on evolution to be reflected by state-run schools.

Weighing in on the subject of evolution when asked by reporters about the Dover fight gave the president an opportunity to signal to supporters that he is "okay" on the subject: "I think that part of education is to expose people to different schools of thought," Bush said. "You're asking me whether or not people ought to be exposed to different ideas, the answer is yes." Supporting intelligent design is a low-risk proposition for the president. He would never go to the mat for it, never order his Department of Education to impose it, and his views hold no statutory sway over any school system in the country. It is the kind of statement that makes his liberal opponents livid, comforts and reassures his conservative Christian base, and changes absolutely nothing.

"Teach the controversy" is a demand heard in a lot of the curriculum debates over evolution, not just from President Bush. Even atheists and biologists who oppose the teaching of intelligent design as science reply, "By all means." However, teaching the controversy does not mean introducing intelligent design in science classes, but rather moving the "debate" to civics or social studies.

As a gambit in the debate, "teach the controversy" is meant to demonstrate that the other side is afraid or insecure or shutting out even the smallest bit of contradiction because they simply do not have the facts. Thus, letting in intelligent design would eventually erode the seemingly impregnable fortress of Darwinism. In these debates, an evolutionary approach to natural history is often spoken of as being a religion, a religion that liberals, atheists, and humanists have chosen to favor over conservative Christians' own.

An educator, scientist, and now member of the Dover school board, Bryan Rehm said he knows the difference between religion and science. "My wife and I both attend a local United Church of Christ congregation. In fact, our church is right across the street from Dover High School. We're very active members. My wife is on the church council in charge of the Christian education committee. My wife and I run the children's Vacation Bible School program. I'm codirector of the children's choir. We're quite active in our church and in the community and within the schools, and to—to have this thing sit against us is—it's ridiculous."

Whether it is ridiculous or not, Rehm said he had to put up with quite a lot of personal attack that questioned his Christianity during the Dover trial and his campaign for the school board. "Many people in the community say, 'What kind of Christian are you if you have a problem with this?' 'What religion are you? This is a country founded on Christianity. If you've got a problem with that, go back to where you came from.' And these are things they're shouting out at the board meeting to the public.

"I've gotten numerous hate mailings how about I must be some atheist trying to destroy Christ and I'm going to burn in hell because Christ is the greatest power in the world, and things of that nature. I go door to door campaigning, and I'm getting doors slammed in my face by good Christian folks calling me atheist assholes and son of a bitch and piece of shit, and it's like, okay, thank you!

"They think they say this after they've slammed the door; they forget that it's May and like 78 degrees outside. I can hear exactly what they're saying as they storm away from the door. One of the former board members lives in my neighborhood, and he was going to my neighbor saying, 'You're going to vote for me in the coming school board or you're voting against God.' Right there that says, 'Don't vote for Bryan Rehm because he's not a Christian.' I don't believe that your politics should be based totally upon a religious conviction. Issues should be based upon the issues. They should be based upon what's in the best interest of the community."

The elections of 2005 swept out the entire Dover board that introduced the disclaimer and the *Pandas* textbook. After the ruling in the court case, the "losing" school board was gone and the new board was putting back the old science standards. Evolution supporters paradoxically wanted the new anti-intelligent-design board to appeal the opinion in order to force a higher court ruling on the matter and set a legal precedent against the incorporation of intelligent design into science curricula. Rehm and his board colleagues said there will be no appeal. The first legal battle cost the school system a great deal of money, and it will be hard enough just to replace that. Then the Dover School Board voted in early 2006 to pay just over a million dollars in legal fees to the attorney who successfully argued against the old board's intelligent-design standard. The board had to pay under orders from the judge after he found that the new science policy was religiously motivated.

Continued legal action might be in somebody's political interests, said Bryan Rehm, but it wouldn't be in the interests of the kids of his area. "I'm sorry, our community can't afford it. Unfortunately for the rest of the United States, there's a number of districts that are still willing to pursue it and we're of the mind-set of let *them* pay for it. The amount of evidence that's out there that state intelligent design is religion and people who want to teach it are doing it for religion reasons is absolutely overwhelming. My honest opinion is that no matter where this comes up, it can't go through as an acceptable policy."

One place where this battle continues to simmer is Kansas. In 1999, the state got the attention, first, of the nation and then of the world to its state school board's order that evolution be removed from the science standards entirely. The ferocious fighting that followed, coupled with the embarrassment of many Kansas, first resulted in a Dover-like turnover of the school board: its antievolution majority was turned out in the next election and the science standard restored. But in later elections an antievolution bloc re-formed on the board and introduced a new standard, one that resembles Dover's in not making a frontal assault on Charles Darwin. By a 6–4 vote, the state board adopted new standards calling parts of evolutionary theory into question.

Board members' statements on the day of the vote reflect the splits inside Kansas and the country. Janet Waugh of Kansas City said, "This is a sad day. We're becoming a laughingstock of not only the nation, but of the world, and I hate that." Using that parallel with religion mentioned earlier, board member John Bacon of Olathe said, "It gets rid of a lot of dogma that's being taught in the classroom today."

Other individual schools and school systems will continue to look for approaches to chip away at the primacy of Darwinian theory, motivated by religious sentiment among members of school boards and the religious fervor of the often small share of the voting public that gets involved in school board elections. The Frazier Mountain School in Lebec, California, north of Los Angeles, is one school that tried to test the new limits. It sought to introduce a course first called "The Philosophy of Intelligent Design," which became "The Philosophy of Design." Instead of trying to insert the materials directly into the mainstream of the science curriculum, the earth-and-species-origin course was designed as a four-week elective. The course description given to students said, "This class will take a close look at evolution as a theory and will discuss the scientific, biological, and biblical aspects that suggest why Darwin's philosophy is not rock solid."

Watch out for the minefield! In three lines there's the strategic reference to evolution as a theory, the biblical refutations of Darwin, and the reference to Darwin and his successor's scientific work as "philosophy." Taught by a young-earth creationist, that is, someone who believes the Genesis account of the creation to be literally true, the course immediately attracted challenges to the school administration and later in court.

Theory means one thing in science, and another in everyday parlance or coming from the mouth of a prosecutor in an episode of *Law and Order.* No matter how many times that discrepancy is explained, antievolutionists fall back on "It's just a theory," bolstered by Christian conservatives and the megaphone squad of talk radio and the Internet. Kenneth Miller, professor of biology at Brown University and an expert witness for the plaintiffs in the Dover case, explained in court that a theory in science is "not just a hunch. It is a strong, overarching explanation that ties together many facts and enables us to make testable predictions." Detective Lennie Briscoe may use it that way as well, but antievolutionists do not.

In fairly short order, upon examination of the teaching materials and testimony from the teacher, school authorities, and outside experts, a court order was entered in the case, stipulating that "No school over which the School District has authority, including the High School, shall offer, presently or in the future, the course entitled 'Philosophy of Design' or 'Philosophy of Intelligent Design' or any other course that promotes or endorses creationism, creation science, or intelligent design." [12]

For some watching these court and school battles, along with the bare-knuckled rearguard action fought on the radio and cable TV, both the fight and the outcome are perplexing. Anglican theologian the Reverend

Martin Smith finds that Christian fundamentalists who insist on a literal reading of the Genesis creation story "are just as faithless as scientists, since they are just as unable to passionately embrace myth as liberal secularists. By basing all belief about the origin of life on the rigid literalism of the Book of Genesis, they prove themselves to be equally incapable of mythic belief—all the while excoriating their enemies for their inability to perceive the Divine at work in the world."

In the real world, Martin Smith said, both "science and Scripture find it difficult to have the complete autonomy they want." He bridles against the notion that we must be forced to accept in its entirety one story of the world's origins or another. "Why can't scientific advance unveil the beauty of creation?"

Perhaps the Reverend Martin Smith's speculations are more relevant to the world of adults. It is harder for children to operate from the fortress of a made-up mind. Children are presented with material, encouraged to master it, and then expected to demonstrate that mastery in exams. Telling them to master evolution in biology class and then winking about the material is odd, but it is not the only mixed message children get.

It is clear from much of the debate swirling around evolution in recent years that parents think the job of the schools is to confirm their own biases in the education of their children. If they think the earth is six thousand years old, that is what their children should be taught. If they find Holden Caulfield a dangerous nihilist, devoid of respect for adults and without deference to authority, then *Catcher in the Rye* should not be used in schools. If they think premarital sex is wrong, then their children should not be taught about their sexual selves.

The decision to follow popular belief on these subjects is not without consequences. Maybe you can get away with missing Holden's interior monologues, but not knowing conventional biology might make things more difficult in college and in the job market. Not understanding the functioning of a teen and young adult body can have even more serious consequences in the form of unwanted pregnancy and sexually transmitted disease.

Once again, the warriors on both sides behave as if they have never been to school themselves, or if they did go, managed to get from kindergarten to twelfth grade without knowing any children. Secularists underestimate the ability of children, especially once they are in high school, to consider different sources for material and organize them into a hierarchy of value and credibility. Conservative Christian supporters of creationist and intelligent-design-based lessons maintain that the very nature of the evolutionary theory, describing a multitude of unplanned events across millions of organisms and million of years, makes children shoot up their schools, commit suicide, and engage in sexual promiscuity.

In this context, a repeatedly heard phrase is "evolved from slime." In 1999, Congressman Tom DeLay, in a speech on the Columbine shootings in Littleton, Colorado, told his audience "Our school systems teach the children that they are nothing but glorified apes who are evolutionized out of some primordial soup."

The anger from parents stems not from recent DNA discoveries validating evolutionary theory or even the forms of evolution supported by intelligent-design theorists. The very idea that modern humankind was not created in its current form is reduced to the proposition that we "evolved from slime." There is often a fevered tone to these declarations, a sense that evolutionary theory is a cocked pistol, burning dynamite, a notion so explosive that its effects cannot be exaggerated. No consequence is too far-fetched, from rape and murder, to suicide and drug addiction. The implication is that our children are so sensitive that learning evolution will reduce them to nihilist, materialist, self-seeking beasts.

It is unquestionable that teen sexual activity is both more common and more dangerous than it was in previous generations. Parents are thus presented with the daunting moral challenge to encourage children to make the right choices in what they do with their bodies—while at the same time worrying about how to respond if they do not.

In an age of incurable AIDS and far more widespread sexually transmitted disease, we owe it to our children to discourage teenage sexual activity. However, stopping there, knowing what we know about teenagers in the 2000s, would appear to be immoral. That subtle challenge would appear to be a call to all Americans of every religious stripe and political orientation to come together and forge commonsense public policy that both keeps children safe and recognizes real life in real high schools.

The conservative Christian movements have been tremendously influential in this regard, but not tremendously helpful. The age at first menstruation, the age of sexual maturity, has declined in years over the last century, at an average of three months per decade.[13] The age at first marriage during that same century has risen steadily, recently reaching its highest-ever median age at twenty-five years, three months, a full five years older than in 1950, when it was twenty years, three months.[14]

So, all our religiously driven political party has been able to give our children at school is a message that is extremely unable and unlikely to carry them from sexual maturity to their wedding night. The message advocated by Focus on the Family, the Family Research Council, and others is abstinence only, encouraging all teens, but especially young girls, to delay what researchers call their "sexual debut" until marriage. With the gap between sexual maturity and first marriage now approaching 13 years (and with the age at first sexual intercourse somewhere between 16½ and 17½ for boys and girls), "Just don't do it" does not appear to be sufficient.

Everyone agrees, from left to right, that holding off starting sexual activity would be better for everyone. There would be fewer pregnancies out of wedlock, fewer infants abandoned by their fathers, fewer sexually transmitted diseases, fewer exploitative relationships, and fewer abortions. There is now plenty of evidence to suggest that "abstinence-only" education does not work.[15] Young women who have taken chastity pledges in the high school years are more likely to engage in risky sexual behavior, such as intercourse without condoms, and less likely to seek treatment after infection with an STD.[16] One sociologist, Peter Bearman of Columbia University, told USA Today, "It's difficult to simultaneously prepare for sex and say you're not to have sex . . . The message is really simple: 'Just say no' may work in the short term but doesn't work in the long term."

No one is saying this is easy. The problem is that crafting public policy in order to meet your convictions about what should be, rather than about what is, may not serve the vulnerable people you say you are worried about. If you are most concerned about maintaining your public image, being consistent, and being seen to defend "traditional families" and "traditional morality," your choices in this area of human life might be clear. But addressing the real needs of America's children does not yield such easy answers. Religious groups should be helping government answer this question: Is there a sexual ethic, a theology of the human body, that teaches self-respect and self-protection while recognizing that millions of American minors have sex every year?

Can we get them to treasure themselves and protect themselves, with an eye toward delaying first sexual intercourse, while at the same time recognizing that teens need not be strangers to their own bodies, their own feelings, and blind to the ferocious pressures of the culture. Jesus asked his followers to be "in the world, but not of the world." That might not be a bad goal for our teens and young adults. We can teach them that the real world, the place they live, is full of temptations and snares, but they need not surrender themselves to the danger of sex with people with whom they share no long-term commitment . . . or as happens far too often, someone who doesn't care for them at all.

When that long stretch between sexual maturity and first marriage was much narrower, the prospect of making it all the way to the wedding night a virgin seemed a much more achievable goal than today. With the heightened danger of sex, sexually saturated pop culture, and more opportunity created by wealthier, more mobile teens and mothers being more involved in the workforce, parents need more backup than ever.

But backup of what kind? To reinforce the notion that the wedding-night virgin is still a relevant social ideal? To assume that the aspiration to chastity inevitably ends in failure, so we must be prepared for the fall from grace? This is one area of social reality and social response in which churches of all stripes, liberals and conservatives, and culture warriors all across the spectrum have very little to show for their efforts.

Instead of a group of unified voices and broadly shared messages, American teenagers hear a cacophony of voices in the culture pulling them every which way and leaving them unsure, conflicted, and often ashamed. Conservative Christians have decided to allow no licit choice of sexual expression before marriage, though a relatively small number of their own congregants choose that path for themselves. There has been a reluctance on the part of more liberal and secular voices in the culture to acknowledge that early sexual debuts constitute a failure on the part of families, schools, and peer groups. While liberals have not advocated adolescent sex, their lack of condemnation is construed as a tacit endorsement by their opponents on the right.

The rhetoric from conservative Christians often seems drained of compassion, a pitiless peal of thunder about what is wrong and what is right. Little provision is made for the virginity pledger who fails. The overemphasis on women leaves boys with too few tools with which to construct a positive notion of manhood and, for most of them, what could be a lifetime of loving relationships with women. Judging from the lame "raging hormones" alibis to the overt "Just Say No" commands to women, the job of the adolescent boy appears to be to try and try until someone gives in.

In Montgomery County, Maryland, the state's largest and wealthiest, a long-running battle over sex education has left what is also one of the state's largest school systems without an approved curriculum. Michelle Turner began a lone battle and is now backed by Christian and conservative groups from around Maryland and the country in working to scrap the standards for eighth and ninth grade in a variety of topics in human sexuality.

Turner wants to teach her own children about human sexuality in order to have it taught in accordance with her own religious values, those of the Church of Jesus Christ of Latter-Day Saints. She said, "I made the commitment to be their mom, and to be here to teach them things that my husband and I wanted them to learn. To teach them about church, about God."

She is a stay-at-home parent and a tireless campaigner against the county's sex-ed curriculum, but it turns out one issue in particular concerns her most of all: "God has given us the ability to procreate, to bring children into a family. And as far as the homosexual issue goes, our bodies are not meant or created to be used in that way." [17]

Turner's idea that homosexuality is not part of the natural order is widely held in the United States. Again, as in so many areas of religious involvement in debates over public policy, the forces of wishful thinking clash against the forces of what is. The Citizens for a Responsible Curriculum (CRC) said in its publications that this was not a fight it sought out, but "The Montgomery County Board of Education was irresponsible in promulgating the revised sex-ed curriculum: it was willing to sacrifice the physical and psychological health of children for a political agenda."

In CRC's view, the county had surrendered to political correctness and the homosexual agenda, and the CRC's mission is merely to stand for science against politics, "to stand for medical accuracy, parental authority over the moral and religious instruction of children, and inclusion of all viewpoints and students in the public school system."

Their point is that homosexuality is a choice and that to teach children, especially at the highly impressionable and vulnerable time of puberty, that homosexuality is innate and part of the variety of the human family, is dangerous. Turner and Montgomery organizations have argued to the board that its new standards alleged that homosexuality has a genetic source, and they believe it is more likely a choice. The curriculum, they said, ought to teach multiple, competing views including theirs; that it is possible to stop being gay.

Leave aside for a moment the somewhat contradictory idea of voluntarily joining a despised, marginalized, discriminated-against sexual minority if you also have *not joining it* as an available option. Organized conservative Christian groups insist that gay people make a lifestyle choice, and that with prayer, counseling, and hard work, they can go on to live as heterosexuals. This is a cornerstone position of conservative Christian organizations when issues like sexual-education curriculum arise. If they were to accept that homosexuality is part of God's plan for nature, the unremitting hostility shown toward gay people would be difficult to maintain. Senator Rick Santorum, in his famous "man on dog" interview with the Associated Press, repeated an often-heard response about the lives of gay people, which is that it is not the people or their orientation that offends, but their sex acts. Gay people are beloved; its just their homosexuality we can't stand.

Homosexual people are by their very nature deeply subversive to the conservative Christian worldview. They are not obliged to be yoked in marriage or burdened with children. They are not locked into the rigid economy of sex that places all sex acts only within marriage and all marriage only within heterosexuality. For Christian conservatives already pinned down in battle by a society of riotous sexual irresponsibility, of railing against sex among the young, the unmarried, and the contraception user, the gay person provides a sexual rebel beyond tolerance and beyond the pale.

The conservative Christian organizations may have painted themselves into a corner. Their fight against abortion is so intertwined with a fight against contraception and, indeed, against sex itself that a faithful and sex-positive approach to youngsters seems to be off the menu. The binary stop/go, good/bad bludgeoning of the young over sins of the flesh would have been one thing if it had stayed in church. The conservatives have long since flooded out the church doors and into the halls of the legislature and the school board to put religiously convinced politicians into the position of making moral choices for us all.

In Kansas, Attorney General Phill Kline, an antiabortion politician allied with Christian conservative organizations in his state, is pushing to criminalize sex between young people. First, Kline attracted attention in Kansas for his lengthy battle to force access for his office to the records of family planning clinics around the state, for the stated purposes of investigating sex crimes. Kline wanted to see records of all abortions performed in Kansas.

His emphasis was on young women. In the attorney general's view, any pregnant minor is a rape victim or a sexual abuse victim, thus clinics that have treated girls who have been sexually active are holding records that could be useful in the investigation of a crime. Rebuffed on the first records quest, he has now changed the terms of his search. He has demanded the medical records of any minor that show "compelling evidence of sexual activity is present." Kline said from the beginning, his stand is based firmly on Kansas law. The age of consent in the state is sixteen, so consensual sex is simply not a relevant concept for people under sixteen.

Still, Kline's collapsing of the age of consent into rape has brought strong response from many quarters. "Sexual abuse is not synonymous with consensual sexual activity," said Bonnie Scott Jones, lawyer for the Center for Reproductive Rights. "Consensual sexual activity is not inherently injurious. It is a normal part of adolescent development."

Here again, anything but an outright prohibition is criticized as soft and unrealistic, while the absolutist stance is seen as clear-eyed and responsible. Arguing the case in Kansas, Assistant Attorney General Steve Alexander said, "Illegal sexual activity by minors can lead to STDs, unwanted pregnancies, abortion, depression, and mental illness. To pretend otherwise is foolish." And to pretend that the other side of the question is pretending otherwise is called . . . ?

The attorney general thus accuses his opponents of favoring adult-child sex. "Plaintiffs are arguing that the Constitution does not allow the state to require people to report child rape. We differ. Prosecuting and investigating child rapists depends on such laws, and if the plaintiffs believe that adult-child sex should be legal, they need to take that debate to the Legislature rather than initiate litigation."

The letter of the law would seem to indicate that there is no consent before the sixteenth birthday. But the reality of life in America would further indicate that a full 30 percent of teens under sixteen have had sexual intercourse, and an additional 20 percent have tried oral sex or genital fondling. Is it better public policy to find an approach that tries to take into account both the real social costs of early sexual activity and the reality that it is continuing anyway, or to hide out from the unpleasantness in the simple, unequivocal truth of the Law?

The Kansas court proceeding about the medical records was a bench trial, argued before a judge and an empty jury box. One expert witness, Professor Allan Josephson of the University of Louisville, told the judge that the "distress" that might come from the threat of disclosure "could force change" among adolescents. U.S. District judge J. Thomas Marten questioned the professor sharply about adolescent sexual activity, at which point Professor Josephson chided the magistrate for indicating that teen sex has been going on for ages. Marten shot back that no one had suggested it is good for young teens to be sexually active. However, "it is going on—and to deny that is going to happen is a totally fantastic view of the world."

Dr. Robert Blum, of the Johns Hopkins Bloomberg School of Public Health, testified that exposing sexually active youth to legal scrutiny would have "a chilling effect on youths seeking contraception or treatment for sexually transmitted disease—ultimately leading to more teen pregnancies, more abortions and more disease spreading."

Dr. Blum further testified, "Youths will be less likely to seek treatment for sexually transmitted diseases, and therefore more likely to spread them to others. Untreated, they would also pose significant health consequences to themselves." How you respond to testimony like that depends on whether you are really against abortion, or want to pass laws against abortion. They may be two different things. Dr. Blum told the court California had tried to institute a legal architecture like the one contemplated for Kansas by Attorney General Kline. It failed. State offices, Blum said, were "flooded with irrelevant and obstructive material."

At that point, one might assume, it becomes the responsibility of the state to dispatch law enforcement personnel to further investigate evidence of young adolescent sexual activity. Try to imagine Joe Friday's squad car rolling up to a burger joint to begin a quick interrogation of a suspect. "Did you achieve penetration?" and "In her statement to Police Officer Jones, Miss Perkins said you ejaculated; is that your recollection as well?" might rope Kansas peace officers into pathetic reenactments of the Monica Lewinsky deposition. At present, Kansas Social and Rehabilitative Services has a policy of not investigating what is reported as consensual teen sex unless there is evidence of a crime.

The attorney general's attempts to remind Kansans that teenage sex is a crime may, in its overreach, mask a terrible and challenging reality. Many teenage girls engage in sexual activity and enter ongoing sexual relationships with men much older than they are. As the assistant attorney general suggests, these men often get teenagers pregnant and give them STDs. They also show a staggering unwillingness or inability to provide for the resulting children once they are born.

We also know something about these children themselves. They interrupt and often end their mothers' educations, thus limiting their mothers' future earnings as well. Even if the mothers are eventually pushed into the workforce by welfare reform, the life trajectory for their children is not especially promising. So "liberals" have plenty of common ground with Phill Kline. No one seems to know what the next step is.

It is far more productive, it would appear, to fight over the Pledge of Allegiance.

A Baptist minister, Francis Bellamy, wrote the pledge to accompany a patriotic ceremony marking the four hundredth anniversary of Columbus's first voyage to the Americas. His slightly amended version left out "equality," since so many places in America found that a controversial concept when it came to blacks and women, so it read: "I pledge allegiance to my Flag and to the Republic for which it stands, one nation, indivisible, with liberty and justice for all." Pretty simple, really. I promise loyalty to the flag and the country the flag stands for. Less than thirty years after the end of the Civil War, asserting that the nation could not be divided and was a free and just place seemed appropriate.

Thirty years later, the American Legion and the Daughters of the American Revolution lobbied for "my flag" to be changed to "the flag of the United States of America." Fair enough. You never know when some joker is going to pop out the flag of Luxembourg or Nepal.

Yet another thirty years later, under the pressure of a lobbying campaign from the Catholic fraternal organization the Knights of Columbus, the U.S. Congress added the words "under God." The change, according to one historian of the pledge, now made it both "a patriotic oath and a public prayer." [18] He might have added, "and fodder for court cases."

If you are an adult, it is up to you whether and when you say the Pledge of Allegiance. I still say it from time to time, mostly at Boy Scout functions and occasionally at congressional events. Children, blank canvases that they are, get the choice made for them. Pledge recitation is compulsory in many school districts and some states. Even when it is not compulsory, it is led by a government employee, that is, the teacher, with the full backing of the school and the local government. It is an open question just how much of a fuss any one kid is going to make before placing his hand over his heart and proceeding with the Pledge.

Michael Newdow, a California father, raised religious objections to the words "under God" in the Pledge, since it coerced his daughter into daily prayer. As an atheist, he reasoned this interfered with his right to oversee the religious upbringing of his daughter and violated both the free-exercise and establishment clauses of the First Amendment to the Constitution.

The Ninth U.S. Circuit Court found for Newdow, which made him and that court immediate rallying cries and the blackest villains to God's defenders in the United States. It was frequently heard—from politicians, pundits, and pastors—that an out-of-control court had "made the Pledge of Allegiance unconstitutional." What the California federal court had done, in fact, was make mandatory recitation of the Pledge unconstitutional with the words "under God" included. The predictable results ensued: conservative religious organizations made it sound like the End of Days was at hand because God was not going to be mentioned in the Pledge of Allegiance, even as the rest of the country went about its daily business, saying the Pledge unimpeded.

President Bush criticized the court. Court-haters used the decision as just one more piece of evidence that the country was heading straight to hell. Few asked, "What would change if we didn't say the Pledge with the words 'under God'?" Even fewer asked, "What would change if we didn't say the Pledge of Allegiance at all?" The furor over the first Newdow case became a self-fueling wildfire that eventually burned far beyond the original questions one might ask around the court case.

- Why do we make children say the Pledge of Allegiance?
- If we are standing in a public school, should we be making children pledge to a country under God if they don't want to?
- Does saying the Pledge make us love the United States more?
- Does it make us love the flag more?
- And what does it mean to be allied to a flag, anyway?

- Since the words "under God" were not original to the Pledge, how important are they to have in there?

No matter how you come down on any of these questions, it would have been a good thing for us to have a lively debate about what a pledge to a flag means in the twenty-first century. We proved ourselves incapable of that debate. Instead, we had a debate about just how bad a guy Michael Newdow was.

The president had himself photographed and videotaped saying the Pledge of Allegiance, with crowds shouting out the words "under God" for emphasis. How God responded to all of this is not yet known. Next stop, Supreme Court.

The highest court in the land kicked the can down the road. Rather than ruling on the issues raised by the Newdow petition, it based its ruling on Newdow's standing to bring the action. Since the physician is a divorced, noncustodial father, the Supreme Court said his complaint did not belong before them (though he got high marks from reporters who cover the court for arguing his own case, a high hurdle even for experienced advocates. He has a law degree, but has never worked as a lawyer).

The status of the Pledge is still under debate. A group of Hawaiian Buddhists from the Honpa Honwangji Mission, one of the oldest Buddhist groups in America, passed a resolution supporting a return to the pre-1954 version (without "under God" added). In response, President George W. Bush sent them a letter explaining that when Americans recite the Pledge, "we affirm our form of government, our belief in human dignity, our unity as a people, and our reliance on God." Not exactly constitutional. Not exactly fair game for compulsory recitation, according to Newdow and others pursuing these cases.

In Virginia, a court heard a challenge to the state's compulsory morning recitation of the Pledge. A Mennonite Christian, Edward Myers, whose children attend public school, complained that "the combination of God and country approaches a civic religion that is in competition with my religion."

This argument catches conservative Christians in their own snares. They are generally pretty aggressive in their defense of the Pledge of Allegiance. But at the same time, they are pretty aggressive critics of public schools and ferocious defenders of parents' rights to shield their children from teachings that contradict their own religious beliefs. This particular time, Myers's right to protect his children from the Pledge was completely swamped by its value as a symbolic issue.

To her credit, the trial judge, Karen Williams, conceded that the words "under God" were not meaningless, as has been contended in other separation cases. She wrote, "It is demeaning to persons of any faith to assert that the words 'under God' contain no religious significance. The inclusion of the two words, however, does not alter the nature of the pledge as a patriotic activity."

EIGHT

Now, in the Center Ring . . .
Abortion as the Main Event

WE MAY DISAGREE on when life begins, but it's clear when the abortion battle begins: at conception. From the moment that an ambitious little spermatozoon finds a waiting egg, the womb changes from the most private of private realms to the battleground in a multigenerational battle over pregnancy.

The leadership of the Republican Party is publicly and unanimously opposed to the *Roe v. Wade* decision and increasingly devoted to using faith statements in everyday politics. Some, like Senator Rick Santorum of Pennsylvania, have made public piety and opposition to abortion rights centerpieces of their political appeal, and others, like Dennis Hastert, the Speaker of the House, seem to add "God talk" in a manner that resembles the obligatory tacking on of legal disclaimers to prescription drug commercials. This is not to say Senator Santorum is any more sincere or religious than Speaker Hastert; the young Pennsylvanian has chosen to catch the confessional winds blowing through American politics more than the old suburban Chicago veteran has.

Any examination of the tightening relationship between religion and politics has to pay special attention to the politics, and theology, of pregnancy. The right to legally end a pregnancy is tightly entwined with very old and deep questions about personal sovereignty, ownership of children, and the male prerogative and interest in offspring. The antiabortion groups like to portray all these questions as settled, governed by fixed values, rather than as ones that have changed repeatedly over time along with the rights of women and the shape of marriage, not to mention medical science. The church had weighed in from time to time, and before that, rabbinical bodies, to try to fix the point in pregnancy when the fetus possessed a soul and separate personhood. Not only did gestational ages change over the centuries, but women took matters into their own hands, making their own decisions, and passing on knowledge through the generations on how to stop pregnancies.

The ferocity of the battles fought by the prohibition forces and the abortion-rights supporters obscures a basic and unremarkable fact: abortion has become a widespread phenomenon shared by women across geographical, class, race, and age lines.

- Just over half of all women who end a pregnancy in any given year are under twenty-five years old. Most of the under-twenty-fives are no longer teens. Just under a fifth of all abortions are performed on women under twenty years old, and a third are done on women over thirty.[1]

- Two of every three abortions are performed on women who have never been married. Just under two of every three are performed on women who already have one or more children.[2]

- Though American women are likely to get an abortion while young, the cumulative experience of abortion since *Roe v. Wade* has been very broad: of all women under forty-five, it is estimated roughly a third will have or will have had an abortion.[3]

- Blacks and Latinas have much higher abortion rates than whites.[4]

- One of every four abortion recipients self-identifies as Roman Catholic, nearly half as Protestant.[5]

- There has been a tremendous decline in abortion over the last decade, and a huge overall decline since abortion became legal in all fifty states. Much of the decline, nearly half, can be attributed to the availability of emergency contraception.[6]

- Before you conclude the problem or the battle over abortion is going away, remember this: Half of all pregnancies in the United States are unplanned, and of that half, nearly half again are ended by abortion. From the time of *Roe v. Wade* through 2002, 42 million pregnancies were ended by legal abortion.[7]

- Women are more heavily represented than men at both poles in the debate. More women than men strongly favor and strongly oppose further restrictions on access to abortions.[8]

So there's where we stand. The "strongly favor" and "strongly oppose" wings of the argument carry it forward, decade after decade, in American political life. Many of the battle lines allow no compromise. Abortion cannot be legal and illegal at the same time. Abortion without spousal consent cannot be legal and illegal at the same time. For minors, abortion without parental consent cannot be legal and illegal at the same time.

Religion plays a huge role in all of this. Many of the national antiabortion groups have a frankly religious affiliation or root their motives for going to war against abortion deep in religious conviction. In a 2004 Pew poll, the researchers sliced and diced the sentiment every which way, by race, gender, age, and religion. Of all the big population blocs in society, a majority of only one told pollsters they favor making it harder to get an abortion: white evangelical Protestants. Among those white evangelicals, weekly church attenders supported abortion restrictions at a higher rate than occasional attenders. As opposition to abortion restriction flattens out among generations, the highest support for making it harder to get an abortion comes from the youngest white evangelicals. In the Pew survey, more than two out of three of these eighteen- to twenty-four-year olds said they want more restrictions on abortion access. That made evangelical young adults very different from other young Americans, who expressed majority opposition to making it harder to get an abortion.[9] The young evangelicals were antiabortion at rates far exceeding those of their American over-sixty-five elders, only 44 percent of whom favored making abortion laws more restrictive.

These numbers should not come as a surprise. While *Roe v. Wade* was a galvanizing moment for religious conservatives, it is the youngest adults who have come to maturity with this issue as a top political priority. Older Americans, men and women alike, remember what it was like to have no legal access to abortion. They remember young women disgraced, hastily married, or who went away rather than face community judgment over single parenthood. They remember women sterilized or killed by so-called "back-alley" abortions. This lived experience did not lead older Americans to a lopsided support for either a permissive or a restrictive environment for legal abortion, but to a roughly split decision. Men and women eighteen to twenty-four have grown up knowing that if a woman, her family, or an unmarried couple decided a pregnancy could not proceed, it could, as the saying developed, be "taken care of." Like women who simply assume the victories of the women's movement as givens and proudly say they are not feminists, young evangelicals can blithely choose between the Blue Team and the Red Team. They know who they are by what they are against.

One important thing the abortion battle has done is give national Republicans a handy organizing principle for appealing to the evangelical vote, fueling the fire with one hand while counting the votes with the other.

This has worked so well for Republicans during the thirty-plus years since *Roe* that some Democrats have started to wonder if the GOP really wants to have the law overturned at all. This may be a comment on the cynicism of modern politics or an unsentimental recognition of how coalitions are built and maintained. The Republicans have succeeded richly by mobilizing discrete portions of the overall electorate, harnessing their votes in thumping supermajorities, and, given the overlay of tiny two-senator states and solid GOP house districts, won control or majority influence in all three branches of government.

Abortion has been a handy club for beating divided Democrats over the head every two, four, and six years for various national offices. The sharp edge of the debate has chased away nuance and subtlety, and the Democrats have been particularly ham-fisted over time in their attempts to make the public understand that they are closer to where the public is when it comes to abortion.

What the Pew poll results and countless others quietly reflect is that the majority of Americans have no strong desire to prohibit abortion. Even proposals that would stop far short of prohibition by making the procedure harder to get cannot muster majority support. From years of covering the debate and sifting the data, to me this much seems clear: Americans are as uncomfortable with unrestricted abortion available right up until labor as they are with outlawing abortions entirely. The campaigners who see any restriction as the first step down the long, slippery slope to prohibition are not where Americans are. The activists who seek to ban abortions and all drugs and devices that prevent pregnancies, who make no distinction between a pinpoint-sized cluster of cells and a baby are not where their fellow citizens live on this issue. The battle continues as if each side in this massive tug-of-war has the majority unequivocally on its side.

AFTER A LOUD and vicious demonstration outside a clinic providing abortions in Chicago in 1989 (the clinic provided many services, including contraceptive advice, pelvic exams, and prenatal care, in addition to abortions), Joseph Scheidler, back in his organization's office and plotting future legal strategies, ran down his legislative agenda for me.

Scheidler wanted most forms of contraception made illegal, since he considered them covert forms of abortion. He wanted all abortions made illegal, and doctors and patients who participated in them prosecuted. Finally, he wanted any politicians who tried to fudge on the issue held to account and punished at the polls.

He reserved special scorn for the counterdemonstrators and escorts who helped women run the gauntlet past screaming demonstrators to the clinic doors. In a long conversation with me he compared them to ghouls and vampires: "They love blood. They can't live without it. They aren't fulfilled unless they can help these women murder their babies. To them, that's a success. When they can kill babies."

By the lights of 1989, the language seemed excessive. Almost two decades later, it does not sound extreme at all. Starting in 1986, Scheidler squared off with the National Organization for Women and abortion clinics in a federal prosecution that tied him up for much of the 1990s.[10] He originally prevailed in lower courts, but the case was sent back down by the Supreme Court in 1994. After a trial in 1998, Scheidler and his Pro-Life Action League defendants were found guilty of federal racketeering charges, a verdict overturned by the Supreme Court in 2003.

Scheidler has moved from the fringes of the antiabortion movement to, if not exactly its center, at least its more respectable circles over the past twenty years. While all of the antiabortion firepower was once trained on ending pregnancies through surgical procedures, the movement now leads side battles against a wide array of contraceptives.

For example, President George W. Bush's 2002 nominee for chairman of the Advisory Committee for Reproductive Health Drugs of the Food and Drug Administration, Dr. W. David Hager, was instrumental in a rearguard action blocking the approval of Plan B, emergency contraception, for over-the-counter use.

When Dr. Hager was first picked by the president to chair the committee, the administration was met with a firestorm. The ob-gyn was associated with Focus on the Family's Physician Resource Council and was well-known for his opposition to abortion. After the heat died down, Dr. Hager was seated as a member of the committee rather than its chairman. When the committee sat in judgment of the petition to move Plan B off the list of drugs available only with a prescription, Dr. Hager was outvoted in a lopsided 23–4 ballot.

Normally, when the FDA advisory committees approve a drug for over-the-counter use, it heads to final approval. In the case of Plan B, Dr. Hager's own opposition moved him to keep the fight going. He filed an unusual "minority report" very similar to the document he helped prepare for Concerned Women for America condemning Plan B. The FDA has not fully explained why its then-head, Dr. Mark McClellan, broke precedent and rejected the committee's approval, though it did confirm that it requested no report from Dr. Hager. But the Kentucky physician has said publicly that his brief helped sway the final FDA vote against over-the-counter approval.

The drug levonorgestrel, marketed as Plan B, has passed all the clinical trials for safety and efficacy required by the nation's drug gatekeepers.

The drug has been used safely as a prescription drug for years, with side-effects in a tiny percentage of cases among users overall.[11] Meant to be taken in the seventy-two hours following unprotected sex or contraceptive failure, the compound prevents pregnancy from beginning. If an egg is fertilized, it cannot implant in the uterine lining and begin its journey from egg to blastocyst to embryo to fetus to child.

If you are not a frontline soldier in the abortion wars, Plan B might look like an approach that would allow everyone the chance to lower the racket and see what happens. The women who take levonorgestrel do not get pregnant in the first place. It may sound like hairsplitting, but that fact should loom pretty large in a fight over abortion.

However, those Americans who define life fully invested with legal rights and recognition as beginning with a fertilized egg, taking Plan B is no different from aborting a fetus at twelve, twenty, or thirty-six weeks. Make no mistake, the blood sometimes expelled after emergency contraception does not resemble in any way the chopped up human bodies favored by abortion protestors and annual marchers on the Mall in Washington, D.C. The grisly illustrations of collapsed skulls and tiny feet-first deliveries that became a feature of House and Senate debate in the partial-birth-abortion laws have nothing in common with most women's experience of Plan B.

The fact that Plan B, if used properly, prevents pregnancy from occurring in the first place, might take it out of abortion politics altogether. The clinics, the dilation and extraction, the saline, the blood, the discomfort, and the human in miniature at the heart of the abortion debate are simply absent. But for some the debate over abortion can never be removed from the debate over sex itself, and Plan B cannot be assessed apart from abortion. That might help you understand why an evangelical physician and public opponent of emergency drugs used to control fertility would be appointed by the president of the United States to a committee judging the safety of such drugs.

It might further help you understand how this same doctor, after his nomination to chair the committee was quietly dropped, could still speak publicly of his lobbying in favor of the drug's rejection even after an over-whelmingly favorable vote to approve. And it might help you understand why, years later, Plan B is still not approved for over-the-counter use.

The main objection raised by its opponents had to do with the health of young teenagers. Though the drug has proven safe and effective in re-peated clinical trials in countries around the world, how a high dose of hormones contained in Plan B might affect a fourteen-year-old is keeping it out of the convenient reach of millions of other American women.

When I interviewed Wendy Wright of Concerned Women for Amer-ica and Gloria Feldt of Planned Parenthood together, it was clear Wright's case against Plan B was not strong. It did not matter.

Wright said, "We can also look in five states in the United States where it's available through a pharmacist, that means there's still counseling in-volved, there's still a little bit of intervention to make sure that the person who is buying it understands that there could be risks in taking it. And in Washington state, there has not been a significant decrease in the number of abortions. The only decrease that they've had in the number of abor-tions represents the same decrease we've seen nationwide, so that would show that there is no effect in having the morning-after pill available." If you follow Wright's logic, Plan B should not be approved until we do more research into why the abortion rate in Washington has not fallen more than it has.

Feldt then got to the heart of the matter: "I think it is so disingenuous of Wendy and the organization she represents, because I don't believe you would find that they would support emergency contraception under any circumstances. Their goals are to take away choices that women have to prevent unintended pregnancies and to be able to make their own deci-sions about what to do about pregnancies if they have them.

"So it's really disingenuous to be able to claim that they are in a great concern about women's health right now; that is simply not true. If you're concerned about women's health, then one of the things you want to do is ensure that women can have pregnancies when they're ready to have them, because no one knows better than a woman whether she is, in fact, ready to have a pregnancy." It is the kind of statement that is getting harder to hear over the absolutist din of the abortion debate.

That abortion rights defenders are "proabortion" is a central tenet of faith among religious conservatives. The carefully worded rebuttals from those who would keep abortion legal—explaining that they would be happy if abortions did not have to occur as often, that abortions often show that other things have failed—are dismissed or unheard. In turn, defenders of abortion rights mock the antiabortion forces for being more "pro-pregnancy" than they are "pro-life." Each side refuses to grant the other side the privilege of working from goodwill. More often than either side would care to admit, their opponents are seen as not only mistaken, but bad people.

In this, Martin Marty sees a retreat to a social landscape described by sociologist Georg Simmel a century ago. In his essay "The Stranger," Simmel lays down a diagram that might have been written for twenty-first-century Americans, in which identifying your own position helps you figure out who is a "friend" and who is a "stranger." For modern humans, knowing yourself starts with pointing out the stranger. Simmel writes, "spatial relations are only the condition, on the one hand, and the symbol, on the other, of human relations." In Simmel's and Marty's view, knowing the stranger as a "mainline Protestant" or a "pro-choicer" or an "immigrant" or a "liberal" fixes that other person's place in space and time as surely as knowing the person is a Kenyan, a Chinese, a Chilean, living somewhere specific on the other side of the globe. Seeing the stranger, by subtraction, makes your own circle easier to identify and love.

Granted, it is written in deep "socio-speak," but Simmel's elegant description of the "social other" gives a brilliant insight into the mechanics of bustling, chaotic American social conflict. "The unity of nearness and remoteness involved in every human relation is organized, in the phenomenon of the stranger, in a way which may be most briefly formulated by saying that in the relationship to him, distance means that he, who is close by, is far, and strangeness means that he, who also is far, is actually near. For, to be a stranger is naturally a very positive relation; it is a specific form of interaction. The inhabitants of Sirius [Simmel is referring to the star, not the satellite radio service] are not really strangers to us, at least not in any social logically relevant sense: they do not exist for us at all; they are beyond far and near. The stranger, like the poor and like sundry "inner enemies," is an element of the group itself. His position as a full-fledged member involves both being outside it and confronting it. The following statements, which are by no means intended as exhaustive, indicate how elements which increase distance and repel, in the relations of and with the stranger produce a pattern of coordination and consistent interaction."

Every year, on the anniversary of the *Roe v. Wade* Supreme Court decision, large groups of "inner enemies" confront one another in the public spaces of Washington, D.C. When police let them pass within hailing distance of one another, they shout, "Murderers!" and commands like "Keep your laws off my body!" The large crowds are counted and interviewed and photographed by waiting journalists, who read great significance into their presence.

These demonstrations, with their fleets of rented buses, handmade and printed signs, dueling strollers and placarded toddlers, are two things at once. They are in the first place a strong endorsement of the American notions of free association, petitioning the legislature for redress, and the need for us to continue to try to persuade one another, even in the longest-running battles.

The vast parades are, in the very same moment, a disheartening moment. Two armies assemble, repeat the chants, wave the signs, show off their kids, and grant the TV interviews, listening to speeches laden with threat and dread, and never give any sign of understanding the other side's argument. The 2006 march could have been the 1996 or the 1986 march. Two throngs come to Washington to see their "inner enemies"; we Kremlinologists of capital demonstration see who was standing where on the podium, and inner identity is reinforced. Even though holders of the argument are, in both cases, your neighbors, relatives, co-workers (though there are persistent whispers in new data that communities are becoming more uniform), the strangerness on the other side of the police barricade is reinforced. The mock "battles," of dueling chants and signs, seem almost made for that night's television news. Though I know it does not happen, I can imagine news directors meeting with the cops the night before, making sure the line of march allows one opportunity for *faux* social drama to play out.

The stranger in Simmel's essay is dangerous in part because he or she is free . . . free of the history, free of the assumptions, free of what we today might call baggage, and therefore suspect. The people you shared the ride to Washington with from Cherry Hill, New Jersey, or Murfreesboro, Tennessee, or Florissant, Missouri, are bearers of that shared "history," even when the pickup spot for the charter bus is a newly completed subdivision somewhere way out on the metropolitan edge. In these political movements, people find deep fulfillment in the mechanics of display—handing out the signs, the hymn sheets, making the National Park Service deposit for trash removal, and making sure the public address system is installed results in satisfying success for our sets of inner enemies—quite apart from the cold touch of speculum, the blood test result, and agonizing personal dramas that often surround pregnancy.

Both political parties are trapped. To maintain the goodwill and support of their conservative Christian backers, elected Republicans in much of the country cannot drop their guard on abortion for a moment. In almost equal measure, Democrats are boxed in by Republican prohibitionists and find themselves going to great lengths to fight or block any restriction on performing abortions, even in the face of solid ethical and political logic.

Some, like Senators Sam Brownback of Kansas, Rick Santorum of Pennsylvania, and Tom Coburn of Oklahoma, have made abortion one of the centerpieces of their entire political program. There are times when it would be tempting to drop the state references or such newspaper shorthand as "R-KS" for "the senator from Abortionland." Democrats appear trapped into being just as ferocious in defense as their opponents are on offense, which has elevated abortion's prominence as a political issue to the status of "Great Moral Issue of Our Time," to the detriment of many other worthy, moral, and important questions.

If both sides valued winning less and reducing abortions more, the way religion gets used and misused in this debate might eventually let both sides win something like a victory. (Cynics who accuse the Republican Party of using abortion as a convenient cudgel to pound Democrats can get many of their suspicions confirmed by watching the battle.)

Abortion is used to raise funds, build crowds during campaigns, tap mailing lists for street troops and phone banks for "GOTV" (get out the vote) efforts right before election day. It is such an effective tool for putting the Democratic Party on the defensive that you might wonder if those who wield it so effectively as an issue really want abortion made illegal. You might also wonder if its real value lies in keeping religious organizations active in politics.

After thirty years of this, with the fight stuck in place and both sides hostage to the issue, it might be useful to ask, Isn't anybody tired of this?

Democrats might want to change the subject, since some of the very voters they feel they have a message for—economically pressured seniors, less-educated manual and production workers who have not prospered in the globalizing labor marketplace, students watching college costs rise while starting salaries flatten—have become single-issue voters in a way that disadvantages the "right-to-choose" party.

Father Thomas Reese is a familiar face to American news viewers, as a "guide" to the Catholic world. He was, until recently, the editor of the Jesuit public affairs magazine, *America*.[12] As a Catholic priest, he has little patience for the old alibi, "I'm personally opposed to abortion, but I cannot force my personal views on others."

During the 2004 national race, he watched as Catholic Democratic politicians especially tried to find a way to talk about the issue that would have had some integrity, and in his own view, failed. "What they should have said," Father Reese told me, "goes more like this: 'I am personally opposed to abortion, and I will do everything possible to reduce the number of abortions short of putting doctors and women in jail.'

"Now, if I was writing the sound bite, that's a much better position than what Kerry said. Then you start talking about the fact that there have been more abortions under Bush, under the Bush presidencies, than there were under the Clinton presidency and things like that. As the Clinton people said, it's the economy that's doing it. And that the programs the Republicans are gutting, like things to help children and mothers, those are the things that are increasing abortion. So they're really not pro-life.

"But when they start talking that way, the proabortion group goes crazy, starts criticizing, and you just can't get them. For them having an abortion is practically a sacrament. They're insane over it. I think the Democrats and Congress want to break away from that, but that lobby is still very, very strong, and very vocal in the Democratic Party."

The former magazine editor said the media had to bear its share of the responsibility for the centrality of abortion in the national debate: "Now, I'm not one to beat up on the media, but it would be fascinating for some-one to do a doctoral dissertation going back and looking at, say, the state-ments of John Paul II, and which one made headlines and which one didn't. And I'll bet you whenever he said anything about sex, it made the front page. Or abortion. But when he calls for forgiveness of third world debt, when he talks about aiding the poor, et cetera, if it made the news-paper, it would buried somewhere in the back.

"Now that says something about American media as much as it says something about the Catholic Church. And I don't quite understand it or know why that is, except that maybe it's such a simpler story to cover than the more complicated issues of poverty and social justice."

True enough. Abortion easily surrenders to black/white, yes/no, stop/go coverage. What Catholic politicians might have to say about other parts of Catholic social teaching is hard to illustrate with a quick sound blast of chanting demonstrators or a wide shot of the Capitol Building.

Maybe Democrats are getting the message. It may be the wrong mes-sage (more on that in chapter twelve), but also a reflection of how dissatis-fied the stasis in the abortion wars have left many voters. In 2006, Senator Hillary Clinton of New York, in a speech to abortion-rights supporters in New York's capital, Albany, said, "We can all recognize that abortion in many ways represents a sad, even tragic choice to many, many women. . . .

The fact is that the best way to reduce the number of abortions is to reduce the number of unwanted pregnancies in the first place." She called this position possible "common ground" with antiabortion forces.

Almost predictably, she was slammed by abortion-rights absolutists for, in their view, walking away from a political lifetime of pro-choice support and mocked by prohibitionists as acting out of political expediency, pandering, and heading to the center from her perceived perch on abortion's hard left.[13]

The Reverend Richard Land is offended by the suggestion of the Reverend Jim Wallis, editor of *Sojourners* magazine and author of *God's Politics,* that conservative Christians rode the emphasis on two issues, abortion and gay marriage, into power. Land reflects the widespread conviction in the conservative leadership that broadening the appeal is important, while the opposition to abortion remains as clear as ever: "I think it's an understanding of the mandate from Jesus of Nazareth to be salt and light. To be the salt of the earth and light of the world. And an understanding that that impels us to reject the hunker-down-in-the-bunker mentality and to go out into the society and to seek, as salt, to stop decay and degeneration and death, and, as light, to eliminate the darkness and penetrate the gloom. That would impel us to involvement on the abortion issue. It would impel us to involvement on euthanasia. It would impel us to involvement on protecting marriage as being between a man and a woman. It would impel us to speak out on international human rights, which we have."

In 2005 and 2006, America found that religion and *Roe* have seized the process of nominating and confirming judges to the Supreme Court and lower federal courts. Listening to its expression in Justice Sundays or in the ferocious ad wars and pundit smack-downs surrounding high-court seats, you could be forgiven for coming away from the confirmation debates thinking that judges have only two jobs: judging abortion cases and deciding whether or not to "legislate from the bench."

In 2003, religion and the judiciary came surging forward as an issue, when Republican senators began to say, consistently and publicly, that Democratic senators were discriminating against Bush administration judicial nominees because of their religious belief. The rationale went that since Roman Catholic and evangelical Protestant jurists belong to churches that oppose abortion, Democratic senators would not approve them for the federal bench. That point flared up during the hearings over Alabama attorney general David Pryor's elevation to the Eleventh U.S. Circuit Court of Appeals based in Atlanta.

Alabama senator Jeff Sessions wondered if a Catholic could win confirmation: "The doctrine that abortion is not justified for rape and incest is Catholic doctrine. It is the position of the Pope and it is the position of the Catholic Church in unity. So are we saying that if you believe in that principle, you can't be a federal judge? Is that what we're saying? And are we not saying then good Catholics need not apply?"

Illinois Senator Richard Durbin fired back: "As a Catholic I sit here and resent what I'm hearing. People who are not Catholics are speaking for a religion they do not belong to. There are many Catholics who see this nomination much differently than those who support Mr. Pryor. I believe that his position should be addressed on the merits, and I would hope that you would instruct members of this committee to expunge references to religion from this point forward. This is beneath the dignity of this committee."

Senator Sessions was not backing down: "I would just say it this way. Yes, we have a prohibition on a religious test for this body, and I don't think any member on either side would be prejudiced against a person because of the faith that they have. But what if their personal views are consistent with that faith? What if their personal views are sincerely to the fact that abortion is morally wrong and it's the taking of innocent life, need they not apply?"

"I deeply resent this new line of attack from the right wing," returned Durbin, "that anyone who opposes William Pryor is guilty of discrimination against him because he is a Catholic."

The Bush administration did not help, putting religion firmly on the table after maintaining just weeks before that it was not and should not be part of the conversation at all. When Judge John Roberts was nominated to be an associate justice to replace Sandra Day O'Connor, the questions began about the impact of his status as a devout Roman Catholic in judging cases involving many Culture War cases, including those on abortion.

Senator Richard Durbin came in for a particular throttling after revealing his plans to discuss a shared Catholic faith with nominee Roberts. Connie Mackey, of the Family Research Council, wrote Senator Durbin one of the many critical letters he got in the summer of 2005: "It has been our concern over the past few years that one who is orthodox in their religion, whether it is Catholic, Protestant, Jewish or any other denomination, will be discouraged from seeking a position on the court or for that matter that a chilling effect is being placed upon anyone seeking public office who is devout." Mrs. Mackey also wrote, "It is the intention of the Family Research Council to encourage legislators not to pit nominees' faith against their fitness for public office."

For Mackey, the bottom line was an assumption that Durbin would hold Roberts's fidelity to Catholic teaching against him in his aspiration to join the Supreme Court. Tony Perkins, also of the FRC, told Fox News that Durbin's questions would be totally out of line: "He's clearly implying that people who believe that there should be some restrictions on abortion in this country are out of the mainstream, and that's an extreme position. There should be no litmus test because people have a religious conviction, that somehow they're disqualified from serving either on the bench or some other public office.

"I mean, that line of questioning or reasoning has a very chilling effect upon our process here in this country." Perkins continued seconds later, "I think when you look at someone and whether or not they're Protestant, they're Catholic, or they're Jewish, they have every right to be involved in this process. And our Constitution guarantees there'll be no litmus, religious litmus test. I mean, if anything, I think we need a tolerance test for some of these senators." [14]

For conservatives, especially Christian conservatives, a Roman Catholic United States senator, a member of the Judiciary Committee, could be declared out-of-bounds for a desire to ask a Catholic jurist how he is affected by his membership in a church with very specific views on how the faith should be practiced and very specific requirements about the public responsibilities of Catholic public figures. As America demonstrated in the case of Catholic presidential candidate John Kerry, believing one thing personally and not making law for others based on it was seen as at best an immoral straddle, at worst a public countenancing of grave sin in the case of abortion.

Ten months or so had passed since Catholic bishops had been promising not to give Kerry communion, but John Roberts's assertion that he would simply apply the law without regard to his own religious faith had now passed the conservative sniff test and provided another opportunity to make an issue of the supposed orthodoxy deficit on the Democratic side of the aisle.

The issue quickly whipsawed when a few months later, after the death of Chief Justice William Rehnquist created an opening for Judge Roberts, presidential counsel Harriet Miers was named to the vacant O'Connor seat. Word quietly spread through Washington that the nominee was not only a friend of the president's but a member of Valley View Christian Church in Dallas. America did not know much about what kind of justice Harriet Miers might be, but it knew what kind of Christian she was.

President Bush tried to explain why a citizen, or a member of the Judiciary Committee, might want to know where she spends her Sunday mornings: "People ask me why I picked Harriet Miers," the president said to reporters in the Oval Office. "They want to know Harriet Miers' background, they want to know as much as they possibly can before they form opinions. And part of Harriet Miers' life is her religion."

Dr. James Dobson, founder of the evangelical research, lobbying, and communications group Focus on the Family, did not have to wonder about Miers or wait to see what she had to say at a hearing that would never come. People like Dr. Dobson get a call from the White House. Deputy Chief of Staff Karl Rove might later have wished the powerful and influential broadcaster had been a touch more discreet. He had said publicly that he supported the Miers nomination to the high court because of something he could not divulge.

Then, he divulged: "When you know some of the things I know, that I probably shouldn't know, you will understand why I have said, with fear and trepidation, that I believe Harriet Miers will be a good justice." Dr. Dobson said Rove had assured him that Miers, an adult convert from Roman Catholicism, belonged to "a very conservative church, which is almost universally pro-life, that she had taken on the American Bar Association on the issue of abortion and fought for a policy that would not be supportive of abortion, that she had been a member of the Texas Right to Life. In other words, there is a characterization of her that was given to me before the President had actually made this decision. I could not talk about that on Monday. I couldn't talk about it on Tuesday. In fact, Brit Hume said, 'What church does she go to?' And I said, 'I don't think it's up to me to reveal that.' "

Dr. Dobson dropped some tantalizing details about his "secret" phone conversations with the president's political adviser. "We did not discuss *Roe v. Wade* in any context or any other pending issue that will be considered by the Court. I did not ask that question. You know, to be honest, I would have loved to have known how Harriet Miers views *Roe v. Wade*. But even if Karl had known the answer to that and I'm certain that he didn't, because the President himself said he didn't know, Karl would not have told me that." [15]

You can believe that if you want—that one of the most powerful conservative Christian opinion-makers in America, a leader whose approval will open another front in the struggle to get Miers confirmed, never discussed *Roe v. Wade* with Rove. President Bush cannot admit to having a litmus test, but Dr. Dobson can. Abortion is at the core of the conservative Christian ambitions surrounding the courts. You did not have to read between the lines. The Focus on the Family leader said, "If I have made a mistake here, I will never forget the blood of those babies that will die will be on my hands to some degree." Memo to Senate: If Harrier Miers isn't pro-life, babies will die.

The same Dick Durbin who'd had his ears boxed back in July now found that religion was not only a fit subject for speculation, but vital to understanding who a nominee is. He pointed out the obvious: "The White House is basically saying that because of Harriet Miers' religious beliefs, you can trust her. That to me is a complete reversal of not only the history of choosing Supreme Court nominees, but of where the White House was weeks ago with the nomination of John Roberts."

The Bush administration learned not to respond to observations like Durbin's. Just keep moving forward, do not climb into the pit with your critics, because you then must stand on level ground with them and give away an advantage. It is a lesson many politicians have learned over the years, but few have applied it with the discipline of President Bush and his team, even during the terrible year of 2005.

There are other life issues that tend to line up the iron filings of American public opinion in much the same way as the magnetic force of abortion. The issues repel and attract many of the same people and institutions. Senator Sam Brownback is a member of the Judiciary Committee that openly doubted Harriet Miers's likelihood of Senate confirmation and quizzed both John Roberts and Samuel Alito closely on their attitudes toward life issues, and, as an outspoken opponent of embryonic-stem-cell research and physician-assisted suicide, he has warned supporters of both of dire political consequences.

The Kansas senator, who has also been testing the waters for a 2008 national run, is in touch with pro-life groups nationwide. But if you try to stretch the pro-life coalition too far, will it break? Ardent abortion foe Senator Orrin Hatch of Utah is, at the same time, a supporter of stem-cell research. More than 80 percent of Americans told pollsters they were offended by the Republican leadership on Capitol Hill's attempts to keep Terri Schiavo alive, a far higher percentage than that of those supporting unrestricted access to abortion. That Schiavo number did not decline when, a few weeks later, it was revealed that Schiavo's brain, as many doctors had asserted over the years, had long since become an unresponsive mass.

Congressman Tom DeLay had angrily told reporters and partisan crowds that Michael Schiavo had not gotten his wife speech therapy. Senator Bill Frist, who will leave the Senate at the end of his sole term and is also contemplating a presidential run, diagnosed the severely brain-damaged woman from television depictions of old videos taken by the

Florida woman's parents. The heart surgeon-turned-politician rejected years of diagnoses from neurologists and took to the Senate floor to cast doubt on the conclusion that Schiavo was in a persistent vegetative state. "I question it based on a review of the video footage which I spent an hour or so looking at last night in my office," Frist said in a speech that also cited medical texts. "She certainly seems to respond to visual stimuli."

Big majorities also reported having the impression that House and Senate Republicans played politics with Terri Schiavo's life. Trying to compel her appearance at a hearing, reasoning that she could not be removed from life support if her presence was demanded by Congress, drew legislators from both parties into a last-minute series of debates that left the public angry and backfired on the Republican leadership. At the time, Republican pollster Tony Fabrizio told the *Washington Post* that Frist had made a risky move. "If you want to confirm your bona fides" with one group, Fabrizio said, "this is a good way to do it. But while you're pleasing one segment of the party, you may be setting yourself up for trouble with conservatives who say, 'We don't want more federal control over this stuff.'"[16]

States'-rights-loving conservatives are not the only group Frist will have to worry about after the Schiavo tragedy and his role in it. Boomers with aging parents, caretakers of chronically ill family members, moderates with living wills and end-of-life directives, watched Congress members rush back to Washington on a weekend to create a legal rationale for interfering in a much-litigated Florida case that asked for no legislative input.

In the John Ashcroft-era Justice Department, the attorney general recanted states' rights broadsides printed in such publications as *Southern Partisan* to pet causes of Christian conservatives. As a U.S. senator, John Ashcroft of Missouri wrote ringing endorsements of states' rights. Trying to win confirmation as U.S. Attorney general, he recanted. Then, as America's top law-enforcement officer, Ashcroft went after the repeatedly voter-affirmed doctor-assisted suicide law in the state of Oregon under federal drug laws, trying to catch doctors in the snare of penalties passed to catch pushers. The Supreme Court, while not ruling on the merits of assisted suicide itself, spanked the Bush administration for its overreach, ruling 6–3 that the Controlled Substances Act did not apply to doctors in Oregon prescribing a lethal dose of drugs.[17]

While various Republican politicians are in the habit of assuming that life issues are electoral winners, they may find more subtle coalitions forming for and against abortion, stem-cell research, and end-of-life law. Reliable antiabortion voters on Capitol Hill, like Missouri senator Jim Talent, may have some hard choices ahead. Senator Talent did not come right out and say how he intended to vote on stem-cell research, but instead came up with a GOP version of the common Democratic straddle on abortion: "I'm opposed to cloning, but I support stem cell research. The technology is changing all the time and so I'm always considering whether there is a better way to strike the balance."[18] Missouri's Christian conservatives want to criminalize stem-cell research that involves somatic-cell transfer, often called therapeutic cloning, using the altered nucleus of a human egg.

The difficulty with Christian conservative allies who have carried politicians a long way is the danger that comes with all single-issue or "single-issue-cluster" voters. They are not particularly wedded to you, just to the ideal. You may have all kinds of great ideas in other areas, but it turns out they do not care about that other stuff. Sam Lee, director of Campaign Life Missouri, did not give Talent much wiggle room: "If he doesn't take a clear position on the pro-life side, it's going to hurt him, no question about it. People are just not going to work for him."

Lee told the *St. Louis Post-Dispatch,* "The cloning issue is separating the true pro-life Republicans from the politically pro-life Republicans. It is coming down to a battle within the party over which will take precedence, money or moral values."[19] Clearly, the signal has been sent that banning cutting-edge stem-cell research is more important than reelecting Jim Talent.

"This issue has been very divisive in the Republican Party," said Pam Fichter, president of Missouri Right to Life. "You can't help but extrapolate that and say it would hurt the Republican ticket at all levels."

At a time when Missouri's Republican incumbent U.S. senator was running very close to a challenger State Auditor Claire McCaskill, who was campaigning for stem-cell research, none other than former Missouri senator and Republican John Danforth took to the airwaves in paid spots to work against the stem-cell criminalization measure.

Is the Christian-based right-to-life movement ready to tease apart the threads of the current debates and back compromises to create larger and more effective coalitions? Or will purity be valued above victory and leave Christian organizations facing electoral punishment for misreading the "saving babies" argument for "saving eggs and embryos?"

In chapter nine we'll take a closer look at one historically large partner in the right-to-life movement, the Roman Catholic Church. Has its twin "insider-outsider" role in American history pushed it to make the right choices in recent battles over its role in American politics, and American life?

NINE

From Al Smith to John Kerry

AMERICA'S ROMAN CATHOLICS ARE a success story. Not only have they moved from the margins to the mainstream of American life, but they have proven the very reality of the American Dream itself. Catholics have been at home in what is now the fifty American states for five centuries, tromping through marshy south Florida looking for a fountain of youth and crossing the desert Southwest in search of lost cities of gold. But before Spanish-speaking North America was swallowed up into the American empire, the United States was a Protestant enterprise.

Oh sure, there were Catholics in much of the thirteen colonies, with Maryland founded as a place where Catholic immigrants from the British Isles could find a degree of tolerance not common at home. French in Louisiana, Bavarians in Pennsylvania, Irish in New England . . . Roman Catholics were a small but substantial minority in early America. They were also the target of religious-based political suspicion.

In 1864, Pope Pius IX issued a "Syllabus of Errors," setting out Catholic teaching on a number of political questions, in order to leave no doubt where the full weight of the church lay in regard to a number of political and cultural ideas sweeping the industrializing world. The pope denounced as errors all of the following propositions:

- "Human reason . . . is the sole arbiter of truth and falsehood, and of good and evil" . . . "hence reason is the ultimate standard by which man can and ought to arrive at the knowledge of all truths of every kind."
- "In the present day it is no longer expedient that the Catholic

religion should be held as the only religion of the State, to the exclusion of all other forms of worship."

- "Protestantism is nothing more than another form of the same true Christian religion, in which form it is given to please God equally as in the Catholic Church."
- "The Church ought to be separated from the State, and the State from the Church."
- "Every man is free to embrace and profess that religion which, guided by the light of reason, he shall consider true," and "it has been wisely decided by law, in some Catholic countries, that persons coming to reside therein shall enjoy the public exercise of their own peculiar worship."
- "The Roman Pontiff can, and ought to, reconcile himself, and come to terms with progress, liberalism and modern civilization."

Thus in the space of a few pages the Supreme Pontiff rejected religious freedom and tolerance, ecumenism, freedom of conscience, and humanism. Oh, and by the way, it is an error to expect that the Roman pontiff can, and ought to, reconcile himself to modernism. Anti-Catholic agitators, especially in the English-speaking world, went to town for decades on the papal encyclical *Quanta Cura* and the "Syllabus of Errors," its accompanying rundown of the errors of modern life. For a long time before and after Pius's throwdown to the modern world, non-Catholic and secular governing classes and intellectuals speculated about whether Catholicism was compatible with liberal, secular democracy. Now, where have you heard that before?

A striking political cartoon of the late nineteenth century captures that suspicion beautifully, as European Catholic bishops enter the Atlantic and become alligators on their way to America, their miters, their bishop's headgear, morphing into snapping, sharp-toothed jaws. It was the allegiance to the clergy and the role of the clerical hierarchy in communal life and the reverence for the Pope, the Vicar of Christ on Earth, that fed generations of American anti-Catholics ready ammunition.

Catholic America—rapidly gaining education, clout, and numbers in Boston, New York, Baltimore, Philadelphia, and Chicago—responded in a way that makes perfect sense: they self-consciously presented themselves to the rest of the country as true-blue American. Their salutes were snappier, their flag-waving wavier, and their anti-Communism even anti-er.

You see it in Father Francis Patrick Duffy's statue, a brooding man's man in the middle of Times Square, or just a stone's throw away, the statue of George M. Cohan, song-and-dance man, Broadway star, and composer of "The Yankee Doodle Boy" and "You're a Grand Old Flag." The cardinal-archbishops of the great Catholic metropolises of the Great Lakes and Northeast were as tough as any elected official in their denunciations of America's adversaries in the Cold War (countries that also, coincidentally, suppressed the Catholic Church in Czechoslovakia, Poland, the Ukraine, Cuba, and Yugoslavia).

The descendants of men and women who arrived emaciated and illiterate at America's "Golden Door" had built a stunning institutional life that took children from elementary school to university, sustained widows and orphans, built libraries, hospitals, and churches. By mid-twentieth century they had come into their own in finance, law, medicine, education, and public service. But one set of doors was still not open to what had long been America's single-largest religious denomination by far—the doors to the Oval Office of the White House.

Governor Al Smith of New York became a hero to Catholic families across America with his run for president in 1928, on the Democratic ticket. The chief executive of America's most populous and powerful state, the kid from the slums of lower Manhattan, had already proven plenty about how far in life a Catholic could go. He might have underestimated the sheer amount of anti-Catholic prejudice that still remained in America's Protestant rank and file. The most solidly Democratic region in the country, the states of the Confederacy, voted for political novice Herbert Hoover, as did Smith's own state of New York.

Sure, he was carrying plenty of nonreligious baggage from the moment he accepted the nomination: his ties to the Tammany political machine, his unpolished manners and speech that still bore the mark of the slum, and his strong opposition to Prohibition. Any one of these would lose him potential friends across the South, the Midwest, and the Great Plains. He took on the religion issue in speeches and articles, appealing to the idealistic strain in the American character:

> I believe in absolute freedom of conscience for all men and equality of all churches, all sects and all beliefs before the law as a matter of right and not as a matter of favor. I believe in the absolute separation of church and state and in the strict enforcement of the Constitution that Congress shall make no law respecting an establishment of religion or prohibiting the free exercise thereof. I believe that no tribunal of any church has any power to make any decree of any force in the law of the land, other than to establish the status of its own communicants within its own church.[1]

This declaration, in an *Atlantic* article, was one Smith made because he had to. It was written in response to a broadside earlier that year from a lawyer and Episcopal layman, Charles Marshall, who, when surveying papal encyclicals and historic Catholic doctrine, concluded:

> It is indeed true that a loyal and conscientious Roman Catholic could and would discharge his oath of office with absolute fidelity to his moral standards. As to that in general, and as to you in particular, your fellow citizens entertain no doubt. But those moral standards differ essentially from the moral standards of all men not Roman Catholics. They are derived from the basic political doctrine of the Roman Catholic Church, asserted against repeated challenges for fifteen hundred years, that God has divided all power over men between the secular State and that Church.

Marshall was technically correct. The Roman Catholic hierarchy had suffered through a rough nineteenth century and hadn't quite caught up: the loss of the Papal States to a unified Italy, the rise of the modern industrializing state across Catholic Europe, and the accompanying modern nationalism that supplied citizens with an identity to rival that deriving from their religious faith. Writing in the spring of 1927, Marshall was writing in the trough between the papal backlash against modernizing citizenship and the later acceptance and even endorsement of a Catholic citizen's fidelity to both church and state. The papacy had not even reconciled with Italy over the loss of its country. Fifty years of standoff would finally end in 1929 with the concordat signed with Benito Mussolini's fascist government.

But Marshall's widely read and widely quoted article did get to the crux of Protestant America's misgivings about a Catholic chief executive: "Thus the Constitution declares the United States shall hold in equal favor different kinds of religion or no religion and the Pope declares it is not lawful to hold them in equal favor. Is there not here a quandary for that man who is at once a loyal churchman and a loyal citizen?"[2] For many Americans, the imagined choice facing Catholic politicians was stark: when a church teaching conflicted with American law or custom, which would win out?

Governor Smith called on two important allies for help in crafting a response, Judge Joseph Proskauer, a Jew, and the same Father Duffy whose glowering stare surveys Times Square. Duffy's emigration from Canada to the U.S. to teach in Catholic schools, serve as a chaplain in two wars with the storied New York Volunteer Regiment, the Fighting 69th, symbolized the growing acceptance of Roman Catholics as patriotic Americans. By the 1920s, he was probably the most famous Catholic priest in America and ready to do battle both with reactionary members of his own faith and the suspicious American majority.

This ecumenical trio emerged with an answer mirrored by Catholic politicians for decades to come: ". . . I am unable to understand how anything I was taught as a Catholic could possibly be in conflict with what is good citizenship. The essence of my faith is built upon the Commandments of God. The law of the land is built upon the Commandments of God. There can be no conflict between them."[3]

The Happy Warrior did not prevail. Smith even lost his home state of New York. But his losing campaign was an important one for Catholics and eventually for all Americans.

It would be thirty-two years before the Democratic Party would try again. This time the candidate would be one more generation removed from the immigrant cadences and rough-and-tumble world of the ward boss. No matter, John Kennedy again had to take on the issue of his Catholicism and show himself in sync with American ideals, in the face of persisting whispers about divided loyalties: "It is apparently necessary for me to state once again—not what kind of church I believe in, for that should be important only to me—but what kind of America I believe in."

In his widely covered and quoted 1960 speech before the Greater Houston Ministerial Association, the Massachusetts senator made a striking appeal for separation of church and state, and religious pluralism: "I believe in an America that is officially neither Catholic, Protestant nor Jewish; where no public official either requests or accepts instructions on public policy from the Pope, the National Council of Churches or any other ecclesiastical source—where no religious body seeks to impose its will directly or indirectly upon the general populace or the public acts of its officials—and where religious liberty is so indivisible that an act against one church is treated as an act against all."

It was going to take more than just a few finely crafted phrases to sweep away 180 years of encrusted prejudice. In the same speech, Kennedy tried to take the "divided loyalties" argument head-on: "I ask you tonight to follow in that tradition—to judge me on the basis of my record of 14 years in Congress—on my declared stands against an Ambassador to the Vatican, against unconstitutional aid to parochial schools, and against any boycott of the public schools (which I have attended myself)—instead of judging me on the basis of these pamphlets and publications we all have seen that carefully select quotations out of context from the statements of Catholic church leaders, usually in other countries, frequently in other centuries, and always omitting, of course, the statement of the American Bishops in 1948 which strongly endorsed church-state separation, and which more nearly reflects the views of almost every American Catholic."

Kennedy was boldly declaring his independence from the Roman hierarchy and decades of arguments over school funding, and rejects the possibility of diplomatic relations with the Vatican (they would have to wait until Ronald Reagan opened them in 1985). For a Catholic, this time it worked. It worked in part because of the glamour and "vigah" of the young politician and his beautiful wife, his millions, and his opponent. But right along with America, Catholic America had changed. The struggling sons and daughters of Ellis Island arrivals were grandparents now, and their grandchildren were middle-class, college-bound boomers, suburbanites, part of the American whole with fading memories of living on relief, TB wards, and the employment and security that might come courtesy of the alderman and a prized city job.

Cardinal Theodore McCarrick, born in 1930, ordained in 1958, has watched the Catholic Church as an institution and its people as citizens changing throughout his lifetime: "They've become more discriminating. They want to be Americans in every way, yet there are still some things that trigger the Catholic, rather than ordinary American response. The Catholic response has been triggered by the great moral questions. I wouldn't necessarily say that for everyone; it's not true for everyone. But there are still many in the church who when they look at issues like the sanctity of human life, euthanasia, the need for peace, violence, help for the poor—all these questions have great moral value, and they bring out in many of our people a Catholic response. None more than the question of the right to life.

"If they were once likely to vote as a bloc, now they would not. There is a solid number who are moved by the moral values. The Catholics basically have their own moral principles, some so faithful to them that it guides everything they decide to do, including their votes. Some are less likely to be guided solely by those moral absolutes. So they are there in the background." That description sounds more like the American voter in general than the Catholic one in particular.

The old religious coalitions against the Vietnam War, against Southern resistance to civil rights legislation, against Appalachian poverty, and for organizing workers around the country have come apart as the component parts of our common lives have morphed beyond recognition. The straddle John Kerry attempted as a presidential candidate echoes throughout the American Catholic world as old assumptions disappear.

John Podesta was a political strategist and then chief of staff for Bill Clinton, and now runs a think tank called the Center for American Progress. In an April 2005 speech to the Pew Center for Religion in Public Life, he talked about the "two-ness" of being a Catholic and a progressive: "I attend Mass, I take communion. It's a source of strength for me. I think it's really what makes me a progressive. And while—like many Catholics—there are issues where I disagree with my church, I could not help but be touched by what I think really all Americans experienced recently—the life and works of John Paul II. He once observed that America today has what he called a heightened responsibility to be for the world an example of the genuinely free, democratic, just, and humane society.

"That is as clear and precise a statement of what faith has to say to politics, I think, as anything I could come up with. Those moral values not only help define me as a Catholic and as an American; they're the reason why in this time of conservative power, and particularly at a time when I see a conservative abuse of power, I'm standing my ground as a progressive and I am willing to get engaged in this fight and this debate for the direction of our country." That appeal was simple when speaking to the white ethnic church of the last century, even at the time of the Cold War. The memories of discrimination and exclusion were fresh, as were the struggles of starting at the bottom of the American ladder and climbing.

In the last few electoral cycles evidence has popped up of several new ways of looking at Catholic voters. In the not-quite-meshing, not-quite-conflicting data lies a question: Is the transformation of Catholic America complete, or are they still a distinct voting public? And what effect will the country's largest single religious group have on that tightening embrace between religion and politics in America?

Father Robert Drinan was a five-term congressman from Boston and a Democratic Party stalwart, until Pope John Paul II ordered priests to end their involvement in elective politics: "I know lots of Catholics who have become Republican, Reagan Republican, but they do it in part maybe because they're conservative or they're religious but lots of factors are involved. They don't want to pay taxes. They're moving up to the middle-class. Now, even if these people were not Roman Catholic, they might become Republican." A favorite object of derision among conservative Catholics and critics of the Second Vatican Council, he sees, in addition to a more affluent Catholic America moving right, rank-and-file communicants anxious about social change: "A lot of these people are scared. They don't know how to interpret the gays and all the divorce, and abortion, and they'll vote for anybody who'll try to stop that."

Professor Scott Appleby has been writing about these changes for years among his fellow Catholics. He cautions that you cannot look at a post-Kennedy era among Roman Catholic voters in isolation from the other forces in religion, economics, and culture shaping American society. A lot of the scholarship looking at Catholic voters, he says, shows "that they are praying with their pocketbooks. The attempts of the liberal, Democratic, post-Kennedy progressive Catholic wing to teach these folks Catholic social justice, preferential option for the poor, solidarity, and so on, just failed because it was not in those people's economic self-interest. It certainly wasn't a stigma anymore to be Catholic, and they were true-blue patriotic Americans. That had been determined before they came into their own, by that generation of people who are now in their forties and fifties. They see their faith in much the same way some mainstream evangelical Protestants do. They see it as a blessing to prosperity, success, hard work, so on, and they are not reached in the same personal crisis or by a particularly persuasive pastor. They're not reached by the part of Catholicism that keeps me Catholic personally, which is care for the poor, concern for social justice, that asks, 'What are you doing with your affluence?'

"They will be involved in charities—I'm not saying they're heartless folks—but it's just not their personal identity. Their relationship between the political and the religious and the economic is dictated more by the larger environment than by the church itself. To put it better, there are enough people in the church itself and enough bishops and enough propaganda within the Catholic church that they can find some kind of support for their point of view."

Roman Catholic voters chose Bill Clinton in 1992 and 1996. They voted for Al Gore by a slim margin in 2000, and for George W. Bush in 2004, 52 percent to 47 percent. So while conservative Protestant voters form the bedrock, the base of the Bush coalition, slim margins of victory in places like Ohio, New Hampshire, and Florida made the difference in 2004. For example, the swing from 2000 to 2004 in Catholic-voter preferences alone was enough to constitute the margin of victory, given the large number of Catholic voters in Ohio, the state that gave President Bush the electoral college margin he needed to remain in office.

President Bush, and the Republican Party under chairman Ken Mehlman, have worked hard to peel away white Catholics from the Democratic coalition permanently, making them part of a new social-conservative political alliance. (Black and Latino Catholics still pull the lever in overwhelming numbers for Democrats in local and national elections. Getting them to vote Republican is more of a long-term goal.) The president has been consistent on issues of particular interest to white Catholics and Catholic conservatives in particular: euthanasia, stem-cell research, and abortion.

President Bush also took particular pains to revere Pope John Paul II. Though the pope had been a severe critic of capital punishment, of the effects of globalization and capitalism, had stood for the rights of the Palestinians and stood against the war in Iraq until the day he died, the American president headed to Rome to give the dying pope the Medal of Freedom. In a citation that reminds the reader of just how much America and the world have changed, no superlative about the leader of the world's Catholic was too super-:

> *A devoted servant of God, His Holiness Pope John Paul II*
> *has championed the cause of the poor, the weak, the hungry,*
> *and the outcast. He has defended the unique dignity of every*

life, and the goodness of all life. Through his faith and moral conviction, he has given courage to others to be not afraid in overcoming injustice and oppression. His principled stand for peace and freedom has inspired millions and helped to topple communism and tyranny. The United States honors this son of Poland who became the Bishop of Rome and a hero of our time.

The pope was brief in his spoken remarks at the ceremony, but a written text was issued to accompany the medal ceremony that might as well have read, if not for the flowery language of papal diplomacy, "Thanks for the medal, pal. But we're still not friends." It read in part:

> *Mr. President, your visit to Rome takes place at a moment of great concern for the continuing situation of grave unrest in the Middle East, both in Iraq and in the Holy Land. You are very familiar with the unequivocal position of the Holy See in this regard, expressed in numerous documents, through direct and indirect contacts, and in the many diplomatic efforts which have been made since you visited me, first at Castelgandolfo on 23 July 2001, and again in this Apostolic Palace on 28 May 2002.*

Translation: I'm still pretty upset about the war.

> *It is the evident desire of everyone that this situation now be normalized as quickly as possible with the active participation of the international community and, in particular, the United Nations organization, in order to ensure a speedy return of Iraq's sovereignty, in conditions of security for all its people. The recent appointment of a head of state in Iraq and the formation of an interim Iraqi government are an encour-*

aging step towards the attainment of this goal. May a similar hope for peace also be rekindled in the Holy Land and lead to new negotiations, dictated by a sincere and determined commitment to dialogue, between the government of Israel and the Palestinian Authority.

Translation: If you get help, you'll be out of Iraq sooner rather than later, and, hey, get back in gear on Israel and Palestine, will you please?

The threat of international terrorism remains a source of constant concern. It has seriously affected normal and peaceful relations between states and peoples since the tragic date of 11 September 2001, which I have not hesitated to call "a dark day in the history of humanity." In the past few weeks other deplorable events have come to light which have troubled the civic and religious conscience of all, and made more difficult a serene and resolute commitment to shared human values: in the absence of such a commitment neither war nor terrorism will ever be overcome. May God grant strength and success to all those who do not cease to hope and work for understanding between peoples, in respect for the security and rights of all nations and of every man and woman.

Translation: We were right there with you after 9/11, but those Abu Ghraib pictures, yikes!

The pope concluded his public message to the president by acknowledging the terrific work done in the world by American charities, especially Catholic ones, but the accumulated message was clear.

A few months later the president spoke to the national convention of the Knights of Columbus, a Catholic men's fraternal organization, in Dallas. A large picture of the pope and the president was projected above the stage, proof of political advertising's ability to transcend reality with pictures that look just like reality. Though it had been widely reported that the pope had been very severe in his criticism of Mr. Bush's war, the picture of the two of them, a slumping, declining pope and a vigorous American president leaning in to listen, drew warm and enthusiastic applause. The president remembered his meeting in his talk with the Knights, splitting the difference between the honorific *His Holiness,* and his form of address, *Holy Father:* "Two months ago, I had the privilege of visiting His Holy Father Pope John Paul II at the Vatican. It was my third meeting with His Holy Father since I took office, and for those of you who have ever met him, you know I'm telling you the truth when I tell you being in his presence is an awesome experience. He is a true presence. On the occasion, I had the special honor of presenting him with America's highest civil award, the Presidential Medal of Freedom. It was my chance to express our nation's respect for a devoted servant of God and a true hero of our time.

"Pope John Paul II has been a unique and commanding voice for the cause of the poor, the weak, the hungry, and the outcast. He has challenged our nation, and the entire world, to embrace the culture of life. He's called upon us to uphold and affirm the dignity of every person, rich and poor, able and disabled, born and unborn. He's called us to love and serve our neighbors in need." It was a home run. Message to the Knights: Let's forget all the unpleasant things we don't agree on. The pope and I are both anti-abortion. The president could even get a laugh from the assembled Knights about his brother Jeb's progress in the organization. The Methodist president is barred from membership, but his Catholic-convert brother is steadily moving up the ranks.

What made the Bush showing in 2004 even more worthy of careful examination was his opponent. John Kerry was the first Roman Catholic nominee for president since John Kennedy. The surging pride, hunger for validation, and response to decades of bigotry had brought Catholics of many political stripes to Kennedy's side. In four decades the religious landscape of the nation had changed, and Kerry no longer had to explain away being a Roman Catholic, but instead wrestled with how to show whether he was a good enough Catholic. Southern Baptist Al Gore had not had that problem.

As the Democratic nominee, the vice president had told *US News and World Report* of his support for separation of church and state, and, in a more general sense, his view of how an elected official in a religiously diverse country should signal the importance of his or her own faith: "I was raised in a tradition that honors the establishment clause, and I think that puts an extra obligation on those who serve in public office, especially in a constitutional position, to refrain from implying some special guidance by virtue of their relationship to God or religious tradition. And I try never to inadvertently communicate something like that. But at the same time, I think that we have gone too far in conveying the impression that those in public life are obligated to refrain from ever acknowledging that they have a spiritual life and that they have a set of core beliefs."[4]

The Catholic litmus test for one of their own would prove tougher. To begin with, there was President Bush's own steadfast opposition to abortion rights. The "X factor" was Kerry's own apparent discomfort with, and disinclination for talking about, religion. Though a direct and distant relation of the Puritan governor John Winthrop, the senator was also the grandson of a Czech Jew. He had been a regular Mass-goer through much of his life and had apparently thought deeply about the nexus between private faith and public service. He might have combined his interesting family tree and his life experience to form a compelling pitch to Americans across the religious spectrum. Until the waning days of the campaign, it was hard to tell if that had ever occurred to him.

For someone with Kerry's apparently real distaste for too much public airing of private religious concerns, running against George W. Bush presented a daunting challenge. It was like getting to a picnic area late in the day and finding that all the best tables and all the best spots for the blankets are already taken. The other diners relax, and you struggle to make the best of what you have. The senator told the *Ladies' Home Journal,* "I will say I personally would not choose—though I'm a person of faith—to insert it as much as this president does. I think it crosses a line, and it sort of squeezes the diversity that the presidency is supposed to embrace. It creates a discomfort level. You have to balance it, and be very thoughtful about it."[5]

Professor Michelle Dillon, a sociology professor at the University of New Hampshire, calculates that John Kerry's public policy does not put him outside the mainstream of American Catholics. Dillon says a majority of Roman Catholics in the U.S. disagree with church authority when it comes to birth control (93%), divorce (65%), married priests (60%), women priests (60%), and even abortion, with two thirds reporting they are not categorically pro-life and would not support blanket bans on abortion. So, a divorced Roman Catholic who does not support some forms of late-term abortion but also would never legislate a blanket ban might not be a problem, right?

In 1960, the problem was showing you were not too Catholic. In 2004, it was proving you were Catholic enough. In his landmark speech in 1960, Kennedy had to put plenty of daylight between his running the country and his fidelity to Roman Catholic teaching: "Whatever issue may come before me as President—on birth control, divorce, censorship, gambling or any other subject—I will make my decision in accordance with these views, in accordance with what my conscience tells me to be the national interest, and without regard to outside religious pressures or dictates."

John Kerry had to woo regular churchgoing Catholics who viewed him with skepticism while still keeping the more secular part of the Democratic coalition on board. That tightrope walk came to sound like this:

> *I am a believing and practicing Catholic, married to another believing and practicing Catholic. And being an American Catholic at this particular moment in history has three particular implications for my own point of view as a candidate for presidency.*
>
> *The first two follow directly from the two great commandments set forth in the Scriptures: our obligations to love God with all our hearts, souls, and minds and to love our neighbors as ourselves. The first commandment means we must believe that there are absolute standards of right and wrong. They may not always be that clear, but they exist, and it is our duty to honor them as best we can.*

The second commandment means that our commitment to equal rights and social justice, here and around the world, is not simply a matter of political fashion or economic and social theory but a direct command from God.[6]

By late in the campaign season, aggressive polling seeped into the mainstream press showing a majority of Roman Catholics thought John Kerry was not "a good Catholic." Even Gallup disaggregated data from Catholics, breaking out regular church attenders, giving Bush a sizable lead among "faithful Catholics." In every religious group it is regular attenders who are more likely to vote.

By October of 2004, when few voters of any religious persuasion are still believed to be "in play," Kerry came out swinging at the final presidential debate in Tempe, Arizona: "I respect everything that the president has said and certainly respect his faith. I think it's important and I share it.

"I think that he just said that freedom is a gift from the Almighty. Everything is a gift from the Almighty. And as I measure the words of the Bible, and we all do, different people measure different things: the Koran, the Torah or, you know, Native Americans who gave me a blessing the other day had their own special sense of connectedness to a higher being. And people all find their ways to express it.

"I was taught—I went to a church school, and I was taught that the two greatest commandments are: love the Lord your God with all your mind, your body and your soul; and love your neighbor as yourself. And frankly, I think we have a lot more loving of our neighbor to do in this country and on this planet.

"The president and I have a difference of opinion about how we live out our sense of our faith. I talked about it earlier when I talked about the works and faith without works being dead.[7] I think we've got a lot more work to do. And as president I will always respect everybody's right to practice religion as they choose or not to practice, because that's part of America."

All in all, a smart statement politically. In it he affirmed and complimented the president on his faith, reported by members of the public to be an attractive trait. Then he showed where the daylight between the two men was, while highlighting the religious diversity that made it problematic for public servants to embrace a policy based on religious faith alone. In the final month of the campaign, there were conflicting polls, some showing strong preference for President Bush among Catholics, others showing a Kerry surge, especially among those who did not attend mass regularly.

What is hard to gauge is just how one of the most stunning gestures of the campaign season shaped the Catholic vote, and John Kerry's performance. Bishop Michael Sheridan, the bishop coadjutor of Colorado Springs, Colorado, had a message for his people, and delivered it from the pulpit and in writing. Later he said, "I think if I were to summarize what I wanted to say, it's this: When they exercise their very important right and duty to vote, they needed to do so based on clear conscientious convictions, not only as citizens and Americans, but as Catholics, not to reflect sectarian religious practices, to bring to that activity of voting what that faith has taught them about the dignity of the human person, and about the common good. I dealt with specific issues."

In other words, if you are a Catholic, candidates who profess ideas in line with Catholic teaching, especially on matters of life and death, are the best choice. Bishop Sheridan told me he really did not think his remarks were going to set off a firestorm: "It was addressed to Catholics of this diocese. I was naïve enough to think things like this stay inside the diocese."

The episcopal advice did not stay in the diocese. Bishop Sheridan's superior, the archbishop of Denver, Michael Chaput, raised the ante higher, telling his flock and visiting journalists that voting for pro-choice candidates like John Kerry was a sin of sufficient gravity to require confession before coming to the sacrament at the heart of Catholic worship, communion. "If you vote this way, are you cooperating in evil?" he asked. "And if you know you are cooperating in evil, should you go to confession? The answer is yes."

In case you did not get the message, or missed mass that week, the archbishop discussed Catholic priorities in the election in fully half of his columns in the archdiocesan newspaper. In the same election season, forty churches in the archdiocese ran voter registration drives.

As preachers of the Word and translators of Catholic teaching to a vast and diverse flock in the United States, bishops and priests have often spoken out on issues of importance to the institutional church and of religious significance to Catholic teaching.

But never before in an election year had so many bishops spoken so specifically about the connection of politics to issues, most specifically abortion and stem-cell research, and so explicitly linked individual Catholic voting behavior to sin and access to the sacraments of the church.

I asked Bishop Sheridan if he had been worried about so directly advising people on how to vote. He replied, "I did think it would spark reaction in the diocese. I think we all know that people's political feelings override their religious convictions. But I don't know how to talk about issues and then pretend they aren't associated with people. It was not my direct intent to tell people how to vote, but if we're going to take seriously those moral issues that have to do with the rights and dignities, we have to connect people's voting behavior with those policies."

The broad umbrella "Catholic teaching" has a lot more than abortion and stem-cell research under it. The bishops appeared to be giving one Catholic teaching, the opposition to abortion, great pride of place in a campaign between a pro-choice Catholic and an antiabortion Protestant.

Bishop Sheridan said that in principle clerics would be well within their authority and responsibility to also say, "The church has teachings in regards to the death penalty. Here they are, and they cannot be disregarded." He went on to say, "Just to make it clear, people brought a number of questions to me after the statements on abortion. They asked, 'Why didn't you say something about the death penalty, about the war?'

"I isolated issues in a way that falls into a different category. Abortion is intrinsically evil, and there can be no circumstances that can make it right. The act is intrinsically evil. When you're talking about a war, or capital punishment, there are different cases that require a different response. The Church has never categorized all war, or capital punishment for that matter, as intrinsically evil."

The bishop said that was the case, even with the country in the middle of a war clearly opposed by the pope and with very different policies about the war being put forward by the two candidates for president. Bishop Sheridan said there was a key difference, and one that reflected his earlier point about the unambiguous nature of the teaching on abortion when compared with the war in Iraq. In the case of Iraq, the pope had not been speaking *ex cathedral* (literally, "from his throne") as the universal head of the Roman Catholic Church. This is a distinction that might not mean all that much to other Christians, or even to many Roman Catholics, but it was a significant difference for the bishop from Colorado Springs. "Opposition to the war in Iraq is not a magisterial teaching of the Catholic Church. It is the position of the church that the judgment as to how this war is being carried out finally lies with those who define the civil order.

"The pope will not make himself principal political strategist or military strategist of the world. To tell you honestly, I can't imagine any pope ever advising for war. I think it's the pope who always is the voice for the alternative." Later, Bishop Sheridan said, in subsequent columns and in talks in the diocese, he took the chance to talk to people about capital punishment and war: "I despise war, I wish there were never wars, I share Pope Paul's sentiments, war never again. Sadly there must be, there will be wars. The bishops both individually and collectively would be behind the pope calling for any alternative to war, to bring an end to a war already begun."

The archbishops and bishops who publicly declared that both Roman Catholic politicians who did not support church teaching and the faithful who voted for them were in trouble did get a lot of attention. Father Thomas Reese, former editor of the Jesuit magazine *America,* has a modest suggestion: "You know the headlines should have been on that whole thing '180 Bishops Don't Say Kerry Can't Go to Communion.' But of course the headline was about maybe ten or a dozen bishops who just stepped out of line and said these things. Most remained quite silent on this stuff. Those who got their names in the papers did not represent the majority of the bishops, I don't think. They got all the publicity because they were the ones who were standing up and saying something. It's kind of like in the Sherlock Holmes story, the dog that just barked. That's the story that's hard for the media to cover.

"I think most of the bishops didn't want to get into this fight," Father Reese elaborated. "Now, on the other hand, they weren't willing to come to the defense of Kerry because they disagreed with him radically on abortion. They did not want to appear to be coming to his defense and therefore coming to the defense of somebody who was pro-choice. They were, even if they didn't like what the other bishops were doing, not willing to come forward and say so. So it sounded like these few bishops were speaking for the church."

As cardinal archbishop of Washington, D.C., Theodore McCarrick does not lead the largest archdiocese in the American Catholic Church, but he does lead one of the most visible and influential. In his pews every Sunday morning are senators and representatives, ambassadors and lobbyists, leaders and foot soldiers in the federal government and in the international organizations that call Washington home. He has in many ways inherited the mantle of "brother and conciliator" held so long in the American church by Cardinal Joseph Bernardin. Cardinal McCarrick led the deliberations that led to a declaration on communion from the national church that discouraged using exclusion as discipline: "You have to deal with the real world. I took a stand, as did the task force that I chaired. An overwhelming number of the bishops felt they didn't want to have a confrontation at the altar rail. But there were also those who felt they needed in their diocese a stronger point of view, that they needed to act more decisively. The result was unity, rather than uniformity. This is why the documents that the bishops put forward at that time allowed for the difference among the bishops."

The declaration adopted by the bishops endorsed the idea that Catholic politicians who support abortion rights are "cooperating in evil." That statement bolts the doors against the "personally opposed, but not imposing my views on others" formulation long used in political speech by prochoice politicians. The bishops also stopped the march to the dais at diocesan dinners by agreeing that pro-choice officials should not receive "awards, honors, or platforms which would suggest support for their actions." In their unanimous resolution, the bishops did not rule once and for all on whether those politicians should be turned away from communion, leaving the situation as it was before the emergency meeting, with each bishop free to set a sacramental policy for his diocese.

Father Reese looks at the stated beliefs of rank-and-file Catholics and wonders where such a policy could lead, noting that if you were to insist that only Catholics in full agreement with the church's teachings on "life issues"—such as abortion, stem-cell research, and birth control—could receive the sacraments, "I'm afraid we're going to have nobody taking communion. When we start barring people from communion, we get on a slippery slope and we become a church of 'saints,' when we've never been that. We've always been a church of sinners."

McCarrick's critics were not satisfied either. The American Life League saw the agreement as a betrayal of the unborn and of the bishops who were standing strong for the faith. They all said in a statement "Too many bishops like Cardinal McCarrick and Archbishop O'Malley [of Boston] continue to allow pro-abortion 'Catholic' politicians to receive Holy Communion. By doing so, they turn a blind eye to the 1,400,000 babies surgically aborted every year and ignore the clear teaching of Canon Law: 'Those who . . . obstinately persist in manifest grave sin are NOT to be admitted to Communion.' If every Catholic bishop enforced this one simple law, abortion in America would end in short order. Cardinal McCarrick and Archbishop O'Malley—please don't allow 'Catholic' public figures who favor abortion to defy Christ and His Church."[8]

Professor Appleby told me of a speech to a Catholic bishops group in 2002 where he chided them for aggressively taking on abortion, but not contraception, which is accepted and practiced by more than 90 percent of Catholics. He laughed when recalling that they heard his words, but came to the wrong conclusion: " 'You're right Scott, we need to get tough on birth control.' Which was not my point. Their point, and a lot of them are saying this after the sexual-abuse crisis, is that they'd been weak, and it's time to put their fist down and draw a line and say, 'This is what it means to be Catholic.'

"You know to some extent on certain issues I do agree with that, but I just quiver when I see it being applied to communion, and Kerry, and birth control, and a litmus test. The church is a messy thing. It allows for a real range of application of teaching to practice and various points of view, and when you begin saying, 'Here's the litmus test for receiving communion,' it becomes sectarian. The Catholic Church concedes a position it once enjoyed in the mainstream, pluralistic public and says, 'Okay, we're not going to live with that diversity and flexibility with our own church and be players, because (we cannot represent that.) We're going to be pure and sect and smaller and prune ourselves from the John Kerrys and Ted Kennedys.' And I do think that was an important moment, and I think we're still trying to figure out where it's headed and whether or not the church will really truly move more in that sectarian direction."

I put the Notre Dame professor's "sectarian" analysis to Cardinal McCarrick, who responded, "A very fascinating analysis, but it seems to me that what it ignores is this: We are all teaching the same doctrine. I don't know of any one of us who is not teaching the morality of protecting life, and the immorality of taking life. Abortion, stem cells, euthanasia, the evil of treating life cavalierly . . . on whatever practical point of pastoral practice, we all teach the same thing. The difference is not in the teaching. It is in prudential judgments about the here and now. I don't think it is as serious a lack of unity."

Under the "local option" compromise of the bishops, if a pro-choice Catholic politician made his or her way to the altar rail at St. Matthew's Cathedral in Washington, D. C., he would get bread and wine from Cardinal McCarrick: "You have to talk with people who don't agree with you, and you have to teach clearly what the church is teaching."

That same aspiring communicant would not receive the Body and Blood of Jesus in St. Louis, where Archbishop Raymond Burke declared John Kerry would not be welcome at the rail. John Kerry and others should get communion elsewhere, as the Massachusetts senator did in much of 2004, rather than trying to get it in Colorado Springs, where Bishop Sheridan has no regrets: "If you have publicly, obstinately, persistently promoted things contrary to discipline of the church, core teachings that have to do with the dignity and rights of persons, I believe the law says they are to be refused communion.

"Bishops tried to stay out of, and rightly so, what I call partisan politics. Bishops have spoken up at the local level for issues that have to do with the social good. I'm for education, and I don't think there's anything wrong with that when it comes to the issues. That doesn't mean the direct proposal or denunciation of any particular candidate. We're not a theocracy. We're not. There is a legitimate autonomy to the civil order, but that doesn't mean people of faith have nothing to say to the civil order."

The wider civil order had been given plenty to think about by the Roman Catholic Church in the United States long before the bishops got into their argument about the place of the church in partisan politics and voter sentiments.

In the early years of the twenty-first century, newspapers around the country were filled with lurid stories of rape, fondling, and other forms of sexual exploitation inflicted on Catholic children, mostly boys, by priests. What was worse is the number of cases in which it became clear from diocesan records that prominent members of the hierarchy knew about these rogue priests and found it hard to stop their criminal behavior.

With full knowledge of other senior diocesan staff, victims and their families were quietly paid off, priests were counseled and moved to other dioceses or other pulpits, and the number of children in danger grew. In this book-length analysis of religion and religious institutions, and voters and believers, I would be remiss in not mentioning a very important intersection of clerical and state power, and its long, disgraceful unraveling.

There is a strong contrast here to the points made in defense of the threat to withhold the sacraments of the church from candidates and office holders, and the view that voting for certain candidates and parties is a sin that must be repented and confessed. In the case of the bishops who sought to put their stamp on public policy in the run-up to Election Day 2004, there was a defense of an unequivocal view of Catholic teaching and an insistence that any major issue that threatened the life of the flock was a legitimate issue on which the Catholic Church should be heard.

Given the place that religion and religious teaching has in the daily lives of millions of Americans of all religions, you might sympathize with the stated need of bishops not to give wide berth when vital issues of public debate are being put before the whole public, including the Catholic public, for decision making.

The bishops declared that abortion was intrinsically evil. I will also assume for the purpose of this debate that picking cute or vulnerable boys under your authority, separating them from their friends, and raping them repeatedly is also an intrinsic evil.

In the 2004 race, the bishops of the Catholic Church saw such harm to the nation in the form of abortion that they reached out from their pulpits and sanctuaries into the decisions their faithful made as they approached the ballot box. For decades leading up to that election day, dioceses around the country, notably the Boston archdiocese, shuffled priests from here to there, sent high-powered lawyers to do business with wounded, defenseless, and deferential families, and tried to the degree possible to handle a shocking record of criminality "inside the family."

It turned out the separation of church and state was fine only in theory when it came to engaging Catholic faithful in choices that might affect who runs America and how, but separation was dandy when it came to knowingly hiding criminal behavior and moving felons out of jurisdiction. This attitude hearkens back centuries to the days when the church policed itself in many countries, conducting trials and doling out punishment in a parallel legal system to that of the state.

Mix that old idea with the modern psychobabble of healing, hurt, compassion, and the timeless religious ideas of repentance and redemption, and you get a vile brew that victimized untold numbers of children. The district attorney's offices in big urban dioceses around the country treated the local church authorities with kid gloves, putting up with a level of obstruction, doublespeak, and presumed impunity that would have had them using battering rams and the RICO statute to prosecute similar felonies committed by members of less genteel professions.

Church institutions have been pushed to the wall. The faithful seek solace in the mass, turn to their church for baptisms, weddings, and funerals, and still look to the Catholic Church as one of the most effective educational institutions in the country, but a bond of trust between clergy and the flock has been shattered in some places. It will be a long time before we know whether the bond is shattered beyond repair. Long after the churches in Boston, New York, Seattle, and elsewhere have been shaken to their foundations—selling off millions in church property, liquidating insurance funds, and freezing hiring—new evidence is still dribbling out in a Watergate-style "What-did-he-know-and-when-did-he-know-it" fashion.

Church leaders have very successfully manipulated the clash of visions and values that lay at the heart of religion and the operation of the state. In "Church World," it is a tenet of the faith that Jesus died for the sins of humankind. In "Secular World," an offender may or may not admit guilt, may or may not take responsibility for a crime, but once blame has been affixed, culpability proven, saying you are sorry doesn't count for much.

In a shockingly long list of cases, bishops and their advisers became police, district attorneys, judges and juries, determining the validity of the accusations, examining the accusers and their supporters, deciding level of guilt, and punishment, all in-house.

Again, in other contexts, the behavior would be nothing short of shocking. In 1997 Corpus Cristi, Texas, Bishop Edmond Carmody conceded that he had allowed the Reverend John Flynn to continue to work as a priest in his diocese even after he admitted to abusing a fourteen-year-old girl in a San Antonio parish church years earlier. After treatment Monsignor Flynn, an old friend of the bishop's, told people he was not restricted from being around young people. Said the bishop, "It's time to forgive and go on."[9] Monsignor Flynn was eventually relieved of all priestly duties by another Texas diocese.

In the Philadelphia archdiocese in 2002, the then-archbishop, Anthony

Bevilacqua, dismissed six priests who had sexually abused children. The archdiocese continued to employ the priests in administrative jobs and told them to seek reclassification as laymen by the Vatican. Philadelphia also had turned up thirty-five priests who had sexually abused children in the years since 1950. The cardinal, perhaps forgetting that he was not a medieval prince, refused to give the names of the abusing priests to law enforcement, saying he wanted to protect the identity of the victims. He did eventually give in. By the fall of 2005, Cardinal Bevilacqua was gone, but the low points of his reign and that of his predecessor, Cardinal John Krol, were chronicled in a seventy-page report from the Philadelphia District Attorney's Office.

The investigators found lurking in archdiocesan records a litany of terrifying abuse, including an eleven-year-old girl raped and impregnated by her priest, who then took her to get an abortion; a fifth-grader molested in a confessional; a twelve-year-old repeatedly raped by his priest, who was told by the priest that his mother approved of the attacks; and a twelve-year-old who tried to commit suicide after he was raped and sodomized by his priest, and now as an adult remains institutionalized.[10]

In diocese after diocese, the stories were remarkably similar: "bishops helping bishops" by moving and hiding known abusers, families pressured into silence, priests with personnel files bursting with multiple allegations from multiple locations simply moving on, avoiding prosecution and remaining free to find new victims.

And again, in case after case, church officials maintain that the problems have been recognized and are being handled, blame is transferred to the aged, the deceased, and those well beyond the reach of statutes of limitations. In Philadelphia, the old chorus of repentance and forgiveness was discarded in favor of the kind of news release you might expect from a company that just got caught hiding a toxic spill: "Cardinal Bevilacqua's remarkable record of service belies the report's vicious treatment of him. This personal attack against a longstanding leader in our community was neither accurate, nor necessary."

District Attorney Lynn Abraham rebutted that rebuttal, defending both the accuracy of the report and reiterating the culpability of the archdiocese, calling the church's response filled with "all-too familiar denials, deceptions, and evasions" that she said marked the church's handling of the crisis in the first place.[11]

The district attorney is an elected official called by evidence of criminality to investigate and cross the church-state divide. Also feeling compelled to weigh in was Pennsylvania's junior U.S. senator, Republican Rick Santorum. Throughout his career, the senator has been publicly pious, a Catholic ready to talk policy, talk religion, and let the two mingle intimately. Writing in the Web publication *Catholic Online,* Santorum could not resist diagnosing the terrifying malfeasance at the highest levels of the Catholic hierarchy as a symptom of Massachusetts liberalism. He wrote: "It is startling that those in the media and academia appear most disturbed by this aberrant behavior, since they have zealously promoted moral relativism by sanctioning 'private' moral matters such as alternative lifestyles. Priests, like all of us, are affected by culture. When the culture is sick, every element in it becomes infected. While it is no excuse for this scandal, it is no surprise that Boston, a seat of academic, political and cultural liberalism in America, lies at the center of the storm."[12]

At the risk of stating the obvious, the senator's analysis does not help us to understand the abuse cases pouring out of other dioceses across the so-called red and blue states. It is hard to see a motivation for such a conclusion beyond using the tragedy inside one's own church as a chance to score cheap points. As Catholics sift their sense of betrayal, watch their patrimony sold off to pay damage settlements, and listen as their bishops explain away years of jaw-dropping irresponsibility, it is striking for a United States senator to find the real culprit in the media.

Massachusetts senator Edward M. Kennedy, brother of the first Catholic president and a prominent liberal, lashed back years later. Kennedy called for Santorum to retract his remarks and apologize: "The people of Boston are to blame for the clergy sexual abuse? That is an irresponsible, insensitive and inexcusable thing to say."

However, politics, especially in the Culture War skirmishes that reverberate through the Capitol, means never having to say you're sorry. Santorum's spokesman said the senator knows the clergy abuse was not just taking place in Boston. Robert Traynham said that Santorum "was speaking to a broader cultural argument about the need for everyone to take these issues very, very, seriously."

The Santorum-Kennedy dustup is an example of where the intersection of religion and politics can go wrong. Rick Santorum is a famously devout Roman Catholic and uses his faith identity as a tool of political persuasion. Teddy Kennedy, though a Roman Catholic, does not make use of that identity in the same way and would probably not find it a very useful tool after a long public career that has occasionally shone an unflattering spotlight on his private life.

As in so many cases in our common life in this country, there ends up being a difference between whether something is allowed and whether it is wise. As a Catholic layman and a constitutionally protected citizen, is Senator Santorum entitled to have an opinion about the roots of the clergy sex-abuse scandal? Of course he is. You know he is. As one of the two representatives for Pennsylvania in the United States Senate, representing Protestants, Jews, Hindus, atheists, Muslims, and members of every other imaginable faith, is it an important part of his job to be a national scold on moral questions from a specifically Catholic worldview? While he's certainly within his rights, the answer there is less clear.

One of the more unusual encounters between Senator Santorum and reporters came in 2003, when an Associated Press Washington correspondent, Lara Jakes Jordan, asked him about the Supreme Court decision on sodomy laws in Texas and his knock on Boston and liberalism.

First, the senator riffed on the evils of relativism: "You have the problem within the church. Again, it goes back to this moral relativism, which is very accepting of a variety of different lifestyles. And if you make the case that if you can do whatever you want to do, as long as it's in the privacy of your own home, this 'right to privacy,' then why be surprised that people are doing things that are deviant within their own home? If you say, there is no deviant as long as it's private, as long as it's consensual, then don't be surprised what you get." The reporter immediately picked up on the implication of Santorum's sermon: if you guarantee a right to privacy, you get deviance.

She probed a bit more, and asked if there was any alternative to what the senator had called "the right to privacy lifestyle." The senator said, "In this case, what we're talking about, basically, is priests who were having sexual relations with post-pubescent men. We're not talking about priests with 3-year-olds, or 5-year-olds. We're talking about a basic homosexual relationship. Which, again, (according to the world view sense) is a perfectly fine relationship as long as it's consensual between people. If you view the world that way, and you say that's fine, you would assume that you would see more of it."

Jakes Jordan tried again: "Well, what would you do?"

"What would I do with what?"

"I mean, how would you remedy? What's the alternative? I mean, should we outlaw homosexuality?"

Santorum now gets to what for him is the heart of the matter: "I have no problem with homosexuality. I have a problem with homosexual acts." Again, a formulation heard from many opponents of homosexuals and homosexual rights. The bottom line is that gay people should find a way to be gay and celibate. "The question is, do you act upon those orientations? So it's not the person, it's the person's actions. And you have to separate the person from their actions."

Jakes Jordan's tone is of someone who started one interview and realizes along the way that she is now involved in something else altogether. She asks the senator, who has come out against the Texas sodomy case, the right to privacy, and gay sex, to propose a response, "without being too gory or graphic." He didn't listen: "And if the Supreme Court says that you have the right to consensual sex within your home, then you have the right to bigamy, you have the right to polygamy, you have the right to incest, you have the right to adultery. You have the right to anything. Does that undermine the fabric of our society? I would argue yes, it does. It all comes from, I would argue, this right to privacy that doesn't exist in my opinion in the United States Constitution, this right that was created, it was created in Griswold—Griswold was the contraceptive case—and abortion. And now we're just extending it out. And the further you extend it out, the more you—this freedom actually intervenes and affects the family. You say, well, it's my individual freedom. Yes, but it destroys the basic unit of our society because it condones behavior that's antithetical to strong healthy families. Whether it's polygamy, whether it's adultery, whether it's sodomy, all of those things, are antithetical to a healthy, stable, traditional family.

"Every society in the history of man has upheld the institution of marriage as a bond between a man and a woman. Why? Because society is based on one thing: that society is based on the future of the society. And that's what? Children. Monogamous relationships. In every society, the definition of marriage has not ever to my knowledge included homosexuality. That's not to pick on homosexuality. It's not, you know, man on child, man on dog, or whatever the case may be. It is one thing. And when you destroy that, you have a dramatic impact on the quality . . ."

Santorum is on a roll here. Here the reporter interjects with one of the great interview lines of all time: "I'm sorry, I didn't think I was going to talk about 'man on dog' with a United States senator, it's sort of freaking me out."

The senator does not miss a beat. Interrupted mid-exegesis, Santorum is going to finish his thought with a flourish: "And that's sort of where we are in today's world, unfortunately. The idea is that the state doesn't have rights to limit individuals' wants and passions. I disagree with that. I think we absolutely have rights because there are consequences to letting people live out whatever wants or passions they desire. And we're seeing it in our society."

The conservative Catholic critics of the John Kerry candidacy were right when they said some of the senator's own views clashed with the traditional teachings of the church. In the view of priests and bishops all the way up to Pope Benedict, part of the responsibility of a Catholic public servant is to be an advocate for justice and human rights. A surrender to the beliefs of the wider culture when an issue like abortion is at stake is not any more licit in plural democracy.

As Lara Jakes Jordan might ask at this juncture, "What's the alternative?" Senator Santorum does not express a single thought in his "man-on-dog" riff that runs afoul of Catholic principles. Yet the zeal to make sure others are not doing anything you may not like personally has, in long American practice, had strong borders built around it. In *Lawrence and Garner v. Texas,* the Supreme Court ruled private sexual behavior to be no business of the state. The decision extended the protection of private sexual behavior from *Griswold v. Connecticut*'s implicit protections of heterosexual people.

If you are going to extend religious sanctions on private behavior to the legal code that governs us all, a line has to be drawn somewhere, as our AP reporter understood. Your religious conviction may lead you to one opinion about whether a behavior is *advisable.* Once you wish to extend that religious view to govern the lives of people of the same religion, other religions, or no religion at all, your opinion of my behavior better have more substantial ammunition than "I don't like it" to enforce legal constraints.

The question of where your preferences end and my rights begin is likely to continue to challenge lawmakers at every level and judges all the way up to the Supreme Court. Today there are five Roman Catholics on the nation's highest court, a remarkable thing given the history of the last two hundred years. Americans have, with little notice, watched as a religious minority once viewed with suspicion has come into its own in the professions. Now five Catholics, a court majority, will sit in judgment on the issues fueling the Culture Wars: homosexual rights, marriage, abortion, birth control, stem-cell research. Five Catholics reached that pinnacle in a short span of years because we have gotten beyond religion to other forms of definition and association to appraise judicial skill.

Antonin Scalia, Anthony Kennedy, Clarence Thomas, John Roberts, and Samuel Alito, Jr., have their jobs because of ideological (and in the case of Thomas, an adult convert, racial) assessments made by the presidents who appointed them. Someday in the future, a Democrat will appoint a Roman Catholic to the high court, and that model of ideology and experience as master statuses, as opposed to religion, will be even more firmly established.

• • •

AT THE CORE of the Catholic clergy sex-abuse scandals there is a religious issue, involving men entrusted with the care and nurture of human beings who have betrayed that trust in some of the cruelest ways imaginable. How to preach about what has happened, how to teach about it, and how to understand God's intentions and purposes in the face of both the abuse and its mishandling is a profound and Catholic challenge.

Also embedded at the core of these incidents, taking place over decades and now unfolding around the country in a short spasm of difficult years, is how the legally constituted authorities who represent all the people are going to deal with crimes. That part of the story does not belong only to American Catholics. It belongs to us all. Raping someone in a rectory is not a fundamentally different crime from raping someone in the locker room of a public school.

For a long time, Catholic authorities removed themselves from the judgment of the wider society, making a bad situation worse by placing institutional self-preservation over the lives of those in their care. From the earliest days of the United States, a large separate sphere was carved out of American life for religious institutions. But it was never imagined that "otherness" might someday be used to mask a large criminal enterprise.

The clergy sex-abuse scandal was an aberration, a blip in a centuries-long march out of the exotic and into the mainstream for American Catholics. The challenge of being a religious person in the wider marketplace was understood twenty centuries ago by Jesus himself when he asked his followers to be in the world but not of the world.

In our next chapter, how the church comes to struggling communities and walks that line between church and state is our focus, along with a look at how the political establishment longs to get its hooks into the highly organized, active, and revered church in America's communities of color.

TEN

Shifting Battle Lines and the
Browning of America

REPORTERS DO KNOW HOW to add. So give them some credit for noticing, in 2006, the hundreds of thousands of demonstrators on the streets of American cities decrying the threat to declare them criminals and send them home. Naturally, with the long shadow of the 2006 midterms stretching across the calendar, the news business tried to understand what the political blows and counterstrikes over a large, nonvoting, illegal-immigrant population meant to the conventional two-party game.

Relatively fewer tried to understand how Latinos fit into the wider strategy of Republicans and Democrats for the future, what African American bystanders were going to make of the whole thing, and how this would mesh with both big party strategies to make their tent the cultural home of black and brown Americans.

African Americans? The most uniformly church-affiliated population of all the major demographic groups in the country. Latinos? The largest and fastest-growing minority population in America. Together, they make up roughly a quarter of the population of the United States. Their families are poorer than the average Americans'; they have fewer years of schooling than the average American; they are less likely to own a home than the average American and less likely to have any household net worth. The Democrats, with their focus on palliative social policy and bread-and-butter issues, say both Latinos and African Americans are "natural Democrats."

At the same time, both Latinos and African Americans are more hostile to abortion and gay rights, more likely to question sex education in public-school curricula, and easily roused to support voucher programs in public schools (if not more likely to use those vouchers once offered, a story for another day). Latinos, depending on the way the questions are asked, are not any more likely to support bilingual education than other Americans or support amnesty for illegal immigrants. They are, at the same time, the Catholic bedrock on which the huge archdioceses of Los Angeles, Chicago, and New York now stand, and a fast-growing component of both mainline Protestant, and evangelical populations. Church-affiliated Latinos, with their economic aspirations and their horror of the American social norms they see on television, are believed to be "natural Republicans." So are the most church-affiliated African Americans, with their disdain for homosexuality, out-of-wedlock birth, and their enthusiastic embrace of the president's "faith-based initiative."

Could RNC chairman Ken Mehlman's bet about the strong appeal of social conservatism pay off in a different kind of Republican Party? Or can the Democratic Party's toying with their traditional message successfully add a "faith and values" component to the party's bread-and-butter focus?

For Methodist pastor, political scientist, and Democratic activist the Reverend Andrew Hernandez, there is some logic to the Republican pursuit of Latino voters, but the numbers do not support their conclusion: "It's hard to explain why those districts that are predominately Latino, overwhelmingly end up electing liberal Democrats." Add in the overt pressure of the church, he said, and things do not improve for the Republicans. "You've had occasions where the Catholic church has come out and said 'Don't vote for this candidate.' The Latinos vote 70 to 80 percent for that candidate. And this has been going on for the last thirty years."

"There's a lot of evidence laterally to suggest that whereas Latinos may agree on certain issues like, you know, limiting the ability of gays to enter into marriage, it's not the most relevant issue when it comes time to vote. And I think the most compelling argument for that viewpoint is that when Latinos get a chance to elect someone, they tend to elect people that are more liberal than most non-Latino mainstream people do, period. Here in San Antonio, at all levels, you have a district, City Council District 5, that's

93 percent Mexican American and poor. They elect a liberal, almost counterculture Anglo woman, Patty Rado. And she beat a moderate, a pro-life, Mexican American politician."

The other side of the argument comes from Bishop Harry Jackson, leader of a two-thousand-strong African American congregation, Hope Christian Church in College Park, Maryland, in the suburbs of Washington, D.C. Bishop Jackson was one of a small, but growing number of black clergy who supported George W. Bush for reelection in 2004. The bishop was also a fixture in the Justice Sunday programs, appearing as the only black speaker on the program for Justice Sunday II (like Super Bowls and popes, Justice Sundays get Roman numerals).

When we talked about politics and faith, the pastor told me that the right way for a clergyman to approach both realms is something he had gradually been rethinking and was coming to some new conclusions: "It's something I've probably evolved to, and changed on over time. I coauthored a book called *High Impact African-American Churches,*[1] and George Barna and I looked at model churches around the country, and tried to come to some conclusions about how and why the black church works so well."

What Bishop Jackson said he realized was that the black church had been a political institution long before the civil rights movement, long before Jim Crow and abolition, back to its earliest days. "The black church has always been disproportionately involved in the political realm. When blacks were still held in slavery, it was a center of the community, a keeper of cultural treasures. Later on it would be the founder of the original black banks, and mutual-aid and protection societies. I had never realized that this was a part of the heritage of the African American church."

What Bishop Jackson, a Harvard MBA, is doing with his pulpit and growing public profile presents an interesting middle course between the Reverends Al Sharpton and Jesse Jackson, at one end of the pastoral continuum, and Pastor Ted Haggard of the National Association of Evangelicals, at the other end. He appears to be stopping far short of an open and public embrace of the Republican Party and the Bush administration while using his access to raise specific issues. In that straddle, Bishop Jackson upends decades of black politics in America, forging church alliances across racial lines and presenting the GOP as a real option for church-aligned black voters.

"I think the goal would be to start with things that are consistent to what the Bible teaches, then make allegiances with like-minded Christians. The National Association of Evangelicals, thirty million strong, is a predominately white organization. I am a pastor from an alliance of predominately African American churches, the High-Impact Leadership Coalition. We speak with a voice that would reflect the issues that I deal with a lot, having to do with justice as the foundation of God's throne, as in Psalms 89 and 97."[2]

There is a difference, the bishop said, between black and white conservative Christians. "The evangelical movement in America has veered into righteousness issues, a lot of these issues that deal with personal righteousness, personal-conscience issues. While the black community has been more involved with justice issues, social-justice issues." Having said that, the pastor is still open to overtures: "When I get invited by NAE, to come preach, to speak at events, I think I should take that step. It's bridge building. It's eye-opening, for instance, speaking on Dr. Jim Dobson's radio program, which is heard by millions." That does not mean there are not lines that must be observed with care, and boundaries that must not be crossed. "The thing that I should not be doing is violating basic 501c3 rules, or using my church as a sponsorship organization for a specific party. If I stand outside the pulpit, I can still get involved in significant ways in the political realm. Christians are interested in the wider issues confronting the community and we should be addressing that." For all his support of George W. Bush in the last national election cycle, he would not put his church in harness to further the reelection effort. "We don't bring dollars and contributions to the table. I say this at a time when more and more of the Christian political-action committees back their issues with money."

Bishop Jackson and his fellow conservative black pastors overlap with white conservative Christians in some ways, and part company with them in others. The High Impact Leadership Coalition has developed a Black Contract With America, their own version of the GOP document that

Newt Gingrich and Co. used to such great effect in the 1994 midterm elections. While the coalition commits itself to repairing the moral compass for all America, the Black Contract calls for policies that would attract few "amens" at the NAE: African relief, prison reform, community redevelopment, and other policies that white congregations might in less-generous moments hear as more "special programs for blacks." But one agenda item in the Black Contract would get ringing support: "The family is the first biblical institution and the foundation of society. The family must be supported by the protection of the traditional institution of marriage (one man and one woman, protection of the unborn, and the adoption of children separated from their biological parents)."

Combine the urgency conservative black Christians feel over gay marriage with their misgivings over the criminal justice system, and you get Bishop Harry Jackson walking to the pulpit at Justice Sunday and telling the crowd, "I believe that what God is doing today is calling for the black church to team with the white evangelical church and the Catholic church and people of moral conscience. And in this season, we need to be able to tell both parties, 'Listen, it's our way or the highway.' " That is a line to send shivers up the spines of strict separationists and Democratic Party political activists. The bishop continued, "We're not going to just sit back and let America go down this ramp of moral decline. I'm not black alone, I'm an American. And, beyond that—praise God—and beyond that, I am a Christian. You and I can bring the rule and reign of The Cross to America, and we can change America on our watch, together. Do you believe it?"

The almost exclusively white crowd at Justice Sunday II ate it up. The dreams of GOP strategists are fired by the prospect of using influential black ministers to peel away the overwhelming black support for the Democratic Party. The bishop hinted at that tantalizing prospect in his Justice Sunday address: "Many African Americans are afraid of the word conservative. They think it's a code word for racist. They think that what it means is that we're going to go back to some antiquated system of doing things and they're not going to get a break." The bishop is not sure America's ready for social justice. He says, "The truth is, if we don't have process in this nation, then those who are the least, and they're not necessarily empowered, will always have a problem with the winds of change bringing in somebody new."

Away from the cheering and the TV cameras, Bishop Jackson does not sound so sure that black and white Christians will bring about the reign of The Cross any minute now. Conservative Christians and their allies in the Republican Party, he said, are "not dealing with racial profiling, with uneven sentencing in the criminal justice system, and the resulting black loss of faith in the legal system. With education, there are a lot of problems with black dropouts from high school. We still want the statements of support that could be made around affirmative action in the higher education realm. These are frontier areas where in order to be successful, I say to you without any shame, they're going to have to make some improvements. If they stick with what they've been doing so far, that will not get African Americans and their votes.

"If they're willing to make some modest adjustments, they'll see a huge movement of Bible-believing black Christians to their party. I'm just not sure that it's going to happen."

Bishop Jackson is frank in his assessment of the black American political landscape. The vast majority of African Americans do not trust Republicans to take seriously their worries about the justice system and the use of the government to open and guarantee economic opportunity. At the same time, he insists that the deep social conservatism of black Americans make gay marriage a deal-breaker politically. "If you buy the argument that the institution of marriage and the social structure can be distorted to such a degree that it doesn't work anymore, that little girls are not dreaming of what their children will be like, that boys are not looking ahead to being providers, then you are overseeing nothing less than the destruction of the foundational definition of family."

It has been a long time since a majority of black children were born to married couples living together. Black women get abortions at a higher rate than other women. Bishop Jackson told me that black pastors' embrace of these issues is not paradoxical at all, but a logical outgrowth of the emergency in the black family. "We're more conservative about the institution of marriage even if we don't practice it correctly anymore. Our congregations are still open to gay individuals. But black clergymen are very, very conservative when it comes to their treatment of gays and lesbians."

Outside his hometown in Queens, New York, Floyd Flake was probably best known as a veteran member of Congress, a Democrat who stressed issues having to do with the economic empowerment of black Americans. All during his years in the House of Representatives he was also a pastor, at the helm of the enormous and influential Allen African Methodist Episcopal Church in the Jamaica neighborhood of Queens. Along with pastoring his black megachurch, he is also president of his alma mater, Wilberforce University in Ohio.

When I asked the former congressman to define a right relationship between church and state, he said the changes in America have challenged the notion of the U.S. as a Christian nation: "The changes in America make that a very difficult and limited definition. What we have to do going forward is acknowledge we have many people of many faiths, while the vast majority believe in God. Religion is a very large part of our life, but how that informs our politics becomes a different issue."

Floyd Flake has often had his loyalty as a Democrat questioned, since he was always willing to make strategic alliances with Republicans in power to serve greater goals he had for his city, his district, and his church. Standing as he did for so long, at the intersection of religious vocation and political influence, he got an intimate view of the tightening embrace between the them: "The two are being connected in a way that hasn't before existed in the history of our republic. I think that it's getting a lot of attention because it's linked with a particular part of the faith community and a particular party." But he sees that connection, for all of America's secular traditions, as a natural one. "You can understand the appeal of it. I'm not sure that it's so far-fetched given that those who shaped the Constitution, they put God in everything. Money still bears the statement 'In God We Trust.' They go hand in hand with one another."

While he is clearly not one of those Democrats allergic to a familiarity between religion and politics, he said he is not sure America is getting the balance right. "People still think their particular religious persuasion should carry the day. Republicans for the most part believe they have the correct tilt, that their politics are in line with what God has spoken, and what would be best for all people. There's an evangelical class that I think has taken over a significant portion of faith definitions, defining what faith means for everybody else, especially with the current leadership in place.

"My Democratic friends act as if they don't believe there should be a definition, or if they say anything at all, they should make only the most liberal of faith statements and try to say something that will offend no one. It's a very definite weakness for the Democratic Party. Democrats have looked almost exclusively to the African American church when they have reached out to religious bodies. They haven't done much reaching out to other denominations, other faiths. The problem with that is homogenization of approach. Look at Bishop T.D. Jakes, Eddy Long, and churches like my church. Those churches are more aligned with religious conservatives." Floyd Flake, veteran Democrat, lines up with Bishop Harry Jackson, the Bush supporter, when assessing the GOP's chances of making inroads. "If blacks believed conservative Christians really understood what they were up against, it could change the relationship with the Republican Party."

The Reverend Floyd Flake echoes Bishop Jackson's analysis of the black church's agreement with white conservative denominations on issues having to do with personal morality. The pastor and college president adds a particular interest and track record in community development to his perspective on the two parties. The Jamaica, Queens, church does far more than minister on Sunday morning. It has become a vast enterprise encompassing education, housing development, employment, and training. Twenty-thousand-member Allen AME has a $100-million portfolio, and is the sixth largest employer in Queens, a borough of 2.2 million people.

A strong component of Allen's appeal to its faithful is its emphasis on personal growth, empowerment, and self-improvement, given out in large helpings along with Scripture, prayer, and a strong music program. Listen to the Reverend Floyd Flake for a while and his impatience with both parties and their common insufficiency in answering the needs of black Americans is clear. Of his own Democratic Party, he said, "Making religious appeals, and doing so across denominations, is not in their habit of mind. They have generally looked at African American leaders and worked with and campaigned with African American leaders who are elected and hold a liberal world view. That's getting skewed by the reality of the populace in megachurches, and they tend to be conservative and are more frequently stressing economic justice in their preaching. Stressing home ownership, good schools. They have become not only voices of that, but practitioners."

However, he felt a particular irritation with the strong Republican wooing of black social conservatives: "Their problem is they are not inclusive enough, and they aren't going to get significant buy-in until they are more realistic about differences between Americans, the daily lives of people in places like New Orleans. Until they are ready to show some support, and disengagement from the kind of rhetoric you sometimes hear. I don't think Republicans know how close they are to making a real breakthrough.

"Just being right on gay marriage won't be enough. It's not a big enough issue. If they were more proactive making sure they were producing housing, for instance, making sure they were more supportive on opportunity questions, that would mean a lot.

"I think the greatest criticism of the conservative Christian movement is the fact that there is a refusal to talk about social-justice issues. It's almost as if there's a belief that we're living in paradise when that's not the case. They overlook a significant portion of people who are part of the American landscape and not enjoying all the benefits the country has to offer."

Ken Mehlman, of the RNC, may travel around the country apologizing in African American churches for the Nixon-era Southern Strategy that helped the GOP take control of the South, but he is not proposing undoing its long-lasting effects and starting over. Mehlman's Democratic counterpart Howard Dean may berate Democrats for their ineffective efforts to talk about faith and the way the values religions teach become public policy. Neither seems poised to make the internal changes that will speak to a group that is more socially conservative than the country as a whole and perceives itself as more in need of effective government to guarantee their liberties and open America's opportunity structure.

Encouraging black churches to get politically mobilized around gay marriage, opposition to sex education, and abortion will not be enough to permanently distract black Americans from the fact that they on average die younger, make less money, amass less wealth, get worse health care, lives in worse houses and school districts than their fellow citizens.

The Democrats are ready to speak to the economic human, but unsure of how to widen that definition without scaring off other parts of the loose coalition. But the Republicans are equally loath to alienate any of their loose confederation, and an overture to African Americans on issues outside the moral/social realm risks losing the Republicans as many voters as they gain, losing among Americans who think black citizens have already received a disproportionate share of the country's attention.

Does that, in demographic terms, make Latinos the jump ball that decides the whole game? Analysts like Bush-supporter and Republican senatorial candidate Linda Chavez and advertising executive and Republican consultant Lionel Sosa have suggested that Latinos are not any different from other, earlier, mainly Roman Catholic immigrant groups. The Irish, Italians, Poles and others came to this country, began their American journeys in manual trades and built their neighborhoods around churches that reflected their aspirations in their soaring spires and loving craftsmanship. In a few generations, they were just the people next door, as American as anyone else.

You do not have to work too hard to point out the differences between Mexicans and Poles. Unlike Polish immigration that rose, spiked, and subsided, Mexican immigration never subsides. For much of the country, outside areas of large Mexican settlement, there is little interest in figuring out who came to America this morning and whose forebears were already in what is now the U.S. when the country came to them.

Latinos from everywhere in the hemisphere are moving into new places in the country that have never known large-scale immigration from non-English-speaking people. Latinos put the roofs on new subdivisions in northern Georgia, kill cows in Nebraska and chicken in Delaware, and run sawmills in North Carolina. As they spread across the great American middle from the coasts and the borders, Latinos are also becoming Protestants in a way that might have been hard to predict. Sure, the massive immigration of Spanish-speaking workers and their young families have filled the pews of Catholic churches in Los Angeles and Florida and Chicago. However, in the last few decades, older church buildings in central cities across the country have become the homes of burgeoning Pentecostal, Baptist, and Assemblies of God congregations.

Jennifer Lopez may be gyrating and reminding you her love don't cost a thing on MTV, but elsewhere in the five-hundred-channel universe, blow-dried Latino televangelists remind praying, swaying, and weeping congregations of the threats to their eternal souls. Univision and Telemundo may have a high jiggle-factor, but modestly dressed girls in Chicago's Humboldt Park, Los Angeles's Boyle Heights, and Miami's Opa-locka are still heading out on dates with chaperones or taking their dates to midweek, multihour church services.

Daniel DeLeon is pastor of Templo Calvario, an Assemblies of God congregation that, at 6,300 members, ranks as one of the largest Latino Protestant churches in America. He knows well that both political parties covet the 75 percent of his home congregation that is native-born or naturalized and able to vote. I asked him about the assumption, like Lionel Sosa's, that Latinos are "natural Republicans" because of their social conservatism and church affiliation. He responded, "I think that's a statement that has little merit. I think they are assuming too much because of the following: Yes, we are against abortion. We are against homosexuality. Some of those values are very dear to us. Even a lot of people in our camp who are Democrats will say that. We are conservative, almost by nature. And still the majority of our people are Democrats."

Pastor DeLeon is a second-generation Protestant. Born and educated in California, his English is, of course, flawless, though he speaks it with the residual lilt of a man who still grew up in a Spanish-speaking milieu. He has made a smashing success of Templo Calvario, and spun off mission churches around Southern California, ministering to fifteen thousand weekly worshipers in all. As his church has grown, so has the political interest in speaking to his flock. "They've all sought, our endorsement, especially at the local level, county candidates, candidates for state office. Jack Kemp visited the church when he was the Republican candidate for vice president."

All the candidates, at all level of offices, from all political parties, DeLeon said, get the same treatment: "You're welcome to come and sit in the audience; I will acknowledge you, ask you to stand; and we will pray for you." Would he ever endorse a political candidate, from the pulpit or publicly? "Absolutely not."

"We are getting more and more requests. Before, none of the candidates, Hispanic or Anglo, looked for us. Now they're calling us, setting up meetings for us, want to hear what we think and tell us where they stand."

Just as he has watched the Latino student body at his seminary grow from 2.5 percent when he was a student to 25 percent today, he has watched his denomination, the Assemblies of God, change in what it teaches its clergy about politics. "Years ago we were taught in seminary to stay away from politics. We were told that it's not appropriate for pastors. For one thing, it's dirty, and you can't trust politicians. A lot has changed. The new generation in the church is saying, 'We need to say who we are and why we're here.'

"We are taking a more proactive role today. I for one have gone to Washington many times, since 1982, under President Reagan. I've been asked to set up a White House conference so our ministers could experience a level of involvement with the White House staff and politicians on Capitol Hill. You see more and more ministers going to Washington, encouraging people to write to their congressmen and senators. I think it's positive; I think it's healthy for our people. The church has, throughout the ages, found itself an instrument in the hands of God."

I pressed DeLeon. All they want from your church in Washington is an interesting exchange of opinions? He replied that no one has ever overtly tried to make a deal with him. If they asked and he agreed, DeLeon insisted, for the churches and for the politicians, it would be a big mistake:

"If we as churches fall into the idea that someway, somehow we can get something from Washington that will be a benefit for us, that we can sell ourselves to get it, it would be terrible.

"The white evangelical churches are at the right side of the church. I think the Hispanic side of the church leans more toward the Democratic Party, yet they are conservative in their values. At the same time, they feel the party is more in line with some of their needs. They can't see themselves as part of the Republican Party because that party has done nothing to reach out to the Hispanic. But for us to receive some benefit from that would be entirely wrong.

"I saw that happen in the 1980s under the Reagan administration. The white evangelical church sent the wrong message to the church in general. They said, 'This is time to go to Washington. Go and create some ties. Let's see what we can get out of Washington.' " DeLeon said it has not worked for the church.

The issue engaging pastors of large Latino congregations now is immigration, which exploded into a national issue in the months leading up to the midterm election in 2006. Pastors like DeLeon believe they can still be tough on an administration that is trying to court them, since they have not gotten too close. "If we sell ourselves to this present party, then we have to play the political game. You scratch my back, I scratch yours. And before you know it, the benefits have dissipated before your very eyes. It's a scary scenario that none of us want to be a part of."

His lobbying in Washington on immigration has convinced DeLeon that keeping his distance while keeping the channel open to both parties was right. "We don't agree at all with what the president has been saying on immigration. And we are adamantly against the House bill [the immigration bill that passed the House in 2006 concentrated on border security and punishment of illegal entrants to the US, and made no provisions for eventual legal status]. I was able to tell members of the Bush administration and the GOP leadership, 'You lose this, you lose the Hispanic vote. You've been trying to get us to become part of the Republican coalition. Well, you want to lose us, be careful how to treat this issue.'

"I said the same thing to Attorney General Gonzales regarding federalizing local sheriffs and police forces to round up illegals. Had we sold ourselves to the party, we couldn't do that.

"We must be people that stand our ground as Christians and follow our conscience based on our theology," DeLeon concluded. One of the hallmarks of conservative Christian congregations, across racial and ethnic lines, and across denominational lines, is a deference to legal authority and respect for law and order. It is an interesting juxtaposition of impulses that propel Daniel DeLeon to support the rule of law while showing sympathy for millions of illegal immigrants. The problem, he said, is not the undocumented workers, but the law. "Let's go back to the 1960s in the black community. What was happening in this country was terribly wrong. To me, this is an issue like unto those. And the Italians? The Polish? When they came everybody was upset. They were often sent into ghettoes, and they stuck to themselves. This is a different situation. We have the border right here. That's coupled with the fact that Latin America is in a very bad state economically.

"I'd be doing the same thing to save my family. These are hardworking people, and like them, I'd do whatever I had to do to save my family. We haven't really talked about who is the real lawbreaker? Is it the person who comes looking for a job, or the ones that give them the job?"

In much the same way that gay marriage exploded into view as a national issue in the months after *Lawrence v. Texas,* immigration may end up a national wild card, decisive for all sides of the question in different states with different populations. Some portion of that innumerable army of undocumented workers will end up staying in the United States legally, and voting. The complete inheritance of this debate may roll out over decades rather than one or two elections.

The Reverend Andy Hernandez said a decisive stage of political power is being able to shape how people think of themselves politically: "For example, if I think I'm a conservative, a moral conservative, before I'm a Latino worker, that's who I think I am. I mean, that's my identity. I'm going to vote against my own economic interest. Because identity creates interest. And people tend to vote along interest lines.

"So if you can control identity and manipulate identity, you control people's perception of their interest. And if you control the perception of their interest, you are able to influence the way they vote. It's not just the Republicans that have done it. Conservative forces have done this over the years.

"At the turn of the last century, there was a huge populist movement in the South. It was religiously and evangelically based, by the way. And this populist movement of poor whites, mostly farmers, tenant farmers, and blacks took over a lot of state legislatures. The reason we have such progressive legislation in Texas, railroad commissions and all that stuff— it's because of populists. That movement of black and white workers and tenants farmers were saying, 'You know, we have something in common.'

"It was at that point that the Ku Klux Klan and the racial supremacists began emerging again. Then white workers became, not workers, but whites who had to protect themselves and their culture and their women from blacks. And then you had this kind of racialization of the movement, so that you began to have a different kind of populist whose contemporary expression was George Wallace in the '60s. You know they were liberal in the economic stuff and social stuff, but segregationists and everything else when it came to blacks.

"So that happened at one time, and then you look over and over again—White women, the biggest beneficiaries of affirmative action have been white women in this country. But if you ask white women who do they believe is the most discriminated against group in the country? They say white males. Really. Surveys have shown that. You know, for me that's power. They don't think of themselves as women, they think of themselves as whites.

"If you can get people saying, 'I'm a moral person and this is the way I define my morality and my spirituality as a Christian,' that has political consequences. There's a group of Christians, in my experience as a pastor, who use religious language and the Bible and their faith to justify positions they already hold. In other words, even if they weren't Christian, if they were Buddhists, they'd still hate gays. You know they just look for reason and the Bible gives them the cover they need. Same thing happened with slavery.

"There were theological arguments for slavery, and there was preachers who preached for slavery. So these were people who probably—they weren't owning slaves because the Bible told them to. They were owning slaves because it helped them economically and it was in their interest and it gave them a sense of power, and they just used the Bible to cover it. That's all. So that's one group. And I think a big chunk of what we call the religious conservatives are people that hold positions like this already. And just use faith as a way of justifying it.

"There's another group who've just come into the faith. These are people that are being converted, or people who are having a new religious experience. They're being brought into the evangelical church through services that they provide. You know, youth programs, support groups, entertainment, music entertainment, all these large evangelical churches that have these, you know, five- and ten-thousand-member congregations and provide a whole host of really cool services. People are being brought into those churches through these services they provide, the outreach that they have, and the support that they get once they get there. But once they get there, they're being indoctrinated with a certain political identity. A Christian identity that fused with a political, Republican-conservative identity at the same time. That's a—that's a different group than the first one. And we have to make the distinction between those two faith expressions.

"And then there's this other group; I think they're truly sincere about trying to figure out what the right thing to do is, you know, what the moral thing to do is. And that group sometimes, you know, will say, 'Well, you know, the Bible does talk about gays shouldn't be married, but on the other hand, we should be loving.' So that's kind of a torn group, and you can go one way or the other on this, depending on what's happening in their lives.

"The final group is what I call the religious Left. The religious Left makes up about 14 percent of the electorate. These are people that believe in God, that consider themselves Christians, that consider themselves, you know, of a denominational Christian faith, but who are liberal in every other measure. Nobody ever talks about the religious Left."

The Reverend Altagracia Perez cut me off when I used the word *lib-*

eral. She countered, "I am not a liberal, I'm a leftist." Listening to her describe clergy political activism from the other end of the continuum, I had to conclude the challenges were remarkably similar to those conservative activists wrestle with. Perez pastors a congregation in Inglewood, a small city in southern Los Angeles County. It might have been best known as the home of the Los Angeles Lakers,[3] but Inglewood is a community in the throes of social change. This black-majority city is becoming a brown one, and an Afro–Puerto Rican priest from New York finds herself on the front lines of social struggle, trying to talk to both sides.

Unlike Floyd Flake, Harry Jackson, and Daniel DeLeon, Altagracia Perez does not find that black and brown congregations are all that different from the mainstream when it comes to the hottest social issues of the times. Do not assume that her black and brown working-class flock has a different approach to, for instance, gay rights. "I don't think it's a good assumption, for good or for ill. Black and Latino communities represent the broader community. What saves us is that 90 percent of the people think it's right to have a conversation about this. Even when they don't agree, they really see the connection between lesbian and gay people and the black civil-rights movement. This is an extension of human rights, this is what it means to be a faithful Christian."

Perez was called to be the rector of Holy Faith Episcopal Church in 2003. What she calls a diverse and multicultural congregation, Holy Faith wanted to welcome everyone, and she said it did. Then came the General Convention of the Episcopal Church, later in the same year. This meeting of the lay and clerical leaders of the denomination would be the one that ran into controversy over the approval of the Diocese of New Hampshire's election of an openly gay man as bishop. Holy Faith's members saw their new rector on television speaking up for the new bishop.

She told me later, "Gene Robinson is a friend of mine; I have experienced his gifts as a leader. He's himself, he's a human being, he's a good pastor. I spoke in his defense. I really felt I could speak on his behalf with clarity to different parts of the church. I wasn't worried at all about the reaction back home. This is a congregation that's had these conversations; it won't be that bad."

When she returned home to Los Angeles from the convention in Minneapolis, "there were people that were really happy, people proud of their pastor while annoyed at what she was saying. And I had people leave this church. And some of them were people who had taken serious stances in the civil rights movement. It was hard—saying good-bye, needing to let go of people. I kept telling them, 'You can stay, your position is valid and respected. It's okay for us to have differences.' "

The churches of the more than sixty million blacks and Latinos in the United States are as different from one another as are all the people who call this country home. Floyd Flake is working among aspirational blacks in Queens, New York, extolling the virtues of bootstrapping your way into the American Dream, and working with the conservative Manhattan Institute as a fellow. He has no problem with teaching creationism in public schools, hanging the Ten Commandments on their walls, and calls debates over church-state separation of "no value."

Altagracia Perez told me the religious Right has hijacked the national conversation. "People plot on a bell curve; the majority of people are going to be somewhere in the middle, not the radical right, and not the left. They care about people, they want to love God and their neighbor, in this society with all the change we're going through. That Focus on the Family stuff is so simple. Some things are simple, like courtesy, love, mercy, and compassion. I can see why people are so attracted to simplicity. That's what we need to be talking about."

Listen to Andy Hernandez, and it becomes difficult to hear where the politics begins and the religion ends. As Democrats try to claw back the third of the Latino Protestant vote they lost from 2000 to 2004, Hernandez said, "You have to challenge. It's not really a political challenge; it's a theological challenge. You have to support the kind of pastoral leadership that offers an alternative view of what it means to be a loving Christian in the world—what the religious progressives or religious left or liberals don't talk about. It's a war on love, Christian love, that the right wing has created. Because they're against things. They're against gays. They're against, you know, they're against the Arabs, they're against the Muslims. They're against things.

"They're not for something, for love, for peace, for all those virtues and values that are easily found in the scripture. And so I think you have to create an infrastructure of leadership, pastoral clergy leadership as well as lay leadership. We're able to offer an alternative theological paradigm of what it means to be Christian in the Latino context."

Bishop Harry Jackson wrote in 2004 that black Americans had the power to shape the electorate and set the course of the nation for years to come. And there was no question, in his mind, which direction the black church would point: "In my view, God has been preparing the heart of President Bush to take a radical stand for social justice in his next term. This could be the beginning of the development of a 'kingdom agenda' instead of a limited 'conservative' versus 'liberal' approach to the woes of our society. The current political labels have led to bitter divisions that do not serve the nation's best interests."[4]

After the election, Bishop Jackson said his prediction had come true. He cited a rise in the black vote in Ohio for Republican candidates and the slim margin of victory that gave the president the state and the race. He says he has his eyes on a much bigger target: capturing America for Jesus by harnessing the power of the church in elections. "Imagine what would happen if Christians would rise up and take a stand with a specific, unified strategy to restore America's moral greatness? Perhaps this is what was meant by the term used over a decade ago, 'the Moral Majority.' Unfortunately, this group did not understand the difference between personal righteousness and the need to create an atmosphere of justice in the land. They appeared contentious, strident, and petty. We, however, have an opportunity to joyfully present a God who loves sinners and is willing to deliver them from their sin."[5]

No one strategy can hold the majority of black and Latino voters in the Democratic camp. No one strategy can peel away large blocs of these voters for the GOP permanently now that the electoral career of George Bush is over and his personal appeal has passed from the scene. The chairman of the Republican National Committee can count, however, and it is not necessary to capture a majority of black and brown voters to win elections in states where white voters are pretty evenly divided. Targeting the churches, especially conservative Protestant churches, can change the dynamics of gubernatorial and senatorial races across America.

Can these subtly positioned churches—socially conservative but looking for help from an activist government, worried about morals but sympathetic to the underdog—be pulled to one party's banner as effectively as majority-white conservative congregations and denominations have been brought to the GOP's banner? The tale will be told by the state of America in the coming decade.

A legalistic and punitive solution to the tricky policy challenge of illegal immigration or a government that proves unresponsive to the needs of working poor families could easily make supporting conservative politicians appear counterintuitive to black and brown voters.

More-secular politicians will ignore at their own risk the centrality of the life of the church to black and brown neighborhoods. The church, in its dazzling array of forms of worship and theology, brings a kind of solace that you cannot get from an hourly raise or a tax refund. However, if they do the opposite and pander, that strategy also carries risk. Solicitousness can bring out the vote for one election, but never will it make voting the pillar of civil religion for working-class blacks and Latinos that it is for other Americans.

The party that shows it is ready to enter a long period of engagement that really looks as if it will craft policy to change people's lives will manage the trick. Daniel DeLeon's church will approach with caution. Harry Jackson's will look elsewhere if after such a public embrace, his good faith is not returned with interest.

Where is this relationship between church and politics headed? That is our last stop in the book.

ELEVEN

Render Unto Caesar

LET US ASSUME for a moment that you actually wanted to run a state according to what are too often called "Judeo-Christian principles." Would the electorate give you a chance? Would the people who say they subscribe to those principles approve of a legal code that provided for "these, the least of my brethren," or "loving your neighbor as yourself?"

Quite by accident, Alabama decided to find out. The state really could not be better placed to test the proposition of a possible marriage between secular government and religious principles. It is without a doubt one of the most uniformly Christian places in America. Half of Alabama's 4.5 million people are Baptists, more than nine out of ten are one kind of Christian or another. Just 1 percent profess non-Christian religions. Only 7 percent, or just over one in fifteen, call themselves "nonreligious."

Yet after repeated collisions between courts, judges, voters, and the legislature, Alabama has: (1) removed a granite Ten Commandments from its highest court, (2) defeated a proposed Bible curriculum for the state's schools, and (3) defeated a landmark revamp of the state's tax code to reflect what one tax expert called "faith-based principles."

How did that all happen? And if you cannot get an avowedly Christian government going in Alabama, where can you get one?

The Ten Commandments story was covered at some length in chapter six. Since his removal as chief judge of the Alabama Supreme Court in late 2003, Roy Moore has written a book, *So Help Me God,* found success on the conservative lecture circuit, and launched a campaign against the incumbent governor, conservative Republican Bob Riley.

The 5,300-pound granite monument found a home at a church in Gadsden, and Moore promised Alabamans, "I will defend the right of every citizen of this state—including judges, coaches, teachers, city, county and state officials—to acknowledge God as the sovereign source of law, liberty and government."

It appears to be extremely difficult for the former chief judge to tell the difference between the right of various civil servants to acknowledge God as the sovereign source of law and to make such acknowledgments while also carrying out their taxpayer-financed duties to the various governments and institutions of Alabama. I admit I am speculating there about whether Moore knows the difference or not, because he would not consent to be interviewed for this book. Perhaps his inability to tell the difference between professions of faith, never denied, as far as one could tell, to any Alabamian, and making those proclamations at work contributed to his losing at every single level of appeal and being removed from office.

Alabama ranks forty-first among the fifty states in per capita income,[1] a fourth of Alabama's citizens are obese (the worst rate in the country), and a quarter of its children live in poverty.[2] A little more than half the state's incoming ninth graders graduate high school, and its rates for smoking and uninsured citizens both rose during the early 2000s.[3] In 1960, a sixty-five-year-old black woman could expect to live another eight years. Forty years later, a sixty-five-year-old black woman could expect to live another six years.[4] In other words, the state of Alabama has plenty more to worry about than whether or not its chief judge makes the state a safe place to be a Christian, something 92 percent of Alabamians already freely tell public-opinion researchers.

You might also wonder about the correlation between faithfulness and social indicators. The most unchurched state in the union is Oregon. Some 75 percent of Oregonians self-identify as Christian, but at a mere 12 percent its church membership is the lowest in the union, and 24 percent report no religion at all.

Oregon's per capita income is barely two thousand dollars a year higher than Alabama's, but its social indicators are uniformly higher. A fifth of its citizens are obese, and roughly the same share of children live in poverty. About seven of every ten entering ninth graders graduate high school, and it has one of the lowest rates of death on the job in the United States. This does not make Oregon a particularly moral place, or Alabama an immoral one. All it demonstrates is that spending for prenatal and perinatal care is more likely to bring down the infant mortality rate than just praying about it.

In many ways, looking back at the Moore case, the remarkable thing might be that Moore was removed, along with his monument, in the first place. After his first few setbacks, Moore insisted that "God has chosen this time and this place so we can save our country and save our courts for our children." After federal judicial review and the order to remove the Commandments from the court came down, an Alabama ethics panel had to review the situation of the recalcitrant judge and sounded almost pained to have had to do so, pointing out that this was "not a case about the public display of the Ten Commandments in the State Judicial Building nor the acknowledgment of God. Indeed, we recognize that the acknowledgment of God is very much a vital part of the public and private fabric of our country. Moreover, this is not a case to review the judgment of Judge Myron Thompson nor the actions of the United States Court of Appeals for the Eleventh Circuit or the United States Supreme Court. This court does not have the authority or jurisdiction to reexamine those issues."[5]

After running through the circumstances under which they got the case, repeated federal orders to remove the monuments and repeated refusals by Judge Moore to do so, the Alabama panel had to admit the obvious: "Any person who undertakes a solemn oath to carry out a public trust must act in a manner that demonstrates both respect for and compliance with established rules of law of the institution that person serves. Here, however, we are faced with a situation in which the highest judicial officer of this state has decided to defy a court order." So, he had to go.

Not that his elected peers in Alabama had any zest for carrying out the federal order. Several of the state's constitutional officers indicated publicly that they wanted to keep the Commandments in the court, did not want Moore removed, but found a federal order left Alabama little choice. Typical was David Pryor, the state's attorney general and a Bush administration appointee to the federal bench. Siding with Moore would have ended his career outside Alabama. Siding too much with federal authority could have ended his career inside the state, so he split the difference, saying, "At the end of the day, when the courts resolve those controversies, we respect their decision. That does not mean that we always agree with their decision." Not exactly a ringing endorsement of the work of the federal bench you actually aspire to join.

Governor Bob Riley, a former U.S. Congressman and, like Pryor, a self-identified Christian conservative, did not back Moore's attempts to keep the monument and his place on the bench. Facing a $5,000-a-day federal fine for keeping the monument in place, Alabama sent the man now called "The Ten Commandments Judge"[6] on to fatter speaking fees, a governor's race, and the life of, as one Alabama political scientist called him, "a rock star of the Christian right."

By mid-2006, Governor Riley's strategic choice of the First Amendment over the First Commandment was not doing him the damage first predicted: the "Ten Commandments Judge" trailed him by twenty-five points in Republican-primary opinion polls.

The head of the Christian Coalition of Alabama, John Giles, took pains to remind me that his organization endorses no candidates for public office but, as an observer of Alabama politics, gave this reading of the judge's performance in the governor's race: "I would say at the outset of the election, I've always maintained that it was his to win and his to lose. When he started off, according to the polls, he was at 28 percent. And that was a core solid vote. He had been out of the spotlight, out on the speaking circuit. And what I would call myths about pulling the monument out started to circulate. Stories about why he pulled it out. When he stepped into the race, he was stepping into his raw net vote. He hasn't increased that.

"He started with that support and little else. So I would give him an A-plus in building grass-roots organization, a C-plus in raising money, and a D in media."

The fact that Moore is not running against a liberal, a secularist, or a non-Christian might be part of the problem. Some of the most vehement charges he makes against Alabama's leaders and against government in general are hard to stick on one of the most conservative politicians in the state. That may end up being a blessing for Alabamians, even for the most religious among them.

The judge who would not follow the law and denounced the functioning of the courts and the Constitution will likely not ride that disobedience into inauguration as the state's chief executive. If you want to hear Moore poems like *"Our American Birthright,"* you will have to head to a stop on the Christian lecture circuit rather than listening to the governor's speeches. Moore finds little to like in American history since, let's say, 1850:

> So with a firm reliance on Divine Providence for protection,
> They pledged their sacred honor and sought His wise direction.
> They lifted an appeal to God for all the world to see,
> And declared their independence forever to be free.
>
> I'm glad they're not with us to see the mess we're in,
> How we've given up our righteousness for a life of indulgent sin.
> For when abortion isn't murder and sodomy is deemed a right,
> Then evil is now called good and darkness is now called light.
>
> While truth and law were founded on the God of all Creation,
> Man now, through law, denies the truth and calls it "separation."
> No longer does man see a need for God when he's in full control,
> For the only truth self-evident is in the latest poll.[7]

In a fund-raising appeal on her husband's behalf, Kayla Moore told the faithful that the ACLU and Americans United for the Separation of Church and State would "stop at nothing to keep Roy Moore out of the governor's office in Alabama!" But the jurist's wife can only lay that political desire, keeping her husband out of the governor's office, at the doorstep of this rogue's gallery of wedge-issue champions: "They want to continue to promote homosexual marriages, maintain abortion on demand and remove Christ from Christmas. They FEAR nothing more than the emergence of a powerful national spokesperson for Christian conservatism.

"And make no mistake: If elected governor of Alabama, my husband will be that spokesman! But again, he can't get there alone which is why I am hoping you and thousands of other Christian conservatives will join with my husband in his campaign for governor."

Secular Americans probably do not think there is a lot of room to outflank President Bush on the right when it comes to issues of personal morality and human sexuality. But there is. Just as state legislatures moved well right of the president in passing blanket abortion bans, a fracturing coalition may even find the Bush-Rove formula for marriage, so successful in the reelection campaign in 2004, insufficiently pure.

Moore opposes amending the U.S. Constitution to ban gay marriage. While conservative Christian organizations have largely read from the same playbook in their insistence that any change to traditional marriage norms come from the ballot box instead of the courts, Moore said, "I don't think you can make a constitutional amendment for every moral problem created by courts that don't follow the law of their states. If you do, you pretend to do what God has already done and make it subject to the courts. I think it's a problem to establish morality by constitutional amendments made by men when the morality of our country is plainly illustrated—in Supreme Court precedent and in state-law precedent and in the common law—as coming from an acknowledgement of God."

Whoa! Your Honor! At first read it may look like just more outraged boilerplate, pocked with references to God and law and morality. Look again. Amending the Constitution to head off state court actions on gay marriage would be superfluous, since there is already a law against homosexuality: God's law. If you make a constitutional amendment to block individual state court actions, you "pretend to do what God has already done" when American morality is already apparent in judicial precedents as "coming from an acknowledgement of God."

It is unclear how much of this boils down to a states'-rights argument that would have made his removal from office by federal court order impossible, and how much from a real belief that when the Bible has spoken, and gotten general backing in court decisions, that no further law is necessary or desired. We should be thankful that frequent scriptural approval of slavery was not successfully asserted as binding on modern legislatures. Whether you believe the Hebrew scriptures and its Christian descendants are sacred or incapable of error, or just find them to be a culturally significant collection of folk wisdom and fable, you should be able to agree that the Jewish and Christian scriptures are an unreliable law text.

Alabama, called by John Giles "without question, whether you look at secular polls or Christian polls, the most conservative state in the southeast," may still value secular government more than anyone realizes. Even though, according to Giles, "anything defined by the electorate as conservative can happen in Alabama, and anything found to be obtuse to those values can be stopped."

In 1998, a tax-law specialist at the University of Alabama Law School, Professor Susan Pace Hamill, headed off for a sabbatical year of study. Instead of heading to a business school to further bone up on tax law or guest lecturing while pursuing further study in the law, Professor Hamill headed to Beeson Divinity School of Samford University in Birmingham. The school calls itself a seminary with an "explicitly evangelical perspective." The professor is a tough-minded and blunt-spoken academic not given to mushy language or dreamy spiritual speculation. Even religious inquiry in our wide-ranging interview was grounded in real-world challenges and people's daily lives.

She headed off to Beeson planning to contrast corporate decision-making structures to biblical morality. Gradually she was drawn to studying the federal tax code and that of Alabama. "I wasn't attempting to engage in creating new high theory in either piece. I was attempting to sort of define a moral framework that is revealed biblically and then apply it to a very practical issue. In the case of Alabama, it's the disgusting way we treat poor people here. In the case of the federal system, it's much more complicated. Sort of the pull between the middle-class and the very wealthy. Which obviously is both theologically, practically a much tougher question.

"But the analysis in the federal work very soundly condemns the Bush administration trends under faith-based morals and really attacks it as being driven by a form of individualism that's atheism. Which is fine if that's what you are, but the country is supposedly made up of churchgoers, and that can be empirically proven, and then the president himself is very unabashed as far as faith being a big part of his life and his public policy and everything he does. Yet with tax policy, we're going off in an atheistic form of individualism."

Keep in mind that the tax lawyer, who calls herself "one of the queens of limited liability corporation law," did not sit down at the word processor to unleash a statewide debate on government and biblical ethics. "When I wrote the article, I really did not have a clear sense that it could do anything. Remember, this was a master's thesis for a degree that was going to be published in a law review. How much public discourse is there about a law-review article that you've heard of?" I conceded there was normally not much.

"See? None. I was with some law professors when I was speaking about this work. We were at dinner and one of them said, 'So what's your secret? You're the only law professor in America that—that figured out a way to get people to read your article.' "

Or got help figuring it out. A friendly columnist ran a piece about the Hamill thesis, that the Alabama tax code, steeply regressive for low-income people, taxing food while giving a pass to some of the wealthiest landowners in the state, would not pass a biblical test for its treatment of "the least among us." The article appeared in the Sunday editions of the Mobile *Press Register:* "And the Monday I came in my office, it was pandemonium. No, I mean the phone was ringing off the hook, the e-mail box was going nuts, and, I mean, people from the bowels of the state I'd never heard of were calling me up. And I said to myself, gee whiz."

Even early on, politicians and legal colleagues told the professor her overview of Alabama taxation and biblical morality would make one group in particular angry, the Alabama Farmer's Federation, which would not take kindly to her critique of the ways the tax system burdens poor wage earners while benefiting wealthy landowners.

She said nothing prepared her for the firestorm of debate her paper set off in Alabama. Special interests weighed in immediately and began attacking Professor Hamill, her conclusions, and her motives. She recalled,

"The ultraconservatives have done a very good job convincing mainstream Ma and Pa Kettle that we're in it with you and we're into family values and you're into family values and blah, blah, blah, and meanwhile, economic policy issues are not favorable to the mainstream. But that sort of gets lost in America and apple pie and family values, and 'Why would you want to be part of a latte-drinking liberal freak show?' Do you see what I'm saying?"

It helps if one of the readers of your scholarly paper is the new governor of Alabama, who holds Bible study classes in his chambers in the state capital and has one of the most conservative voting records of the chamber during his time on Capitol Hill as a U.S. Congressman. Governor Bob Riley came to office in January 2003 to find the state cupboards bare and a looming deficit of almost $700 billion. As was mentioned earlier, Alabama has never been a proponent of "maximalist" government, and the horror of taxation had created a budget without lots of obvious cuts.

The state already has one of the lowest-performing education systems among the fifty states, and somehow got twenty-seven thousand inmates into state prisons built for twelve thousand. Because of the mix of a low dollar threshold to reach the highest tax rates, the property tax structure designed to benefit big landowners, and taxes on food, the overall tax burden in Alabama falls unusually heavily on the poor. The governor called the current tax structure immoral and, armed with Hamill's paper, headed out into the state to campaign in favor of a state referendum to both restructure Alabama's taxes and raise more money to support government services.

Time magazine called him courageous and a GOP heretic. He ran infomercials on television channels throughout the state. He appealed to aspirational Alabamians, noting that if he raised just enough money to address the budget shortfall, the state "would still be last in education, last in social services, last across the board." The governor appeared to have learned the lessons of his predecessor, Democrat Don Siegelman, who campaigned heavily on raising the prospects of the poor and campaigned for a lottery to fund state spending. Siegelman ran afoul of conservative Christians, who loathed the lottery as much as higher taxes.

Riley kept moral and biblical appeals at the center of the campaign, along with the ones that might appeal to Chamber of Commerce members as well. It did not work. Elected with strong support from wealthy and upper-middle-class voters, Riley was swimming upstream against his own party, and the Christian Coalition of Alabama.

Coalition president John Giles does not think you should spend too much time dwelling on the rich irony of the Christian Coalition working to defeat a faith-based tax bill. "We opposed that amendment. It just doesn't fit one of our tenets. We are for easing the tax burden on families. We are for tax reduction. We are not going to support easing taxes on one class by raising burden on another class.

"We had this law professor out of the University of Alabama pushing it. The bottom line about her thesis was that Alabama needs to give a tax break down at $4,600, that people who earn that little shouldn't be paying the top rate of tax. She also said that it was immoral and a sin. But the way we viewed it was, listen, we are all for giving relief to those at the $4,600 level. But the amendment wasn't a reduction only for those people. That was the way it was sold and marketed. It was trying to make that moral appeal, *we need to raise taxes*. We supported giving tax relief to the poor. We would phase in raising the threshold."

I asked Giles if raising the threshold and lowering the taxes of low-income Alabamians without raising any taxes would not eventually give the government less money to spend? He responded, "Here's the deal. We have maintained all along that growth is the way to go. If we keep Alabama's economy growing, then the government will have the money it needs." The Christian Coalition's supply-side gospel might appear in the quadrennial Republican Party platform and in the theories of Arthur Laffer, but it appears nowhere in the Bible.

True to his consistent identity as a sometimes cryptic and always challenging moral teacher, Jesus' opinion of taxation boils down to two words: *pay them*. Taxation, governments, emperors, road-building projects, public-employee pension plans, and all the trappings of the modern state are all part of a world quite apart from his Kingdom of God. Jesus and the followers he knew in his lifetime spoke in verb tenses that signaled their own belief that the end of the world they knew was coming fast. What that means to people trying to discern what Jesus would do today is not clear.

Or is it? "Scripture is clear," Giles said, " 'Render unto Caesar what is Caesar's, and render unto God what is God's.'[8] The average taxpayer feels as though they're paying plenty already, and they feel like they can't trust the legislature. You pick up the newspaper and see a state senator has his family on the payroll. There's corruption and bad judgment. The voters soundly rejected Amendment One because they didn't buy in. All these different goals were bundled up in one vote. Had the governor broken it out and said, 'Let's give these people tax relief,' it would have passed. But when you start talking about raising people's taxes across the board, that's another question altogether."

Professor Hamill concedes that a "cleaner" bill might have passed. But she finds far more significance in the state's voters' inability to approve anything. "There was a referendum on the ballot to remove the racist language from the Alabama 1901 Constitution, the requirement that we have separate schools for blacks and whites in particular, and removing the 1956 amendment that states that there's no public constitutional right to an education. That was put there in 1956 in response to the *Brown* decision. Where removing that language would have done nothing, I repeat nothing." First of all, Hamill said, separate but equal schooling was rendered illegal in all cases by the *Brown v. Board of Education of Topeka* decision, and second, removing the denial of a right does not create a new one in its place.

"So this referendum was merely cosmetic. It was an attempt to—fifty years too late—save some embarrassment. And it failed by a hair." The law professor's conclusion is not flattering to Alabama voters: "But then, you might ask, why did our people, why did the special interests spend a lot of war chest money fighting this? And why did our people defeat something that did nothing? And the answer is the special interests view any change, even if it's cosmetic, as the camel's nose under the tent. Any attempt to change anything, they will fight to the core."

When I asked Giles about the issues that attract the Christian Coalition's political program in Alabama, I admit I was a little surprised by the answer: "Typically what you might call the black-hat guys are funded by the teachers union and the gambling interests. The white-hat guys, let's say, are business, agriculture, and the faith-based community." I guess surprise came from the fact that it's rarely put to me in such naked terms, and without the slightest shred of irony, that the followers of a first-century preacher with a special love for the poor and scorn for the rich might list business interests as their number one "white hat."

I figured there was little daylight between the "faith-based community" and the Christian Coalition. I then asked Giles if the Coalition's priorities and those of business and agriculture always line up. "Candidates that are strong on moral and social issues tend to be economic conservatives, which makes them pro-business. If you look at our voting score card"—issued around election day as a comparison, since the Christian Coalition does not endorse candidates—"and then take a look at some of the business score cards, and you'll find 92 percent of the time that economic conservatives, pro-business candidates are also right on our issues." You might wonder if Jesus himself, that scruffy Jewish rebel denouncing the wealthy, would have gotten as high a score as 92 percent.

Giles is not encouraged by the more frequent use of religious language and religious appeals in political campaigns. Paradoxically, it makes the Christian Coalition voter guides even more important. "Listen, and in Alabama you'll hear more citing of faith commitment by elected officials. They'll get their pictures taken for the newspapers going to church. You hear them quoting Scripture on the campaign trail, and there is a strong pandering to the Christian vote. It becomes the responsibility of groups like ours to quote their true voting records.

"Don't watch his lips move. See what he does. When you pick up a voter guide, you can see this is the issue. We make no endorsement. This is what we put: Here's how they answered the questionnaire, and here's how their opponent answered it."

Another form of that showy, public religion, in Giles's view, is the recent initiative sponsored in the Alabama state legislature to make a new Bible literacy curriculum available for high schools around the state. The bill was sponsored by state senate majority leader Ken Guin, a Democrat who tried to tiptoe through the minefield of popular opinion and constitutional precedent: "The bill says in Alabama we'll offer a course called The Bible and Its Influence. We'll supply a text of the same name offered by the Bible Literacy Project. It's an elective course, and our bill gives authority to local school boards. They can offer a course or not offer a course. It's completely elective."

Senator Guin told me one of his first concerns was whether the bill, the course, and the textbook could all pass constitutional muster. He read the book at night for a month, talked to clergy, teachers, and lawyers, and decided it was worth a shot. "One of the things I like about it, there's a teacher training program, so teachers can learn how to best use the materials." The senator said the state has long since signed off on local boards introducing their own Bible courses, but left it to local boards to come up with the curriculum on their own. "So the larger systems in our state have already offered this as an elective. This bill would help the smaller school systems, and the poorer ones, to have the same access to the material."

John Giles is not impressed. "We took the position that it was already constitutional, fully legal, without any other legislation required. Even some of the local media dismissed it as nothing more than feel-good election-year legislation. It's on par with putting 'One Nation Under God' on our automobile tags."

The senator thinks the Christian Coalition and its Republican allies did not really oppose the bill, though they worked hard to defeat it. "They're playing partisan politics. They don't want a Democrat to be able to have a faith-based bill. They're saying publicly that they don't like the textbook mentioned in the bill. Now they're asking, 'Couldn't we simply use the Bible itself as the text?' They keep trying to raise the bar."

The Christian Coalition leader shot back, "What we supported is Bible literacy. We backed a nonbinding resolution that calls on school boards to make the courses available. If you want to use the Bible as a textbook, we think you should be able to use it. The bill is not necessary, it's just frivolous." Then Giles zeroed in on *The Bible and Its Influence.* "The problem is, it's a brand-new textbook. It's not being used out there. I don't know of any statewide systems that are using that text. The Bible has been taught relative to its impact on history and literature in several states." Now it feels like we are getting closer to the real problem.

"You're walking a thin line here. The textbook challenges theological ideas held by many students' homes and churches. It gets into issues like, 'Did Adam and Eve get a raw deal?' or 'Was God judgmental?' 'Was God unfair?' It represents an undermining of theological teaching that children are getting at home. This is an elective course in public school. This is not a Sunday school class." Now we were getting somewhere. Giles conceded that the Bible could not be taught in Alabama schools as a divinely inspired revelation. Alabama schools apparently were not ready to give the Bible the same kind of critical reading high school students might be expected to give *Moby Dick*.

Senator Guin still hopes his initial defeat can be overcome. He seems genuinely enthusiastic about the text, and while he is a public and professing evangelical Christian, he insists *The Bible and Its Influence* is not a religious work, "I've sat down with local superintendents and shown them the book. I haven't had one person who's said we shouldn't do this. We had editorials around the state, typically in support.

"*The Bible and Its Influence* pulls together an awful lot of things about how the Bible has influenced our society, our literature, and popular culture. It gives countless biblical references to show specific influences. It does a great job with the civil rights movement, and that's certainly important to us in Alabama. It shows how biblical references have influenced great writers and painters, and shows geopolitical influences."

When I cracked the spine on a brand-new copy of *The Bible and Its Influence* and set aside several hours to wander its chapters, I was not expecting to be impressed. As a paid skeptic, I assumed this effort would be little more than a Christian Trojan horse dressed in the livery of scholarly evenhandedness. The book is instead a pleasant surprise. However, you are reminded what a contested terrain this has been from the very first pages; the cover page to the opening chapter contains a legal argument for the existence of the text: "Academic study of the Bible in a public secondary school may appropriately take place in literature courses. Students might study the Bible as literature. They would examine the Bible as they would other literature in terms of aesthetic categories, as an anthology of narrative and poetry, exploring its language, symbolism, and motifs."[9] How many high school texts contain, in the very first chapter, Supreme Court citations explaining why textbooks of this kind are legal? As a kind of legal inoculation, the book chooses its words and its ambitions carefully:

1. You are going to study the Bible academically, not devotionally. In other words, you are learning about the Bible and its role in life, language, and culture.
2. You will be given an awareness of the religious content of the Bible, but you will not be pressed into accepting religion.
3. You will study about religion as presented in the Bible, but you will not be engaged in the public practice of religion.
4. During this course, you will encounter differing religious views, but those views will neither be encouraged or discouraged.
5. You will never be asked to conform to any of the beliefs you encounter in this course.[10]

In those five cautious clarifications the problem of introducing religion into public education, even in one of the most uniformly religious states in the union, becomes much clearer. The long list of reviewers and consultants covers the waterfront, representing a wide range of religious affiliations, scholarly disciplines, and political convictions. It includes Harold Bloom, the formidable expert on the Western cultural canon, a self-described secularist raised an Orthodox Jew in the Bronx, and Frederica Mathewes-Green, a writer on religion and an adult convert to Orthodox Christianity, and Anthony Picarello, president and general counsel for the Becket Fund, which supplies the legal firepower in many church-state separation cases, on the side of religion.

Much of the book is devoted to illuminating the common cultural inheritance from Judaism and Christianity that makes Americans part of the broad stream of Western culture. The book's definition of culture is broad, and its curiosity is vast. Highlighted boxed articles scattered through 377 pages of text explore the links between the Bible and Dante, Harriet Beecher Stowe, and even J.D. Salinger's *Franny and Zooey*. Lincoln's speeches are dutifully excerpted and biblical allusions cited, and cultural arcana is unearthed from *Time* magazine's cover story on *Jesus Christ, Superstar* to Father Mapple's sermon on the *Pequod* in *Moby Dick* to a bare-chested young Placido Domingo as the doomed Jewish hero in Camille Saint-Saëns' *Samson et Dalila*.

That painfully constructed disinterest is hard to keep up for 377 pages. *The Bible and Its Influence* is, at heart, a believer's text. The book is fascinating, and it's great fun to learn about images of original sin in Nathaniel Hawthorne, the influence of Revelations on William Blake, and Walker Evans and James Agee's use of a phrase from the Apocrypha's Book of Sirach for the title of their stunning Depression-era portrait of Alabama sharecroppers, *Let Us Now Praise Famous Men*.

But the book's kaleidoscopic range, diversity, and thoroughness gradually take the reader (and, one imagines, the high school student) far beyond the borders of the knowledge necessary to be an intellectually full-fledged Westerner. The book's biblical tour eventually becomes something more like a handbook for well-educated, culturally aware, religiously knowledgeable Christians. And to quote John Giles, "This is not a Sunday school class." *The Bible and Its Influence* is a terrific book. Despite the disclaimers, it is a Christian book. That is a strong source of its value, and the difficulty with its use as a public school text. As happens in so many realms, its very integrity as religious education detracts from its value as a tool for public education.

In order to pass constitutional muster, religiously informed value statements and religiously based teaching are asked to perform all sorts of contortions in order to fit through the schoolhouse door. In order for public education to remain nonsectarian, it has to remain vigilant about how religion informs the curriculum. In order to be true to itself, religion should not streamline, smooth down, elide between the difficult places just to pass public-school muster.

A full intellectual journey of this kind, from Genesis to Revelation, can only be meaningful to a believer. A lesson plan that removed large chunks of Scripture would be rejected by those same believers. Even the gentle suggestions of critical reading of the Bible in this text attract the opposition of the Christian Coalition and organizations like Phyllis Schlafly's Eagle Forum. That same subject matter and its presentation, Senator Guin noted, also earned the opposition of the American Atheists chapter in Alabama.

Blair Scott, the leader of the Alabama atheists organization, said elected officials do not slam the door in his face. "They will let you attend committee meetings and voice your opinion. They usually respond to any letters that I send them. They're professional and they're courteous. But at the same time, they're blunt. It usually comes down to not only 'no,' but 'hell, no.' It's kind of like 'We appreciate your opinion, but this is a Christian country.' "

The Christian Coalition tried to rally the public against *The Bible and Its Influence* because it was not religious enough. Scott's atheists were rallying from the other end: "First they try to put a religion class in the high schools under the guise of what they call the Academic Freedom Act. Now, the main point of this was to allow teachers to teach creationism without getting fired.

"Then as an amendment they threw in this Bible-as-literature class, as an elective. When I wrote to Senator Guin, I mentioned that the Academic Freedom Act was not even required because people have religious freedom anyway. There's no reason to prevent a teacher from being fired for having religious beliefs. He was saying the bill would allow teachers to present alternative theories; it's a catchphrase they like to use. But he mentioned this will give you the opportunity for teachers to teach biblical creationism. So it's clear what, what his intention was. And I brought this up in a letter, and his base response was, 'Thank you for writing. I appreciate your opinion.' Then he said, 'I understand your sentiment. I understand the legal aspect that you have brought up. We think that this legislation and the effect it will have on Alabama schools will not contradict any Supreme Court rulings because it does not force the teaching of creationism.'

But it completely avoided the fact that it allowed the teachers to teach it. It's not forcing it, but it's still giving the teacher permission to teach it if they come up with all these just crazy mental gymnastics and excuses and apologetics to get around the real issues."

Scott is not excited as he tells this story. His voice betrays no anger or impatience. He sounds like a man who is being asked to tell a familiar story for the thousandth time. "Anytime I write a letter to them, they never actually address the issues that I bring up. They come up with all this, this crazy mental gymnastics to get around it. But we don't give up. We still write letters. We still call. Sometimes we go down and we actually go to the committee meetings and talk to them, and they'll let you talk, you know, they have to, they're required by law to let you talk, but . . ." and Scott's story trails off.

One interesting thing about Scott's analysis of the use of religion in Alabama politics is where it compliments the head of the Christian Coalition. Scott uses the persistent battles over state standards for teaching evolution as an example: "I think most of the time it's not an effort to push their own religious beliefs, although it does happen. Kansas is a good example. And so is Pennsylvania. Most of the time that we run into it, they're trying to get reelected. It's a way to appease the constituents, what they believe the constituency wants. They believe the constituency is fundamentalist Christian that believes that the theory of creation should be taught alongside evolution. That's what we run into most of the time. Even with separation issues that we run into in schools, a lot of the times it's just ignorance. When we point out the law and point out the ruling and, and educate the principal or the city council or whoever, they go, 'Really? Oh, we didn't know that. Well, we'll stop, sorry about that.'

"Very rarely do we find that it's someone specifically trying to push their religious beliefs, but when that does happen, it's just—it's a brick wall. You have to go to court, and those are the cases we see. It's just when you run into the fundamentalists, the ones that are truly—I hate to use the word *sincere,* but they are. They're absolutely sincere in what they're doing."

Through it all, the head of the atheists organization in arguably the most religious state in the country has not lost his sense of humor. "It's gotten so bad that the biggest fight I had last year was when the mayor asked if people wanted to move Halloween to Saturday because it fell on a Sunday; that was my biggest issue last year. Come on, guys, give me something worth fighting here!"

Trying to move Halloween does seem a little silly. When I look at it as a parent, I find that the every-now-and-then weekend Halloween is a lot easier to manage than the more frequent weeknight ritual. This is not the first time organized religious groups would take on a minor issue in hopes of a quick and symbolic victory, and it will not be the last.

It has become more difficult to think of religion as a personal orientation toward life, separate from the meshing gears and moving belts of everyday life. The two collide with increasing frequency, and in ways that should leave people on opposite sides of specific questions pondering how we will manage a religiously diverse state.

An Alabama appeals court sat in the judgment of a custody dispute between the maternal grandparents and father of a six-year-old boy. The child's mother and father had never married. During the mother's long bout with heroin addiction that ended in an overdose and loss of custody, the boy never lived with his father. In its particulars, *Ex parte GC, Jr.* (the full name not used to name the case in order to guard privacy) is not unusual. The sad case is one of many like it heard every day in family courts around the country.

When the appeals process came knocking at the Alabama Supreme Court's door, certiorari was granted; that is, the court agreed to hear the case. When the justices of the state's highest court handed down their opinion, they unremarkably sided with the grandparents and denied the father's request for full custody. How they did it is the more interesting part of the story. The justices wrote seven separate opinions in the case, quoting liberally from the Bible and even occasionally from Alabama law. Justice Michael Bolin cited the definition for "government" in Noah Webster's 1828 dictionary: "Let family government be like that of our heavenly Father, mild, gentle, and affectionate." Then Bolin moves from his theory of an affectionate and godlike government to the particular case of the father, GC, who has not measured up. "In acknowledging that our Heavenly Father is a loving and affectionate God, I must question where has been the love, gentleness, and affection shown by this earthly father, the appellant in this proceeding, to his child? It is, according to the record, largely nonexistent. The record reflects that the mother and the father never married. They do not live, and have not lived, together. Since her overdose on heroin, the mother does not seek custody. The father has been irresponsible as a parent for the entire life of the child. Under these circumstances, it was the maternal grandparents who offered the only 'family government' support system of which Webster's definition speaks so highly, and which the child in this case so desperately needed."

Justice Bolin might have simply cited family law and Alabama precedent. Instead he invokes an authority that cannot be cross-examined by other parties in the case: "With parental rights, ordained by God, come parental responsibilities, just as much ordained by God. In fact, we can say that the more sacred the right, the more solemn the responsibility. The defaults of the father to his divinely appointed parental responsibilities throughout his child's life can only be described as egregious."

Later, Justice Bolin invokes that angry letter from Thomas Jefferson to King George: "The Declaration of Independence affirmed a God-ordained natural order. I believe in such a natural order. Nothing in God's order or the Declaration of Independence, however, says that the irresponsible, immature, derelict parent in this case, who has in fact abandoned and ignored his child throughout the child's life, has the essential right to remove the child from the care and custody of its maternal grandparents, who have provided the child with the only love and compassion or semblance of hearth and home the child has ever known."

The other justices weighed in, determined not to be out-Jehovahed in this custody case. Justice Tom Parker, who lobbied the Alabama legislature on behalf of Focus on the Family's Alabama affiliates, joined the fray: "Having acknowledged the historic meaning of government generally as well as having recognized the existence of the four particular government spheres, we should next consider how these governments relate to each other. Perhaps their most fundamental connection is that they all possess grants of specific and limited jurisdiction from the ultimate source of all legitimate authority, God (see Romans 13:1–2 ['there is no authority except from God, and those that exist have been instituted by God']), who as the Supreme Judge of the World is the final authority over all disputes among men as well as among all governments of men."

The justices of the Alabama Supreme Court actually took testimony in this matter from the relevant parties and professional experts, though you might wonder why. They could have placed GC and GC Jr.'s maternal grandparents in a room and waited for God to make his desires known in this matter. A bolt of lightning, a shaft of light, a chasm opening beneath the father's feet, any of them would have sufficed. I am not making fun as much as pointing out the obvious. The law is an instrument that brings in parties in dispute on the basis of trust and seeks to use rules understood by both sides and tested over time to arrive at the best outcomes.

Ours is a world where innocent people are sometimes convicted and guilty people sometimes go free. It is thus impossible to understand the will of God and its utility as an instrument of judgment in court cases, and bring that will to bear in a uniform, reliable, and transparent way. The law, that grand abstraction, aspires to be applicable to all kinds of people without regard to personal religious convictions and ethical groundings. If GC were a member of American Atheists, it is hard to imagine him believing in equal justice under the law from justices who quote the Epistles of Saint Paul and allege godly sovereignty over the people of Alabama to deny him custody of his son.

Blair Scott reminded me that in many cases, the legal outcome would be exactly the same. Scott was talking about previous run-ins between American Atheists and Roy Moore. "He ran for Supreme Court chief justice and he won specifically on the Ten Commandments." During his time as a judge in the lower courts, Moore had fought to keep a framed copy of the Decalogue in his courtroom. Scott continued, "We knew the Ten Commandments backed him up, but even still, I looked at his judicial record and I said, 'Will this guy be a good judge? Theology aside, will he make good decisions?' I did the research and if he was going to be a good judge, I probably would have voted for him, 'cause I don't vote for people on a single issue. I vote for the person that's going to do the best job.

"It finally turned out he was one of the worst judges in Alabama history. In Gaston County Court, he was overturned by the Supreme Court like 50 percent of the time. It was ridiculous, and his rulings were just outlandish. I voted against him because he was going to be a piss-poor judge, but you know Alabamians, being as supportive as they are, voted him into office.

"A few months go by and he makes a ruling against this child custody case. And the ruling was against the mother and for the father. There was evidence he was abusive both physically and mentally toward the children. But they ruled against the mother and gave the custody to him anyways. And the reason they did that was because she was a lesbian. Moore wrote the primary opinion, and he quoted the Bible and talked about how it was an abomination to God: 'The state has the power of the sword when it comes to taking children from homosexuals.'[11] And what he was saying was the state has the right to execute homosexuals to keep our children safe." Later, Moore said he was merely describing the power of the law and would never use it in that way.

Scott said this is what really bugs him: "In the opinion he also wrote a legal reason why the mother was denied, and under Alabama law, he was technically correct. Lesbianism and homosexuality is illegal under Alabama law. And that's all he had to do. The only thing he had to do in that opinion was write the legal aspect of it. And whether people are angered or disagree with the law is one thing, but the ruling was legally correct under the current element of the law. So there was no reason to go into all these biblical verses. There was no reason to call her an abomination. There was no reason to say that this state should execute homosexuals. It was not necessary at all, and it crossed the line, and it violated the Alabama Constitution. The judge wants to believe that someone's an abomination by their religious belief, that's fine. They have the right to believe that, but they can't rule that way on the case. That was actually the very first protest we held against Judge Moore."

That is where the difficulty emerges when religion is explicitly used in crafting public policy. Instead of making law that presumes from the beginning to be for us all, open religious reasoning divides us, even when the eventual result is one with which most or all people might find themselves ready to agree.

In the course of a long conversation, I asked Professor Hamill about how, in a religiously diverse society, one can make public policy from a foundation of faith. Can you make law that everyone feels bound to respect? Can you craft institutions that include, rather than exclude? She said, "Christian ethicists have written about ideals of how you engage other people. And guess what, you don't shout at them that they're going to hell. There's a certain level of respect and give-and-take and listening. You can't win people over by force and threat. And that goes back to how faith by force is not faith. It has to be brought along willingly.

"We can come up with a common set of moral principles, even if they're not all faith-based. There's a lot of secular ways of thinking that would agree with everything I said in terms of result. They just might be a little uncomfortable with how I got there. Would you define as justice-oriented that which I would call a Judeo-Christian-guided tax-policy structure? How do you answer the question of what the top rate should be? How do you answer the question of whether we should allow this or that deduction? General moral principles can't give you an exact answer to the question. It gives you a framework to debate them."

A framework. A place to begin the conversation. That could only help. The professor continued, "There are certain moral principles to consider, such as, do we have adequate revenues for reasonable opportunity? Are we imposing a moderately progressive burden that is noticeable as wealth climbs? Then you get down to the blood and guts of compromise. For a person of faith, that has to be Judeo-Christian-guided. For a person who has a different moral compass, well, this is America, you can choose whatever moral code you like."

Susan Pace Hamill may not have won the battle she joined to make faith-based public policy. She is passionate and pointed in making her case, and said without a trace of irony that what interests her is kingdom building, that is, building the Kingdom of God on earth. "I'm not a theologian. I'm not in the business of proving that my way is ultimately the only way. I am in the business of assuming that if you have decided to check into our way, then let's talk about what that means for you.

"In other words, I'm not in the business of saving souls. Other people are in that business; I'm not suited for that business. I am in the business of helping people, once they're in, to realize what it means to be a kingdom builder. Or if you want to put that in a negative way, sniffing out hypocrites."

Stone secularists around the country who say they worry about an American-Taliban style of Christian politics, who recoil at every Pat Robertson gaffe, and grimace when the president of the United States blesses them, might take the wrong message away from Alabama. You might look at it this way: A state with powerful business interests aligned with conservative Christian groups still has no 2.6-ton granite Ten Commandments monument in its court rotunda, can't figure out a way to get a Christian Bible study curriculum approved for its schools or rewrite a tax code along biblical principles. It may be that what is really bugging you is that Alabama is one of the most conservative places in the country, rather than that it's one of the most uniformly Christian. That perceived alliance between Christianity and conservatism does few favors for either a long political tradition in the United States or a two-thousand-year-old faith.

But if Alabama can't usher in an American Taliban, you don't have anything to worry about. We conclude with a final romp through that intersection of American politics and religion, with some thoughts on how traffic might run more smoothly and safely.

TWELVE

Okay, Wise Guy . . . Now What?

PERHAPS WE CAN BEGIN by agreeing on one thing: What we're doing now isn't working. The rising power of religious politics has left winners who complain about being oppressed, and losers who say the sky is falling. How you make a coherent republic out of gladiatorial politics is a puzzle with an elusive answer.

The paradoxes do not end with the fact that both sides see themselves losing in the debates over religious involvement in politics. Through the entire time this book was researched and written, the United States was involved in expensive wars half a world away that our leaders threatened could be long ones, in countries split over how big a role religion should play in societies reduced to rubble. All around the world religion has moved in to fill a vacuum created by the failure of politics. Religious extremism was not the natural state of things in Algeria, Egypt, Iraq, and Indonesia. Once upon a time these countries were among the leaders of the Non-Aligned Movement, a secularizing confederation that offered itself as a counterweight to the two giants facing off in the Cold War.

Now Islamists are shut out of electoral politics in Algeria and Egypt for fear they will win free and fair elections and take control of the machinery of the state. In Indonesia, the world's largest Muslim nation, Al-Qaida allies are eating away at the traditional relaxed brand of Islam, taking advantage of the festering resentments suppressed by decades of authoritarian leadership.

The United States has never needed political Christianity, because it guaranteed religious freedom, had no established church, and was fortunate enough to have self-repairing, operational political institutions. This allowed most people, most of the time, to live without fear of the state.

Americans could live their lives in some confidence that no matter how personally powerless they might be in absolute terms, there would be no knock on the door in the middle of the night.

Yes, religion could become a beacon for the oppressed . . . Israel's flight in biblical times from Egypt comforted the black church before Emancipation, and that power also provided inspiration and comfort for the next century to undergird the struggle for civil rights. Across more than two centuries, religious faith has sustained Americans in struggle and distress, in loss and victory, spurring them to sacrifice and care, and occasionally blinding them to great and enduring sin.

To borrow a page from Abraham Lincoln, both workers and the mill and mine owners who had them beaten and shot prayed to the same God. It was unlikely both sets of prayers were answered. Both Mexican Catholics and the American Protestants who ordered and coordinated the invasion of their country on false pretenses prayed to the same God. Bull Connor and Medgar Evers prayed to the same God, as well. A loudly proclaimed faith is no guarantee of righteousness, as surely as having no faith at all is no guarantee that your cause is wrong. America has never been that way, and you could attend National Prayer Breakfasts from now until, yup, kingdom come and public piety would not transform America's essential nature.

If one segment of one American religious group gets to call the tune in American life, and especially in American politics, then it is proof that our institutions have failed. As I write, an American president chosen and supported by many voters because, among other reasons, he is a man of faith has also convinced millions that he cannot successfully manage this country.

That is the most apparent failing of highly religionized politics: being a man or woman of prayer may give you no insight at all into organizing a cabinet. Reading your Bible and believing its teachings may leave you no wiser about how to persuade, how to lead, and how to competently manage. Voting for the most religious candidate on Election Day or counting a less publicly religious posture against a candidate when making one's decision may make an individual voter feel better, while saddling the entire community with an elected official who is religious, and incompetent. If Americans are interested in building what liberal southerner Congressman John Lewis of Georgia calls "the blessed community" or more conservative Alabamian Professor Susan Pace Hamill calls "the Kingdom," competence in government is more necessary than piety.

After the 2004 election, we were bamboozled as a country by the bogus statistic citing "values voters." Voters leaving the polls told opinion researchers their top issue, and "moral values" came in first. Fair enough. But "moral values" came in first with a whopping 24 percent of those polled, just ahead of the economy and jobs, with 20 percent, and concerns about terrorism, with 19 percent. Scan down the list, and worries about the war in Iraq garnered 15 percent. What the heck does it mean to think "moral values" is an important issue? Perhaps the 34 percent who voted on the combined Iraq War and War on Terror questions (back when the two were more closely linked in the public mind) also thought they were voting on moral-values questions, too. Most of the "moral-values" voters chose President Bush, while the majority of the economy and jobs voters chose Kerry. No matter, the commentariat had a field day. They wondered what it all meant and speculated that the Democratic Party's weaknesses with religious voters had decided the election.

Conservative Christian activist and 2000 presidential candidate Gary Bauer wrote, "After 24 years of active political involvement starting with Ronald Reagan's election in 1980, are America's political, cultural and media elites really this much in the dark about their fellow Americans who were in church on Sunday, at work on Monday and in the voting booth Nov. 2? The answer to who we are is, of course, that we are your next-door neighbor, your kid's teacher and the clerk at the local drugstore."[1]

Writing in the *New York Times* columnist David Brooks called the "moral values" question "inept" and found no cultural-conservative surge for the president: "The fact is that if you think we are safer now, you probably voted for Bush. If you think we are less safe, you probably voted for

Kerry. That's policy, not fundamentalism. The upsurge in voters was an upsurge of people with conservative policy views, whether they are religious or not."[2]

As ideas like this so often do, the "values voter" did not die a well-deserved, properly analyzed death, but instead became even more securely recalled, as the original event, the election of 2004, continued to decline into memory. The "values voter" became a warning from conservative Christians to the rest of the political system, and a sore spot for Democrats wondering how they lost.

The values voter ends up being emblematic of the current operation of American politics around these very issues. With one set of voters alleging that their moral values guided their voting and the press and opinion researchers adopting that nomenclature, the notion was also created that other voters were not voting from their moral values. The voters who chose access to medical care or concern for the poor as top-drawer issues would probably answer that their values guided them every bit as much as those counted as such in the opinion research, from those who told pollsters it was the beliefs of the candidate (mostly George W. Bush) that guided their choice.

Just as God knew in Genesis, when he gave Adam the job of naming the creatures of the ground and the birds of the air, the power to assign things their name is an important one.[3] Calling yourself a "values voter" can imply that other voters who make other choices are not responding to moral values or are making choices that reflect a less-valid or less-moral values system. The conclusion is left hanging in the air: "moral values" trumped other issues and drove the Bush victory, leaving those voters with lesser or lower values to John Kerry. That conclusion leaves Bauer a cheery winner able not only to award George Bush a moral victory, but to further disparage other Americans who make other choices. Thus, we do not have to consider whether it is the very fact of being a "values voter" that drives other respondents to name the Iraq War, poverty, or the environment as topmost issues. The "Year of the Values Voter" conveniently leaves the Party of Religion describing its triumph, and the Democrats licking their wounds and wondering how to attract values voters, too.

Public opinion polls are not great tools for quantifying subtle conclusions in the electorate. They are best at counting binary values: Do you believe this is true? Do you not believe this is true? Should American troops remain in Iraq? Should American troops leave Iraq? A worldview responding to "values" is a tougher thing to measure in the black/white, yes/no, stop/go world of polling. It is nonetheless reasonable to conclude, from looking at the world and the choices the people make in it, that values do send a powerful electric impulse into the operation of our vast and complex country.

University of Chicago ethics professor Jean Bethke Elshtain has noted that all the nonestablishment clause of the First Amendment means is that the U.S. Congress cannot create a state religion. That is all. "For an American president or any other public official to invoke the deity doesn't violate the Constitution per se or as such. You may think it's imprudent, you may think it's unwise, but it's not unconstitutional, nor is it unconstitutional when congressmen and -women, in announcing their reasons for or against a particular policy, voice certain religious convictions as part of their reason given. Again, nothing unconstitutional about that. It doesn't mean that there's some lurking theocracy about to emerge in the United States."

Speaking of what she calls "strong separationists," Elshtain questions the notion that there is a way to shear all religion-influenced speech from civic discourse, that there is a way for the public to use a neutral language when it comes time to enter the hard debate about what a society will condone, encourage, or forbid: "I've never, I admit to you, I'm sure it's a failing on my part, been able to figure out what such a neutral language would be since people always bring strong commitments from religion or some other place to the public square."

In Professor Elshtain's American model, there are a number of ways religion can influence political debate and public policy, each of which attracts and repels different Americans to different degrees. She calls the first model Full-Bore Christian Politics. The assumption in this model is that a Christian rationale has to be offered for every single political issue. Such politics assumes "that a religious approach to all civic issues is not only appropriate, it may even be required. Now, I don't think there are many who advocate this full stop, but it's a tendency, and it strikes me as a very bad idea. Not because it's unconstitutional, but because it threatens to collapse religion and politics into a single project. And I think the danger here is actually danger from the side of religion as much as from political life."

Elshtain's other models move across the continuum from that extreme to the Prophetic Witness position, in which "no one pushes for an undiluted Christian politics, no one is seeking religious saturation of all things political, like everyday political discourse in action—rather, a person's religious response to extraordinary situations comes from the fullness of religious belief." Elshtain uses the public career of the Reverend Dr. Martin Luther King as an example of the way religious conviction fuses with public concern.

A third form of engagement, or in this case disengagement, Elshtain calls Radical Dualism. In it "the religious believer declares that the world is going to hell in a handcart and that true Christians have to sort of hunker down and be faithful within their own group, because the world is just going to go its sinful way. The world is not going to understand. And in an interesting way, this position is a kind of mirror image of the Full-Bore Christian politics." It is similar to her first way of engagement because "you have to religiously name and define every issue here," but at the same time "you abandon engagement entirely, you withdraw from civic life on the grounds that the religious person is invariably and inevitably tainted if they start to engage in that sort of thing. And often in this position nowadays, I detect a kind of contempt for public life and for democracy itself."

That contempt can be seen in a strain of American Christianity called Dominionism. One of that philosophy's leading lights is Rousas John Rushdoony, an American born of Armenian Turkish parents who wrote over a long career of the incompatibility of secular government and Christian faith. Law is the will of the sovereign for his subjects. No man, Rushdoony writes, can value his faith and conform to the laws of the secular state: "Law represents the word of the God of the society. Now whose Law you have, He is your God. So if Washington makes our laws, Washington is our God. As Christians we cannot believe that. For centuries, God's law has functioned wherever God's people have been, whether in Israel or in Christendom. This is a new and modern thing that we turn to the state's law."

Most American conservative Christians hold convictions that stop far short of Rushdoony's contempt for secular government, but at the same time, many of the most influential journals of opinion in their circles readily absorb the dualist notions of the virtuous faithful standing up to a hostile government. Rushdoony sounds the dualist war cry, lamenting a lost America based on Christian principle compared to today's secular republic: "Now we do not recognize God as God over the United States. The oath of office for the president of the United States used to be taken on an open Bible on Deuteronomy 28 invoking all the curses of God for disobedience to His law and all the blessings of God for obedience to his law. Now basically you can have two kinds of law: *theonomy*—God's law, or *autonomy*—self-law. That's what it boils down to and autonomy leads to anarchy, which is what we are getting increasingly."

The final, and preferred, model in the Elshtain scheme is one she calls Contextual Engagement. The historian of Western political thought alleges, in a commonsensical way, that the public can figure out where religion belongs in political debate and where it does not, by asking, " 'What are the stakes here? How important is this? And—depending on what arenas or spheres of human social existence are affected, and who will be harmed, who will be helped?—how should those implicated in this situation address the issues at stake and express their concerns to their fellow citizens?' Now, my underlying assumption is that in a pluralistic society such as our own, with our politics of negotiation and compromise on most issues, that most often the engagement of religious believers with politics does not involve an earth-shattering dilemma. Most of the time, you're being a citizen and there isn't a big religious question or moral dilemma involved; the lines aren't drawn in the sand. And I also assume that it isn't the task of Christianity to underwrite in toto any political ideology or agenda or platform." Right there, at Elshtain's rhetorical pivot point on where the public good and religious faith intersect, more secular Americans who were nodding in agreement at the earlier models might say, "Wait. It just isn't that benign."

Elshtain assumes in her structure that when the day-to-day operation of the institutions of society goes off the rails, there will be a split between government and religious institutions, and faith communities will step up to speak truth to power. The critics of a tightening embrace between state power and religious interests introduced in earlier chapters have said again and again that that is exactly what is not happening now. In the years since the Republicans have solidified control of both the Congress and the White House, conservative Christian leaders who helped make that control a reality have reveled in their increased access and influence and, at least publicly, have used few opportunities to raise an independent voice against the White House and Capitol Hill.

Professor Elshtain wants a politics of conciliation to kick in when the normal operation of politics reaches no durable solution: "On nearly all issues religious believers and those without religious commitments are obliged to continue the discussion, participate in the debate, find ways to find common ground or to assess more clearly what separates them one from the other. So I'm assuming that most of the time one is not obliged to bring the fullness of one's religious faith or religious reasons to a public issue most of the time. Most issues don't warrant that." But surely, professor, many do. Issues that have not split churches from their party allies.

Whether or not to go to war.

Whether or not human beings have a responsibility to keep the planet from warming in disastrous ways that hurt the poorest people.

Whether or not the richest country on the planet is living up to its responsibilities to its own people and the people in the rest of the world.

The rising religious tide in the United States did not bring many issues to the fore, issues a reader of the Gospels might think were central concerns for the followers of a first-century teacher they believe is God's own

Son. Of course a country as publicly and proudly religious as the United States is going to see religious concerns emerge in its politics. But how? And why?

We met the Reverend Altagracia Perez in the last chapter, trying to find a way to keep faithful people who may not always agree willing to stay in conversation and community with one another. She never shies from a direct connection between politics and the Christian church in America: "Personally, I'm kind of rigid on this. I try to maintain this distinction as cleanly as I can: I think it's very appropriate for clergy and people of faith to be political with a little '*p.*' We are called to faith by a God that lives in history and transforms us by coming to us. You can't separate a life of faith from the rest of what you're doing in the world. It's about where you live and where you shop, what you buy and what you drive; the grassroots people who are trying to be faithful to Christ and practice politics with a little '*p.*' 'Politics 'big *p*' is party politics, electoral politics, and campaigns. As a faith community, our only loyalty is the kingdom of God." Reverend Mother, Dr. Richard Land might not have said it very differently himself.

In addition to her service as rector of an Episcopal church in Inglewood, California, Perez is an increasingly prominent voice in social-and-economic-justice debates in the vast Los Angeles metro area. When she raises her voice to counsel or protest, she is hard to miss: a distinctive New York rasp, machine-gun fluency in argument in English one second, and in Spanish the next. She was a central character in the documentary *Wal-Mart: The High Cost of Low Price,* and has been a prominent go-between as social change and shifting ethnic and racial populations send tremors through the south end of the city of Los Angeles and the small incorporated towns in the same part of Los Angeles County.

I asked her if there were tensions inherent in being a parish priest and a community activist. For one thing, could political activity threaten her congregation's tax exempt status, and that of other churches? "People should be able to say what they feel and what they think, and they should follow the law. The statutes make it very clear what's allowed and what's not, and those laws should be followed. I train all my volunteers on those laws, and they're worth honoring."

As far as the tension between her church office and her life as an organizer? "Listen, the church has always been political. The church is made up of people who are living in history; that's what it means to be political."

If there is a difference between the work she does, and similar work on the political right, it's this: Religious-based activists on the left organize around issues with almost anyone who shares their common ground. On the right, the battles are much more often fought by people who are already of like mind. Perez said, "I will also work with others of good faith. If we're going to be citizens here, we're also going to be in conversation with people of goodwill. So we bring the best of our Christian traditions to the struggle. Others bring what they have to offer. It gets sloppy sometimes. It gets complicated for some people in coalition in a way that it's not for me."

That approach sometimes puts Perez's organizing muscle to work with people who are glad she is on their team, happy to work with her, but, at the same time, drawn from backgrounds far removed from her priestly vocation and with a hostile opinion of organized religion. She called winning them over "fun." She feels she knows and understands the garment workers of Los Angeles's burgeoning low-income, immigrant-dominated workforce. "Some are people who go to church on Sunday and are trying to get their kids to church. My function as a priest in the world is to point out the sacred they are already involved with. What they are doing"—fighting for the right to organize, struggling for a union to improve their work lives—"is sacred. They get that.

"They've asked me, 'What are you doing here? Why are you doing this?' They leave satisfied because that is what the church is supposed to be doing. They give me their personal histories of struggle, empowerment. It's what I would call a resurrection. And when they first see me, not preaching at the church about some alien thing, it opens them up. They make a space for God. Many eventually ask me to marry them and baptize their babies."

For Perez, the crucial difference is the great weight she places on how to begin the word *politics*. "Some people accuse me of being political, with a big '*p*.' Most people assume that I'm interested in political office and that's why I do this. They don't always believe me when I tell them the church has enough politics for me already and I'm not interested in politics in that other way, running for office. That distinction means I am able to keep my church open to everyone." And here this most political of parish priests added a view to which Christians on every side of America's many divides should answer, "Amen." "The church needs to be a place where people come together and have conversations that are hard."

Maybe a too-close allegiance with one side in America's political battles is leaving the church unable, or unwilling, to have conversations that are hard. In 2006 the National Association of Evangelicals convened a conference on Christians and the environment. In the face of growing mountains of evidence that human activity is changing earth's atmosphere, which may potentially have devastating effects on the world's poorest people, not to mention the rest of us, the conference punted, kicked the can down the road, and left warning the millions of faithful who attend its churches for another day.

I asked the Reverend James Ball, who leads the Evangelical Environmental Network, why it has been so easy to hear conservative Christians on so many issues, yet any expressions of concern for the health of the planet have been so faint. Part of the problem evangelicals have with environmentalism, he said, is with *environmentalists*. He said it is hard to clear that first hurdle: "We try to get them to distinguish and say, 'Look, regardless of what you think about who you think the environmentalists are, caring for God's creation is a biblical thing.' But I think their kind of default position about environmentalists is, 'Those folks are liberals and a lot of them are kind of a special brand of liberals that includes some types of theological ideas that we think are dangerous to our youth.' " Dangerous to youth? How?

"Like worshipping the earth instead of the Creator. If you look, especially in the Old Testament, there is not a more profound theological no-no than worshipping the creation instead of the Creator. It is the first commandment. So we're not talking about an inconsequential thing here.

"It's a profound problem. If evangelicals think that somebody is kind of teaching pantheism or when people use the language of like 'Mother

Earth,' that will get evangelicals nervous. Because it starts sounding like, you know, you're maybe getting close to worshipping the earth."

I put it to James Ball that many, even most, of conservative Christians' fellow Americans are not Earth-worshippers or anything of the kind, that even the most superficial look at the environmental movement would reveal a broad group of motivations, worldviews, and religious convictions. Did evangelicals have to agree with potential allies about everything else before they could make common cause on the environment?

"If I didn't believe that this was a biblical call, that this was part of being a disciple of Jesus Christ, my Savior, my Lord, I wouldn't be doing it. So I have been thoroughly convinced, and so I want to help others in my community understand this from a Christ-centered, biblical perspective. And I think the case is overwhelming.

"So we first need to continue to educate our own community here and have them understand that it doesn't matter in some ways necessarily what we think about these other folks or what they're doing or anything. We have to decide what is—what should we be doing on these issues based on our own beliefs and values." For this evangelical environmentalist, looking for allies from other religious groups or of no religion at all pales in significance to first getting his own brothers and sisters to buy into the notion that there is a problem in the first place. For many, Ball noted, the environment scans as a "liberal" issue. We are not liberals, the thinking goes, so we are not environmentalists, either.

I wondered aloud during our talk how the modern evangelical political movement squared a love of God, a scriptural grounding, and a strong teaching tradition around the value of stewardship, with the conclusion that care for the planet is "not for us." One interesting counterargument from conservative Christian circles was an accusation of the sin of pride against environmentalists. The rationale goes something like this: God runs the world, not human beings. The reasons for changes in the planet were more vast than anything the human mind could comprehend, and thus it was nothing more than human vanity to believe that individual human beings could change the environmental future of the planet for good or ill. "So what do you say," I asked Ball, "to someone who says,

'Look, the loss of the spotted owl, the loss of the snowy egret, or the blue whale is just part of God's plan. Unless God willed it, it wouldn't happen'?"

"Well, I say there's lots of things that happen in this world that are not God's will," he replied, "and you don't want to make God the author of evil, do you? Go read Genesis 3. There are plenty of things that happen in this world that are not part of God's will. It's very clear in scriptures that God created all of his creatures to glorify him. And that if we snuff out prematurely a creature that's glorifying God, that is a sin."

An environmental organization rallying conservative Christians runs into not only the "cultural" difficulties its leader describes but the contradictions and inconsistencies created by the thorough embrace not only of America, but of capitalism. Scripture may urge Christians to work toward the perfection they see in God, "therefore be ye perfect, as your Father in heaven is perfect," but it flirts with heresy to assert that capitalism is perfect just because so many conservative Christians like its outcomes. Whatever your economic, political, or environmental convictions, it must be agreed that any urgent response to global warming might occasionally mean saying no to corporations, to governments, to individuals. The same voters so fiercely trusted to do the right thing when it comes to gay marriage are not trusted to elect officials who might regulate personal and economic behavior understood to carry serious environmental consequences. The topic of government regulation makes evangelical clergy sound like Milton Friedman in their zeal for deregulation, low taxes, and free markets. Less often heard is any concession to some of the tensions and contradictions within capitalism that might make a Christian take pause, such as hard work at low wages, outsourcing and downsizing, and awarding more favorable tax treatment to income earned from investment than income earned from labor.

In places like South Carolina, a generation of faithful workers and faithful churchgoers have watched the church oppose the dire consequences of globalization *sotto voce* if at all, while celebrating the investment-friendly Bush economic plan. I am not suggesting that the debate inside conservative Christian denominations has one preferred outcome,

273

just that churches whose members are feeling the pleasures and the pain brought by worldwide economic restructuring need more comfort from Jesus of Nazareth and a little less from Adam Smith of *The Wealth of Nations.* There is a conversation to be had, and conservative Christians, deciding to stress the *conservative* and not the *Christian,* are not choosing to have it.

In the early years of this still new century, teasing apart what is Christian from what is merely American, separating what is called for by religious tradition from what is politically desirable, and recognizing where the church must stand apart from elective politics has been proven difficult, especially for those churches that have hitched their preaching and teaching power to one party's wagon. James Ball has not given up hope that the National Association of Evangelicals and other big organizations of conservative Christians will finally come to grips with what he sees as a threatened global calamity: "So when you have kind of centrist-to-conservative leaders like Ted Haggard, the president of the NAE, start saying, 'Caring for God's creation is a good thing.' Now, he may in the same breath say, 'But we're pro-business, too' and 'We want the free market to help us out here' and this kind of stuff. A lot of environmentalists would say, 'Oh my gosh!'

"So we're going to do it a little different. We're going to sound different. We're not just going to be environmentalists at prayer, as Paul Gorman loves to say." When talking about global warming, for example, Ball does not stress commonly cited measures of climate change to drive home the danger, but instead stresses the impact on vulnerable farmers in the developing world who are now getting aid from conservative Christian organizations. "We're going to be different because we are different, but it doesn't mean that we won't be tackling pollution and the extinctions of God's creatures and climate change. Not just as a 'environmental issue' but a human issue, a relief and development issue."

Maybe there is not that much daylight between Jim Ball and Altagracia Perez after all. Both are committed to setting the church on a course to be an impact player in the culture and see no contradiction between their religious vocation and using political means to achieve what they see as

God's ends. Jim Ball wants to break evangelicals out of the stereotyped issues of sex and reproduction and move toward a different worldview for his people, and a different view of conservative churches on the part of the rest of the community. "We have a tremendous obligation, part of who we are as citizens in this country, to express our values in terms of who we are as citizens as well. That includes how we as a country care about the poor around the world. And I think that President Bush showed good leadership in terms of the tsunami disaster. He's shown good leadership on AIDS.

"Where did he get a good chunk of his motivation for dealing with AIDS? He got it from evangelicals—when evangelical leaders started saying, you know, you really need to start doing something about AIDS. And of course that was a big problem in our community in terms of talking about AIDS. The relief-and-development community led the way on that; Franklin Graham gave good leadership to this. And I think in some ways there are similarities between AIDS and climate change in the sense of how we deal with it. It's a fairly contentious issue that you wouldn't think would gain good traction in the evangelical community. But they were able to do it by talking about poor kids and the poor, and focusing on the impacts it was having on children. And so I want us to do the same thing with climate change and help people, not because it's just some sort of rhetorical device, but because it's actually true that the people who are going to be impacted the hardest are the poor kids in poor countries."

Richard Land gets genuinely angry at the suggestion that his Southern Baptists and other conservative churches have ridden abortion and gay marriage to prominence and influence in the Republican Party and the country as a whole. Being salt of the earth and the light of the world, as Jesus commanded, has brought conservative Christians to Capitol Hill to fight against modern-day slavery, to end the civil war in Sudan and work to stop the killing in Darfur. The Gospel mandate also compels the churches, Land said, "to speak out on sex trafficking and prison rape, which we have. To work to get measures passed through Congress to strengthen families and stable family formation, like the child dependent care tax credit, which we were instrumental in helping to get passed, which started the process of revaluing children in the tax system by giving a dependent child-care tax credit."

Land describes a church that lives out its mission in the world by using the tool of politics to further the kingdom. Like many conservative Christians I have talked to in these past three years, he has no apologies and sees no inconsistencies in the way his religion lines up with his politics.

Others do. Ed Pawlowski can see all sides of the question. He is the mayor of Allentown, Pennsylvania, an evangelical Christian, and a Democrat. He is a graduate of Moody Bible College, was a pastor and a preacher. Mid-career, he found a second calling in affordable housing, went back to school and got a master's degree in urban planning, and, through his work in housing, slowly marched toward elective office. Pawlowski looked back at all his careers—as a pastor, a housing administrator, and now a mayor—and told me the alliance between church and politics has not benefited either party: "I've always been frustrated by politicians who use Christianity to promote their politics. As an evangelical Christian, I've been really turned off by it. I ended up as a Democrat because I've been so disillusioned—so many who run on their faith and use that as a badge in their political climb." The mayor looked back at the Clinton years and recalled, "We had everybody complaining about his [Clinton's] morality, and the key players, the people who complained the most, like Henry Hyde, Newt Gingrich, and some others, turned out to be as immoral, if not more, than the original perpetrator."

For all the religious filigree in contemporary political speeches and the increasing use he has seen of openly religious appeals to voters, Mayor Pawlowski told me the national trends have not shaped his time as mayor of a midsize city, even in the battleground state of Pennsylvania. "On a local level, it's irrelevant in most circumstances unless you're making decisions with national implications." He wants voters to be tougher on the religious appeals, assessing their sincerity and real impact on policy: "Look at the record, don't just look at the party mantra."

Biblically schooled, trained by one of the most powerful training institutions among evangelical colleges, Moody Bible Institute in Chicago, Pawlowski sets a higher standard not only for politicians who would seek to use religious appeals to get votes, but for voters who hear those messages and assess a candidate's fitness for office. "There are different characters of God. Again and again in the Bible we see God in his righteousness and his mercy. And you can't have a proper understanding of who God is without looking at both of those, righteousness and mercy. The Republicans seem to have decided to put a lot of their emphasis on righteousness, and discount mercy, while the Democrats, when they talk about these things at all, err on the side of mercy."

Allentown is an old industrial city, and growing again after years of tough economic decline. Starting in 2006, Mayor Pawlowski faced a decision that brought all the strands of his life together in one Mother of All Political Challenges: organized gambling was coming to the Allentown-Bethlehem-Easton metropolitan area. Would this evangelical urban planner, housing activist, advocate for the poor, and, now, elected official be able to square the competing interests in the community and the marketplace?

"There's going to be gambling in the city limits, and it's either going to go to Bethlehem or to Allentown. The Venetian is promising everything, promising the world, but I'm not sure they can get the site they want. On the other hand, I also have a brownfields site, close to the interstate, and the Tropicana wants that. And I'm in the middle trying to figure out what's the best thing for Allentown?

"Looking at it from a strictly business point of view, a casino would bring in about $10 million a year to the city budget. There would also be several million more a year coming in from real estate development and new taxes. The city's entire budget is $70 million a year, so gambling would bring in more than ten percent of our annual spending, and when I came into office, I had a built-in $8 million deficit." So gambling would close the city's deficit, and eventually mean a large infusion of new cash into a city with lots of needs and not a lot of spending power. Easy, right?

"This is where my faith and politics are intersecting head-on," says the mayor. "I'm being torn in different directions. These are decisions with obvious and serious moral implications, and substantial fiscal implications."

Ed Pawlowski, rookie mayor, does not get a lot of time to wrestle with the subtleties. "Everyone's looking to me to make a decision. If I decide no, that ups the ante for Bethlehem. Funny, right? This small city founded by Moravian Protestants. I don't think it's the best location in the Lehigh Valley for gambling." Suddenly he sounds like a mayor again. I ask if he is close to making his decision and where he is leaning. Yes, he is close. As for the solution he favors: "I'm not going to tell you."

When the affordable housing developer ran for mayor, he did not make his Christian faith a part of his campaign talking points. He did not hide it either, answering when asked about his career in the church. "I probably picked up a lot more Republican votes than I would have otherwise, but it's not something that affects my politics." Did that make him a special target of religious appeals when the casino debate started?

"Churches give me moral arguments. But there's no basis in scripture for being against gambling. There are some vague scriptural references about the evils of gambling. At the same time, you have to be honest about the social impact. There will be some problems. The question I have to weigh is this, 'Does that social impact equate to some moral imperative versus the city's obvious need for greater revenue, which is also meant to serve the greater good?'

"If it wasn't for the fiscal situation, would I even consider it? I think it's an interesting example of faith and politics having an intersect. There are not a lot of issues on the local level where that happens. That's where I am right now: religious leaders are trying to pull me away from gambling, and other interests are pulling me toward gambling."

I found it interesting that the mayor did not simply take his own feelings about gambling and make the decision accordingly for the city the voters picked him to run. He was adamant about the church giving people the moral ammunition to choose a moral life for themselves rather than simply taking orders. "I don't see in the scripture where we're supposed to take a crusade mentality and force people into moral behavior. That's a distortion of biblical principle. I see that if we're truly going to make a difference as people of faith, if we live exemplary lives, we will show people by our testimony what living a moral life can accomplish.

"But I don't think those areas should be legislated. I don't think we should try. Governments have been in existence for thousands of years, and so far no one's been able to force people to be moral.

"Others have come to the conclusion that we have to be zealous for righteousness' sake. We have to make sure we're stopping people from having premarital sex. They are forgetting the other aspects of God. There's this constant tension between righteousness and mercy. The God of the Bible has created that tension. Life isn't always black and white, and right and wrong." That is an interesting point, as far as it goes. Mayor Pawlowski concedes that apart from exceptional policy decisions, like those involving gambling, the political battles over morals happen at other levels of government.

"I clearly disagree with the Democrats on abortion. I truly believe you can be progressive and pro-life. But I admit it's a very difficult row to hoe for people like me in the Democratic Party, okay? Someday, some smart Democrat will figure out how to reduce the abortion rate by supporting low-income women, which will both reduce unintended pregnancies and the difficulties of supporting another child. Sometimes it looks like neither one of the parties really wants to solve the issue or address the underlying causes." He said he is as unhappy with his own party's choices on abortion politics as he has been with successful Republican use of the issue: "I've been incredibly frustrated with the whole line of Christians buying into Republican mantra, that if you're pro-life and anti-gay-marriage it must be okay. I've continuously tried to explain to people of faith that having an attitude isn't defining. The Republican Party has had the ability for years to do something about abortion, and what have they done, they've done. Solving it would take that rallying cry away."

The mayor then goes a step further: "I've been very disillusioned personally by churches that buy into this mantra that one party is godly, and of course that means the other one isn't. There are good people in both parties, and there are corrupt people in both parties. I think that there is this balance, not more of good or bad in one or the other. Neither party can be looked at as having more moral high ground than the other."

How did he square his own "hands-off" model for bringing faith concerns to legislation with the choices politicians face on some of the most personal and contentious debates in American life? "A lot of people of faith want their politics, like they want their lives, to fit into neat, orderly boxes. They seem to be especially concerned with social and sexual matters. To me, they don't seem to get the meaning of faith in politics at all. We're back to showing righteousness without mercy."

Is it just as big an error to show mercy, without righteousness? "Of course it can be. But showing mercy is rooted in a much deeper place than just telling other people that you are right and they are wrong. It's rooted in the image of God. It's rooted in who God is." Like so many politicians, Mayor Pawlowski struggles to find that balance between personal sovereignty and wider community interest: "Where does government role end and private accountability begin? There's illegal gambling going on right now in Allentown; I know that. If they want to gamble, they're going to gamble. There's an offtrack betting facility just a couple of blocks away from where I'm sitting. I can use moral arguments and personal freedom arguments in explaining my decision, but then I still come back to that one overriding question: 'Would I even be looking at this option if it wasn't for the money?' "

In the coming election cycles, the mayor's own party may try to match its rivals amen for amen, Bible verse for Bible verse. The mayor said the right answer for Democrats is to show their values in how they lead, not in figuring out what words to say and what messages to send to convince voters of their religious bona fides. Just getting the God-talk right in order to fight fire with fire is, for the mayor, an unattractive option that will not work. At the same time, there is an impulse not just to political success but to self-defense. His fellow Democrats do not want people to think that just because they are not talking about it, they are not religious people. "They don't want to have people conclude their lives are devoid of faith. It's come to this because at the same time Democrats have ignored it, Republicans have distorted it." Furthermore, he said, "both are in error. They don't get the God of the Bible, and anyway, that was never what the Bible was meant for, to be looked at as a political gauge."

That has not stopped the Democrats from trying to get religion and break the Republican lock on the support of religious voters. One state race that got tremendous attention from both parties as a harbinger of their political futures was the 2005 governor's race in Virginia. The popular and term-limited governor, high-tech millionaire Mark Warner, sought to prove he had coattails long enough to drag another Democrat into the governor's mansion of this Republican-dominated state—Warner's lieutenant governor, Tim Kaine. The Republicans nominated the state attorney general, popular with conservative Christians, Jerry Kilgore.

Kaine had a different life story from that of many Democratic politicians. As a young man, he had been a Roman Catholic missionary in Honduras, working among the poor. He had said throughout his elective career that the experience pushed him toward public service. In heavily Protestant, heavily evangelical Virginia, no one could be sure how a stint as a Catholic missionary would strike the average voter. The governor told me early in the campaign he just talked about religion on gut instinct, and heard pro and con feedback. So the Kaine campaign did what modern campaigns do: they focus-grouped their man, not just on religious-faith narratives, but on a number of issues sure to emerge in the campaign. A cross section of voters were told, "Here's who Kaine is, here's some biographical information about him," Kaine recalled. "We did see that that made people's ears perk up a little bit. And so we felt like we were getting some confirmation that, not necessarily for everybody, but for a good number of people including some who wouldn't normally be inclined to pull a lever for a Democrat in Virginia, that me telling my story was a real plus."

For Democrats running in so-called red states, here is where governor-to-be Kaine's story gets interesting. "We always kind of interpreted it as it was a plus for two reasons. One, because most people have a pretty strong faith connection and they appreciated a candidate—and maybe even especially a Democratic candidate 'cause it's kind of counterintuitive—they appreciated a candidate talking about that. The second reason that we felt like it was [that] it seemed to matter to people if a lot of candidates—and again, maybe this is a little more Democratic candidates than others—tend to talk about what their position is on issues—issue X, issue Y, you know, here's what I think about this or that—and less about their motivations:

Well, why am I doing this? What do I want to accomplish by running for office?

"And what we found was it was not only that people responded to the faith message, but they also just like to hear more of what motivates you, rather than 'Here's my position on issue X, Y, or Z.' I didn't know at the beginning that they wanted to understand that the positions I took weren't just coming out of polling or a speech writer, but that there was some connection between the positions I might take and a moral yardstick I had, and even if the moral yardstick wasn't theirs, they appreciated hearing what mine was and that I had one."

That idea—that even if voters disagreed on a specific issue, they might be interested in hearing more if that stand came from a moral conviction—got a powerful test in the Kaine-Kilgore race in one controversy over all others: capital punishment. As attorney general, Jerry Kilgore was a staunch supporter of the death penalty, while the lieutenant governor, Tim Kaine, was against it. Attorney General Kilgore could thus use the issue to great effect in a state like Virginia, where the death penalty enjoyed strong support. The challenge for the Kaine campaign was to find a way to explain their candidate's subtle position and neutralize the death penalty as an issue.

Attorney General Kilgore struck hard, telling voters in stump speeches, on radio and television commercials, not to believe his Democratic opponent. Tim Kaine, Kilgore said, was a death-penalty opponent and would not carry out the ultimate punishment even when the law called for it. When Kaine struck back in a series of effective ads, he said that when the law required death, his own personal views, however deeply felt, were simply not an issue.

Now that Governor Kaine's been in office for a while and the campaign is receding in the rearview mirror, his campaign's gamble looks like a good one. In the middle of the race, it did not seem like such a sure thing. Looking over races going back to the 1970s, Kaine and his team could not find a single example of a southern Democrat winning statewide office while running opposed to the death penalty. "So clearly we knew from the beginning of this governor's campaign that would be a major vulnerability. I had to be able to look people in the eye and not change my position but say something to them that they could appreciate. And why not, just in a no-spin way, look at the camera and just say exactly what I believe, and so when I got attacked on the death-penalty issue, to be able to look people in the eye in a thirty-second ad and say, 'Look, my religion teaches life is sacred, and I'm not going to apologize for my religious beliefs or change them to get elected. But I do take an oath of office like every other person. My church doesn't make me cross my fingers when I take an oath. I'm going to follow the law."

Here was a Roman Catholic Democrat who did not have to worry about church backlash on a hot-button issue. Unlike most Roman Catholic Democrats running for higher office, Kaine was not trying to explain away a policy position that put him at odds with the Catholic church and conservative Protestants. Here a Catholic Democrat was instead portraying his disagreement with the majority of the voters, Protestant and Catholic, as a matter of conscience in which he was in full agreement with his church.

Again, the Kaine team headed to the focus groups. The campaign prepared its own tough attack ads to be shown to likely voters, and then tested different Kaine responses: "There was a period in the spring where we did ten focus groups in four communities, Richmond, Northern Virginia, Hampton Roads, and Leesburg." That choice of state regions provided a cross section of suburban, urban, and rural voters. "The total number of people in the focus groups was about one hundred. And these were all hard-to-get voters. We weren't going for a statistical norm in these focus groups. We were going for difficult-to-get voters. We asked them at the beginning, 'Are you in favor of the death penalty or not,' and of the one hundred, I think it was ninety-nine said they were in favor of the death penalty. We asked them this question, 'Could you ever vote for a governor who's against the death penalty, ninety-nine of one hundred said no, they couldn't. And then we said, 'Well here, watch this tape.'

"And then they just put up the thirty seconds of me saying, 'Look, my religion teaches life is sacred. I'm against abortion and the death penalty, but I'm going to follow the law, but I ain't going to change my religion to get elected.' We showed them that thirty-second clip, and the uniform reaction really surprised us. We asked, 'Okay, what do you think of this guy?' They answered, 'Oh, yeah, we like him fine. Hey, let's talk about education; that's what we really care about anyway.'

"So the death-penalty position seemed almost impossible until we just took it about a centimeter below the surface, and what we found was that people could understand that for religious reasons, folks might have different opinions. But if they believed you when you said that you followed the law, they wanted to change the subject and talk about something that mattered to them more."

Bingo. Kaine was a less well-known lieutenant governor running to succeed his boss and running mate, a very popular governor who was nursing aspirations to run for president. It would be unfair to imply that he was facing an uphill battle against impossible odds. However, Kaine faced a successful statewide candidate in Jerry Kilgore who had carefully tended his links to conservative Christian organizations and big churches in a solidly Republican state carried overwhelmingly just a year before by President Bush. Kilgore hammered Kaine on the death penalty from one end of the state to the other, while also stressing his strong evangelical links on general media and on Christian radio.

Predictably, analysts and politicians want to figure out if the Kaine model is exportable to other southern states and other parts of the country. In light of how the governor pitched his message, it also makes sense to wonder whether other Democrats would be taking a big risk if they tried to copy one of the headliners of the 2005 off-year race. "The polar positions about religion or faith in campaigns, which are somewhat the different partys' positions—not completely—but the polar positions are these: 'I have religion, and my job, by God, is to get in and pass a bunch of legislation to make everybody else follow the teachings of my faith.' That would be one pole. And the other position would be, 'Religion's a personal and private matter. We shouldn't mention it in public discourse.'

"What I was trying to do in the campaign—and what I think is the right thing to do—is share with people who I am. I'm not sharing who I am to proselytize or make people be like me, but I'm doing it so that people will have a basis for assessing my character which will be helpful for them in deciding whether they want to trust future decisions, on issues known and unknown, to my care. So it's fine to use it to share with people, 'Here's who I am and here's what motivates me.' But if it goes beyond that, it's either proselytizing or my goal is to implement every bit of the Catholic Church doctrine in the law of Virginia. If it goes beyond, 'Here's who I am and here's what motivates me,' that's a problem."

As the campaign rolled out and Kaine's talk about matters of faith began to attract attention, the governor recalled, he had to stop his staff from getting carried away: "I came in one day and there were a bunch of bumper stickers that they had printed up that said, 'Christians for Kaine.' And then they had this other set of bumper stickers, 'Catholics for Kaine.' And I said, 'You're throwing all those away.' One of them even had a cross. I said, 'That's sacrilege in a campaign to use a powerful religious symbol like that to get a political edge. We're throwing all those away; we're not using those.'

"So again, I think the appropriate thing to do is sort of a third way between these polar positions. Talk about your faith if it motivates you. You tell people what your hobbies are, you tell people that you're married and how many kids you have and that you used to be a lawyer, so why wouldn't you talk about the thing that's most important to you?"

Governor Kaine well understands the landscape, running as a Roman Catholic in an overwhelmingly Protestant state, running as pro-life in an overwhelmingly pro-choice party, and running as against the death penalty in a state that is one of the top users of the death chamber. To the extent that he has been asked by Democrats for advice about running and winning in red states, he has been willing to give it, along with warnings: "It's been a recurring theme of some Democratic campaigns to go after the 'religious Right,' to attack the 'religious Right' using that phrase as an attack. Somebody who attacks the religious Right—what they mean to be doing is attacking intolerant positions on this issue or that issue. But when you broad-brush attack the religious Right, a whole lot of religious people who I think would be very amenable to voting for Democratic candidates, that have a lot in common with Democratic policy positions, think you're attacking them. And so you push them away from the Democratic party in a needless way."

I asked the governor if he expected to see more Democratic campaigns trying to master the "Kaine Approach," even overdoing it until they got it right. He replied that overdoing it is a real danger. "Maybe there will be some that will overdo it. Lord knows, anything in a campaign can be overdone if it's not authentic. This kind of stuff done in an inauthentic way can be very offensive. But if people do it and try to do it in a way that's authentic to themselves, I think it can be fine. One of the reasons I am a Democrat is I feel that Democrats get the Good Samaritan principle.

"There is a sense in just about any Democratic event, committee meeting, and so on that I've been in, that the way to soul satisfaction is through lending a helping hand to your neighbor—and not just your next-door neighbor but somebody who is in need, and helping them get back up on their feet and get dusted off and helped along the way. That Good Samaritan principle is such a strong core value for virtually every Democrat that I know that I think it ought to be easy for us to talk about. I really do. I don't know why it's harder for a Democrat to talk about it, because I see the Democrats that I deal with as very much believers in that Good Samaritan principle.

"I think a lot of people of faith are—are admirably reticent to be seen as falsely pious. And so I think that leads to some restraint in people who are deeply religious. And I appreciate that hesitancy for that reason. There's a great scriptural tradition that says you ought to be hesitant about it."

Here Governor Kaine echoes the thoughts of Alabama state representative Ken Guin, who said he hopes his fellow Democrats realize they have got to do a better job speaking to conservative Christians in order to stay competitive. He said his party is held back by an old-fashioned idea: "I would say it's true of a lot of my fellow Democrats. I was taught growing up that you just don't talk about faith and politics. It wasn't that we weren't people of faith; we just didn't see it as polite to mix in with political debate. But today it's just something you have to talk about; we now have to defend our faith. If we don't stand up, we'll lose our positions in the legislature, and our policies will suffer—not because then the political values we have are not good ones, but because we won't be there to fight for those programs."

Like the Virginia governor, Guin said he believes his party can do better talking to religious voters standing on a foundation of authenticity. "You have to find a way that's comfortable for you. Some of us are going to be more comfortable than others, certainly. I guess I should say my members are thinking about it a lot more."

What if Democrats start to run to catch this train just as its losing steam? The Reverend Andrew Hernandez, sociologist, teacher, pastor, and political activist, told me he is sure this latest wave of religious-based politics has reached its high-water mark, in part because the conservative Christian winning streak has produced so little of the victory conservatives were told was just around the corner in America and on the global stage. As an example, he points out that the Iraq War has become an enterprise far removed from the values he sees in Christianity: "People don't seem to care that we've killed almost fifty thousand Iraqis. It's amazing to me that Christians don't. I preached about this. I got a lot of push-back on it, but you know, I felt like it was laid on my heart. I said, 'God loves the Iraqis as much as he loves you.' When we first started the war, I first preached that sermon. 'He loves them, and for every child that dies because we bombed them, God would feel for that child as if your child died walking out the church and being run over by a car.' Well, I got a lot of push-back on that one. But it's true. I believe that's true."

Hernandez said the disillusionment that will follow the Iraq War, whenever it ends, will bring opportunity for different approaches to war and peace, and politics and faith. "You know there's a point where stuff just don't stick anymore, because you think, 'No, wait a minute!' So I think it's played out, and I think the religious Left and the religious progressives are starting to assert themselves again. The war has a way of making you less religious. Wars always make you less religious than more so. When you're going through them, you're more so. After them, you're less so. Think about it. Or you have to rethink what you believe to be the way God works in the world."

The shock and fascination that followed the threatened execution of Afghan convert Abdul Rahman might point to the kind of disillusionment Hernandez said is coming. After years as an aid worker with a European-based Christian agency, Rahman converted from Islam. Years after American and international troops evicted the Taliban from power and installed a new Afghan government, Rahman gained worldwide attention when in the midst of a custody battle with an ex-wife, it was introduced in court that Rahman was no longer a Muslim. Afghan religious scholars and legal experts solemnly intoned that apostasy, a rejection of the faith, was punishable by death.

To their credit, American authorities recoiled at the idea of a convert to Christianity facing execution for his faith at the hands of a government put into power by the force of American arms and with the unstinting and unquestioning support of conservative Christians in the United States. President Bush and Secretary of State Rice both pressured the Afghan government for a way out, while more representatives of Afghanistan's independent and religious judiciaries offered little reassurance.

Word began to leak out of judicial offices that Rahman just might be crazy, thus ineligible for trial and death. Religious radio and television in the United States was not satisfied with the face-saving maneuver of spiriting Rahman out of the country to asylum in Italy. The central fact remained: Conversion to Christianity in the "new Afghanistan" bought with American blood and treasure was an offense punishable by death. Hernandez promised there will be more opportunities for conservative Christian "buyer's remorse" when the smoke clears from America's wars in western Asia, and a long road to the conclusion that the U.S. did not win: "There's no way we can win in this sector's mind because they really believed that we were going to be cheered on as liberators. That whole thing, they believed that. You know I remember this woman at church said, 'Oh, did you see the little boy kissing the president, a picture of our president? God is using him as an instrument to free these people.' Well, what these people are going to say is, 'Okay, we're free, but we don't want you to proselytize here in Iraq.' And then back here they're going to say, 'Wait a minute, why would God want us to sacrifice our children if we can't spread the Gospel there? How come God will allow that? What happened?'

"This is supposed to be a model of, when Christians run the country, they can change the world. And what they find out is that when Christians run the country, the world pretty much stays the same, no matter what you do. That's where the problem is. I'm sure they harbor illusions of sending missionaries and missions over there, and harbor the illusion that they were going to come to Iraq and spread the Word. There's no way fundamentalists, individual Christians, think someone practicing their Muslim faith is a good thing. There's no way they're going to believe that. The only reason they tolerate the Jews right now, the conservatives, is that they think at the end all of the Jews are going to get converted anyway.

"So there's no way that you can create a psychological victory on what's going to happen. And do you think there's any way Iraq's going to allow Christians to go in there and set up churches?

"And then we're going to say, 'Well, what the hell did we do this for?' Remember, a lot of fundamentalists, evangelicals, are working-class poor people, white people. One of the reasons they don't trust government is they're always getting screwed because they're poor working white folks. And so this'll just be another kind of proof, more proof: 'Yeah, we were right to begin with. You know, we got snookered.' So I do think this war will have a huge impact on their politics. I really do.

"You know, in a way this war was fought for geopolitical reasons, but the fallout will be that it may push this segment of the population back into its isolationist mode. Now, there's always going to be a group that uses the language as a front for what they already hold to be true. And those people are going to stay politically active. You know those people will stay politically active 'cause those are the same folks that use Christianity as a means to an end. You just use theological language or spiritual language or Christianity to cover what you want to do anyway."

Far, far away from Andy Hernandez on the political continuum, but closer theologically than either of them might realize, is former U.S. senator and ambassador John C. Danforth. An Episcopal priest and a Republican, the Reverend John Danforth is counseling his party to back away from religious politics, not because he is a maverick, but because he thinks the current course is bad for his party and the country. He, too, said the current cycle has almost run its course: "I don't think it's sustainable. I think that this is going to wear thin. I think there's going to be a backlash, first among Republicans and then more broadly in the population, and people are going to be able to begin to speak out against it. I think that one of the things that's very strange is the silence of religious people who feel the opposite. They haven't been outspoken enough. And, yeah, I wrote two op-eds[4] and they're both about the same subject, but one was more political and the other was more religious. Particularly the one that was more political was written for a purpose, and that was to try to generate a backlash. To try to generate more of an expression, an activism from people who felt that we had gone too far in making the Republican Party the party of the religious Right. So I think that this is not going to be sustained."

The former senator insists that backlash is coming, even in the face of widespread belief inside and outside the Republican Party that the public embrace of religion has worked better than anyone could have planned. Republicans have made strong allies in specific churches. Those churches help drive the vote. That organizing creates a feedback loop that also drives fund-raising, enlisting volunteers, and more success in turn. "That's the argument," Danforth said. "I've received an awful lot of comment on those two op-eds and most of it favorable, but I've received some push-back from Republicans who basically say just that, it's working."

Citing Thomas Frank's widely praised book *What's the Matter With Kansas?*, he describes the reaction of people who want him to dummy up rather than risk spoiling a good thing: "People who are the traditional Republicans are willing to put up with this because it gets the votes, from non-traditional-Republican quarters. And how do you argue with success? We want to win the election, so we're willing to do all this."

John Danforth ruefully named what he sees as the paradox at the heart of the current Republican win streak: "If it's the right thing for the country, it's the worst thing a politician can do, the worst thing a political party can do. I mean, if you think about the basic goal of our country, almost its purpose at the founding, it is to answer: 'How do we keep together this one country, all of the diversity that's America?' If you agree, then you're very concerned about anything that is busily creating wedge issues."

For all that, Danforth said, he sees the tide turning. He told me a watershed moment was the Terri Schiavo debate, when Americans across all political lines said they were repulsed by the hijacking of one family's tragedy by a coalition of religious leaders and elected officials. There was, for a moment, sudden clarity about the downsides of religious politics. "I think that there are just an awful lot of people who are saying, 'Wait a second, what's happening here?' But this has to be a public debate. But if the view is: one side is America, the flag, God, the Ten Commandments, and on the other side are, you know, a bunch of immoral orgy participants and baby killers. I mean, that's the way to both, one, create a lot of bitterness and, two, create the sense that there really is only one side."

The inherent contradictions between politics and faith are becoming too difficult to sustain over the long haul while still leaving both sides in full possession of their integrity. The Republicans and their conservative partners both need each other in a way that leaves both sides vulnerable. Having tasted real power and influence, conservative Christians may have to admit to themselves, in order to stay engaged, that they have not yet gotten what they were bargaining for from the alliance with the Republican Party. Otherwise, where can they go? The Republican Party might have to admit to itself that the alliance with conservative Christians has left it unable to pursue strictly political goals with complete freedom of maneuver. The Harriet Miers nomination, the internationally damaging restrictions on family-planning advice and funding overseas, and the difficult corner the Bush administration has been painted into in Iraq, all point to strains in the relationship.

The Reverend Barry Lynn said, "Something has happened over the course of the dialogue America's been having with itself over the last ten or fifteen years; some of the exit polls showed 53 to 54 percent of Americans believe there should be few, if any, restrictions on a woman's right to choose. That has been framed, with the exception of Nat Hentoff, as a purely religious issue. He's the only well-known atheist I know who doesn't believe in reproductive choice. It's all a religious war. Sixty percent of Americans already believe in either civil unions or all-the-way gay marriage. Sixty-five percent, roughly, don't want politicking from the pulpit. They do not want their minister, priest, to tell them who to vote for. Sixty-seven percent believe that if you give money to churches, as in the president's faith-based program, they should not be able to choose employees based on religion. Those are pretty big numbers.

"Where I went to school, they were majority sentiments, and what I say to audiences every time I speak to them is, if you're depressed, 'Look at these numbers.' If the hearts and minds of the people are already convinced on a lot of these issues—not on all of them, but on a lot of these issues—that we're right, then why can't we translate that into a different set of political leaders who accept those principles?—because apparently they are the majority values of America."

If Lynn is right, and these are already beliefs held by simple majorities of Americans, then the operation of politics is what stands between public desires and the public's distilled will becoming policy. Perhaps the term "religious war" is a little strong, but turning religious symbols, language, and sentiments into tools has not aided in turning political convictions held by the electorate into law. If anything, it has made it harder.

In 2006, while preparing for a possible run for the White House, Governor Mike Huckabee of Arkansas told a gathering of conservative Christians that, contrary to public-opinion polls that call for less religious involvement in politics, there was simply not enough church involvement in the state. More, says Governor Huckabee, would be good not only for Christians, but for America as well.

The current laws standing in the way of more open affiliation between church organizations and political parties have not stopped one party in particular from creating a complex web of organizational support, funding, get-out-the-vote activities, and partisan advocacy. Some of the more frankly church-aligned members of the House of Representatives have toyed with amending the tax code to knock down the restrictions that jeopardize a church's tax-exempt standing if it becomes a partisan advocate.

The Reverend George Regas preached against the Iraq War from the pulpit of All Saints' Episcopal Church in Pasadena, California, the Sunday before the presidential election. Regas made the observation that people of faith and goodwill would be voting for Senator John Kerry the following Tuesday and to reelect President Bush. The rector of All Saints also specifically noted that he was not advising a vote for either presidential candidate.

Months later, in June of 2005, the Reverend Ed Bacon, the current rector of All Saints, got a letter from the Internal Revenue Service, advising him that the tax collection agency was inquiring about possible violation of the church's tax-exempt status through its involvement in a political campaign. The rector said, "It was a surprise. It was out of the blue. I never had gotten any kind of attention from the IRS during my thirty years of preaching and rectoring." He called the congregation's lay leadership, got a lawyer, and answered the IRS's inquiry. It did not end there. "The IRS offered to back off, to drop the case, if we admitted that we were in the wrong and would apologize and say that we would never do it again."

Ed Bacon said he could not apologize and could not admit wrongdoing. "And we still really in our hearts feel that we are not in the wrong. We observed what for me, throughout my career, has been a very clear delineation between proclaiming what I call prophetic values, the values of the Hebrew prophets and Jesus, and calling names of presidents and other elected officials who are behind those policies that are not in alignment with those values. We did that without ever, ever crossing what for me is the golden line of separation of church and state, and that is endorsing a candidate, or endorsing a party."

What got the priest particularly worried, he said, was that the IRS made content judgments about the preaching going on at All Saints, for instance conceding that candidates and parties had not been endorsed from the pulpit: "And the IRS comes back and says [in effect], 'Well, that's well and good, but we can tell that was what you were implying.' That's highly problematic to me that they would make a subjective determination of what our implications are, or any preacher's implications. The other very problematic thing is they told us that they had read all of the sermons that we have on the Web site and had found one that I had preached earlier in the year. Had I preached that particular sermon on this particular Sunday [before Election Day], it would have gotten their attention, but because it was not preached during the election season, it did not get their attention. I find that to be totally unacceptable."

I pointed out to him that there are tax laws governing religion and politics, and reading his sermons would be one way to assess whether regulatory boundaries had been crossed. The Reverend Ed Bacon disagreed: "We are called to promote peace and justice season in and season out." He rejected the offer allowing a quiet surrender by All Saints, and the IRS elevated the inquiry to the level of an investigation.

Through the summer of 2005 and into the fall the dialogue was strictly between the church and its lawyers and the IRS. Once the inquest moved on to the next stage, the Reverend Ed Bacon decided to go public, on November 16, a Sunday when a large crowd was expected in the pews for guest preacher Archbishop Desmond Tutu. A *Los Angeles Times* reporter in the pews for the Tutu sermon wrote about the IRS investigation in the next day's paper, and the publicity floodgates opened. All Saints's stance has been endorsed in newspapers around the country and brought in spontaneous contributions from people across the religious spectrum for the church's legal defense fund. The church also attracted interest from conservative Christians and congregations looking for allies in their own attempts to rewrite the laws regarding taxes and the church.

The Reverend Ed Bacon is not an ally of theirs. He said the IRS might maintain that it is pursuing his congregation's preachers because there have been so many cases of preaching it is important to settle where the line is between partisan advocacy and biblically based preaching and teaching. "And if that is the case, I applaud that because I do have deep difficulty with, I think, probably a substantial number of churches and substantial number of preachers taking a politically partisan position." Sprinkled through the letters of support, he said, have been stories from congregants in other churches whose clergy preached they would go to hell if they didn't vote for Bush. "That is obviously crossing the line. And that obviously, I think, needs to be held accountable to separation-of-church-and-state values."

He learned those values, he said, from his father, who had been both a Baptist preacher and an elected county school superintendant. "And he never crossed the line in any way, leading people to believe that he was the answer or that his opponent was not the answer." That is the tension embedded at the core of his convictions about separation and prophetic preaching. On the one hand, there is reverence for his father's observance of the boundaries between church and state, and on the other, what he sees as a responsibility to identify injustice. "If you're a preacher, you must at all costs courageously say, 'These are the values of God. This is where you're falling short.' We must change and call names without ever crossing the line of saying, 'Now, you must go out and vote against a particular person, or for a particular person or party.' "

The Reverend Ed Bacon preached against both the invasion of Afghanistan and the Iraq War. Through various other debates in the Episcopal Church, like those over the blessing of same-sex unions, All Saints has occasionally lost members who decided they were uncomfortable with the teachings of the church. "I guess I've always thought that we've defined ourselves as much as we could. And we had lost all the people we were going to lose, because we lost a lot of people over my position on Afghanistan and Iraq. But with this, we lost another very major donor who said, 'I just cannot go with you and George on this. I don't like your position with the IRS, and frankly I don't like your position on the war.' So I think that's a never-ending journey in the church's life, and I think that for a church like us, that is part of saving our soul and increasing our fidelity and in strengthening our power to speak for the least of these."

After the case became public, this is how the Reverend Ed Bacon explained his position to his own flock: "Our nonpartisanship is a holy space from which we can, without obligation or allegiance to any party or person, bring the core values of our faith to bear on the institutions and culture around us, remembering that faith without works is dead and that we are called to be doers of the Word, not hearers only.

"Faith in action is called politics. Spirituality without action is fruitless, and social action without spirituality is heartless. We are boldly political without being partisan. Having a partisan-free place to stand liberates the religious patriot to see clearly, speak courageously, and act daringly."[5]

That statement would not sound much different coming from the mouth of a conservative Christian preacher defending his right to urge his congregation to action on political and social conflicts of the day. They, too, have always maintained that they have operated from the best and oldest traditions of the church. Ed Bacon told me what sets him apart is that his quarrels, when he has them, are with both the Republican and Democratic parties. In this case, he publicly faults the president for leading the nation into the invasions of Afghanistan and Iraq, and the Democratic and Republican leadership that gave him the legislative wherewithal to do it. He maintains that is a significant difference with the churches that have been in lockstep with the Republican Party.

Conservative Christian congregations and pastors return fire by pointing out that their critics seem prepared to give a free pass to religious politics from the Left while rejecting it from the Right. As a vast congregation headed to after-worship activities in the sprawling Prestonwood complex in Plano, Texas, Pastor Jack Graham told me that striking the right balance comes from maintaining your mission: "I could turn this whole church into a political-action committee. We have people requesting this, that, and the other constantly: endorsements, signatures, petitions. We do a minimal amount of that because that's not our purpose. Our purpose is not to be a political-action committee. Our purpose is to fulfill the mission of Christ on earth and, when it comes time, to step up to the plate and speak out.

"Believe it or not, there are more evangelicals interested in social justice than imagined. More and more evangelical Christians are concerned about poverty and helping the poor and ministering to the poor. We maybe go about it in a different way than some.

"So everybody has to draw their own line. Do people step over the line? Sometimes. I know I'm not interested in controlling government. I am interested in influencing. Sometimes I think some of us are more interested in control than influence, and I think that's when you cross the line. We should give all the influence we can bring to bear in the right way, and then leave the results to God."

Leave the results to God. During the years I have been gathering material for this book, I have been moved by the deep faith of so many people, and their trust in a God who takes an active role in the life of his Creation. I have listened with surprised attention as a pastor described his learning of a life-changing ministry he now runs after God gets him stuck in traffic so he can hear a radio program. That same God of traffic jams and meeting the woman of your dreams must also be the God who allows Mohammed Atta to take the controls of a hijacked jet and fly it into the World Trade Center. He is also the God who is thanked by successful home-run hitters (he seems, in their theology, to float somewhere above home plate) and super-mega-lottery-jackpot winners.

He is the God who, in the view of General Boykin, made George Bush president even after he came in second in the balloting (you may wonder why He did not simply make more people vote for Bush), and the God who used Hurricane Katrina to clean out New Orleans public housing, in the view of Louisiana Republican Congressman Richard Baker of Baton Rouge. In American discourse, that same God is rarely credited with the events of our lives that can make them nasty, futile, and unhappy for so many people.

Perhaps if we gave a little less credit to God, we might demand more of ourselves in running a world that is a better place for 300 million Americans and the other 5.7 billion people with whom we share this planet. God's repeatedly invoked blessings for America did not make Zacarias Moussaoui reveal the coming terrorist attack to his FBI captors, nor have they saved thousands of Americans from terrible deaths in Iraq. The president solemnizes his own policy goals by attaching them to God's will, but ultimately it is our willingness as a people to help other people be free that will determine the success of such a mission. God could do it today if that was God's will.

The world was given to humankind to manage. If American religion were something to "do" instead of something to "say," we might be managing it a lot better. In our politics, and our faith, saying things and doing them have become hopelessly confused. Our political leaders and we the voters might have a lot more success in transforming the world if we actually did the things we have become so good at talking about.

Much of what is talked about in contemporary shorthand as Christian conservatism in America has a lot more to do with American conservatism than it does with Christianity. From a lifetime's reading of the Gospels, I find it hard to imagine Jesus endorsing the hypernationalism and pridefulness that marks so much modern patriotism. It might not be such a bad idea to recall that Love of God and Love of Country are two different things, no matter how mixed up they often seem in the twenty-first century.

In the mid-nineteenth century, British patriots loved their Empire, their Queen, and their religion no less than Americans do today. Today that empire is nonexistent and their church is hanging on for dear life. Were the British wrong about the salutary effect of loving God and Country? Did the British not love God enough, or did God suddenly decide to start loving the United States more?

When former House majority leader Tom Delay resigned his house seat after a convincing win in the Republican primary in his Texas district, he said God no longer wanted him to be the congressman from Sugar Land. My personal theology does not give God a lot of credit in these matters, but I will go to the mat for the right of the man called "The Hammer" by his house colleagues to believe that and declare it publicly. I would hope that any politician insisting that God is deciding the makeup of the Texas House delegation would not stop there. God, in all his mysterious ways, also got Bill Clinton elected in 1992, and reelected in 1996. If you believe God is deciding the field in a suburban Houston district, he must also be helping Democrat Barney Frank of Massachusetts win reelection like clockwork every two years.

The powerful twin narratives of American history, of the Secular Republic and the New Israel, both had a powerful influence in getting us where we are today. It seems legitimate to wonder whether those ways of seeing our country still have the power to move us from where we are today—a country where tens of millions of Americans are not Christians, are not believers of any kind, or do not see a strong connection between their choices in the voting booth and their religious identity.

If tens of millions of Americans are just the opposite, we have found in debate after debate that we eventually reach stasis. Nothing happens, because there is no place to begin the conversation. If we saw our various religions as what we do, rather than what we say, our dueling visions of our shared country would be fought out on the merits. If we returned our policy debates to disagreements on the cases, rather than on the religious identities that bring us to our conclusions, we will always have a place to begin the conversation.

That approach might be criticized as an attempt to artificially exclude God from the debate. When those who see themselves as God's people are in the fray, furthering the outcomes they support because of their discernment of what God wants in the world, how can they say God is excluded from the debate? The kind of faith that finds it must be the answer to every question, the end to every argument, and must be inserted into every conversation is certainly going to be a presence on the American political scene for as long as we have a country. It turns out not to be a very effective tool in creating common wisdom and furthering the common good.

Religion has turned out to be a potent tool in rousing people and driving them to join winning electoral alliances. Religion has been less successful in helping us create the blessed community, the one people on all sides of the hottest debates in our common life hope . . . and pray for.

ENDNOTES

CHAPTER ONE

1. Matthew 25:34–37 (King James Version).

2. O thus be it ever when free-men shall stand

   Between their lov'd home and the war's desolation;

   Blest with vict'ry and peace, may the heav'n-rescued land

   Praise the Pow'r that hath made and preserv'd us a nation!

   Then conquer we must, when our cause it is just,

   And this be our motto: "In God is our trust!"

   And the star-spangled banner in triumph shall wave

   O'er the land of the free and the home of the brave!

3. "At least ten verses from the Holy Bible shall be read, without comment, at the opening of each public school on each school day. Any child shall be excused from such Bible reading, or attending such Bible reading, upon the written request of his parent or guardian." *Commonwealth of Pennsylvania Bylaw,* Public Law 24, Pa. Stat. 15-1516 (as amended in 1928).

4. *Abington Township School District v. Schempp,* 374 U.S. 203 (1963), decided June 17, 1963.

5. "I thought about Mother and Dad and the strength I got from them, and God and faith, and the separation of church and state." (Then later, in the same interview) "If by 'born again' one is asking, 'Do you accept Jesus Christ as your savior?' Then I would answer a clear-cut yes. No hesitancy. No awkwardness." Vice President George Bush, 1988. Campaign trail interview, as quoted in *The New Yorker,* July 12, 2004, and many other publications.

6. Presidential proclamation, April 2, 2005. Office of the Press Secretary, White House.

7. *Roe v. Wade,* 410 U.S. 113 (1973), Justice Harry Blackmun, decided January 22, 1973.

CHAPTER TWO

1. But you cannot easily fit Jefferson's peg into this or that hole. In the very same letter (August 10, 1787) he insists that Moral Philosophy might be something of a waste of time for his nephew, since "he who made us would have been a pitiful bungler, if he had made the rules of our moral conduct a matter of science. For one man of science, there are thousands who are not. What would have become of them? Man was destined for society. His morality, therefore, was to be formed to this object. He was endowed with a sense of right and wrong, merely relative to this. This sense is as much a part of his nature, as the sense of hearing, seeing, feeling; it is the true foundation of morality, and not the το καλον [beautiful], truth, &c., as fanciful writers have imagined. The moral sense, or conscience, is as much a part of man as his leg or arm. It is given to all human beings in a stronger or weaker degree, as force of members is given them in a greater or less degree. It may be strengthened by exercise, as may any particular limb of the body." Not everything, Jefferson says, can be submitted to the unwavering calibration of science. If it could be, the Creator was "a pitiful bungler."

2. The U.S. is not at the very bottom. It is one rung up from the bottom spot held by Italy in percentage of gross domestic product dedicated to poverty alleviation. Pedants call the U.S. the most generous nation on earth, pointing to its overall giving, and purposely failing to note that as a country of nearly 300 million people, U.S. gross foreign aid would of course surpass that of Norway, which has fewer people than New York City.

3. Thomas Jefferson, October 31, 1819, in a letter to William Short: "As you say of yourself, I too am an Epicurian. I consider the genuine (not the imputed) doctrines of Epicurus as containing everything rational in moral philosophy which Greece and Rome have left us."

4. James Madison, Federalist Number 37.

5. James Madison, Federalist Number 52.

CHAPTER THREE

1. "There is no such thing as separation of church and state in the Constitution. It is a lie of the Left and we are not going to take it anymore." Pat Robertson, address to his American Center for Law and Justice, See Rob Boston, *The Most*

Dangerous Man in America?: Pat Robertson and the Rise of the Christian Coalition (Amherst, NY: Prometheus Books, 1996).

2. *Employment Division, Department of Human Resources, et al. v. Smith, et al.* (November 1993), 79. In this case, the Supreme Court decided that a general law against the use of hallucinogenic drugs could be construed to apply to all citizens, even those who use peyote, a mild hallucinogen, in American Indian rites. Because the law was not written specifically to hinder the ceremony, it could not be understood as a violation of the First Amendment protection of the free-exercise clause.

3. "St. Jack and the Bullies in the Pulpit," *Washington Post,* February 2, 2006.

4. Deuteronomy 21, 18–21.

Chapter Four

1. Matthew 10:34 (King James Version).

2. When Constantine bested his rival Maxentius for the emperor's throne, he set what we think of as "The West" on a Christian course, if only by accident. While popularly remembered as making Christianity the religion of the Roman Empire and being the first Christian emperor, his Edict of Milan only brought freedom of religion to the empire by making all religions equal, and returned confiscated property to the young church. Constantine was only baptized on his deathbed, in May, 337.

3. September 20, 2001, speech to a joint session of Congress after the September 11 terrorist attacks. "I will not forget this wound to our country or those who inflicted it. I will not yield; I will not rest; I will not relent in waging this struggle for freedom and security for the American people.

"The course of this conflict is not known, yet its outcome is certain. Freedom and fear, justice and cruelty, have always been at war, and we know that God is not neutral between them. [Applause.]

"Fellow citizens, we'll meet violence with patient justice—assured of the rightness of our cause, and confident of the victories to come. In all that lies before us, may God grant us wisdom, and may He watch over the United States of America." Office of the Press Secretary, White House.

4. Matthew 5:43–45 ("Ye have heard that it hath been said, Thou shalt love thy

neighbour, and hate thine enemy). But I say unto you, Love your enemies, bless them that curse you, do good to them that hate you, and pray for them which despitefully use you, and persecute you; That ye may be the children of your Father which is in heaven: for he maketh his sun to rise on the evil and on the good, and sendeth rain on the just and on the unjust (King James Version)."

5. From Lincoln's second inaugural address: "Both read the same Bible and pray to the same God, and each invokes His aid against the other. It may seem strange that any men should dare to ask a just God's assistance in wringing their bread from the sweat of other men's faces, but let us judge not, that we be not judged. The prayers of both could not be answered. That of neither has been answered fully. The Almighty has His own purposes." Ronald C. White, Jr., *Lincoln's Greatest Speech: The Second Inaugural* (New York: Simon & Schuster, 2002).

6. Acts 4:12 (New American Standard Bible): "And there is salvation in no one else; for there is no other name under heaven that has been given among men by which we must be saved."

7. From the military instructional handbook for chaplains, *Religious Ministry in the US Navy, NWP–01:* "The chaplain conducts divine services, administers sacraments or ordinances, performs rites or ceremonies in the manner and form of the chaplain's own faith group, conducts pastoral visitations and facilitates ministries for personnel of other faiths. Within the task and activities, the chaplain administers the CRP [command religious program] at the direction of the CO [commanding officer], including plans, programs, and budget for the command's religious ministries. The chaplain advises the commander or CO on religious matters within the command."

8. Michael New, "Taking a Stand" (*The New America,* 12, no. 18, September 2, 1996).

9. Bobby Welch, *You, The Warrior Leader* (Nashville, TN: Ball Publishing Group, 2004), p. 97.

10. Ibid, p. 97.

CHAPTER FIVE

1. President Bush, February 24, 2004. Office of The Press Secretary, The White House.

2. From Virginia's civil union ban: "A civil union, partnership contract or other

arrangement between persons of the same sex purporting to bestow the privileges or obligations of marriage is prohibited. Any such civil union, partnership contract or other arrangement entered into by persons of the same sex in another state or jurisdiction shall be void in all respects in Virginia and any contractual rights created thereby shall be void and unenforceable." *Civil Unions Between Persons of the Same Sex,* Virginia Code §20–45.3 (1997, amended 2005).

3. Jonathan Rauch, *Gay Marriage: Why It's Good for Gays, Good for Straights, and Good for America* (New York: Times Books, 2004). Andrew Sullivan, *Virtually Normal: An Argument About Homosexuality* (New York: Knopf, 1995). Bruce Bawer, *A Place at the Table: The Gay Individual in American Society* (New York: Simon and Schuster, 1994).

4. From *The Catechism of the Roman Catholic Church,* 2nd ed. (New York: Doubleday, 2003), . . . article six, the Sixth Commandment: You shall not commit adultery 2362 "Sexuality is a source of joy and pleasure: The Creator himself . . . established that in the [generative] function, spouses should experience pleasure and enjoyment of body and spirit. Therefore, the spouses do nothing evil in seeking this pleasure and enjoyment. They accept what the Creator has intended for them. At the same time, spouses should know how to keep themselves within the limits of just moderation."

Chapter Six

1. "Article 14: Secularity of the State. The Russian Federation is a secular state. No religion may be instituted as a state-sponsored or mandatory religion. Religious associations are separated from the state, and equal before the law."

2. Tex. H. Con. Res. 38, 77th Leg. 6473 (2001).

3. In fact, the state legislature had already declared Jesus of Nazareth "The Prince of Ethics."

4. *The Papers of George Washington,* Presidential Series No. 285.

5. An archaic reference to Islam.

6. Not as in modern usage, in marriage, but a term for lack of religious belief no longer in regular use.

CHAPTER SEVEN

1. The New York State Board of Regents's Statement on Moral and Spiritual Training in the Schools urged wide adoption of the prayer, and the support of individual school boards around the state, "We believe that this Statement will be subscribed to by all men and women of good will, and we call upon all of them to aid in giving life to our program." Cornell Law School Legal Information Institute.

2. From *Engel v. Vitale,* 370, U.S. 421 (1962). The case was argued on April 3 and decided on June 25.

3. *Washington Evening Star,* July 1962. See also Terry Eastland, ed., *Religious Liberty in the Supreme Court: The Cases That Define the Debate over Church and State* (Washington, DC: Ethics and Public Policy Center, 1995).

4. Gresham's Law. "Bad money drives out good if they exchange for the same price." Named for English financier Sir Thomas Gresham.

5. Teacher training colleges, a term no longer in common use.

6. *Intelligent Designs on Evolution,* radio documentary from American Radio Works, January 2006, hosted by author.

7. Scripps Howard/Ohio University poll, November 2005, 1,005 American adults sampled by phone over a three-day period in late October. Results available, news Polls.org, from the Scripps Survey Research Center at Ohio University.

8. Ibid.

9. CBS News Poll, October 23, 2005, Based on phone interviews with 885 adults, October 3–5, 2005. Results available at CBSNews.com/stories/2005/10/22/opinion/polls/main965223.shtml .

10. *West Virginia State Board of Education v. Barnette,* decided June 14, 1943.

11. *Hurst v. Newman,* California Judgment entered January 16, 2006.

12. Wyshak, G., "Secular Changes in Age at Menarche in a Sample of US Women," *Annals of Human Biology,* 10(1) (1983 Jan–Feb): 75–7.

13. Tallese Johnson and Jane Dye, "Indicators of Marriage and Fertility in the United States from the *American Community Survey*" (Washington, D.C.: U.S. Bureau of the Census).

14. "The Relationship between Virginity Pledges and . . ." National STD Prevention Conference, 2004.

15. Ibid.

16. Paul Duggan, "Montgomery Mother's Stand on Sex Ed Begins at Home," *Washington Post,* May 19, 2005.

17. Dr. John W. Baer, *The Pledge of Allegiance: A Short Story* (1992).

CHAPTER EIGHT

1. RK Jones, JE Darroch, and SK Henshaw, "Patterns in the Socioeconomic Characteristics of Women Obtaining Abortions in 2000–2001," *Perspectives on Sexual and Reproductive Health,* 34(5)(2002):226–235.

2. Ibid.

3. National Abortion Federation.

4. RK Jones, JE Darroch, and SK Henshaw, "Patterns in the Socioeconomic Characteristics of Women Obtaining Abortions in 2000–2001," *Perspectives on Sexual and Reproductive Health,* 34(5)(2002):226–235.

5. Ibid.

6. RK Jones, JE Darroch, and SK Henshaw, "Contraceptive Use Among U.S. Women Having Abortions in 2000–2001," *Perspectives on Sexual and Reproductive Health,* 34(6)(2002): 294–303.

7. Alan Guttmacher Institute, 2005.

8. The Pew Research Center for the People and the Press, April 2004.

9. For the Pew sample, evangelical Protestants are those who describe themselves as "born again or evangelical," and mainline Protestants are those who say this description does not apply to them.

10. By bringing the prosecution under the RICO (Racketeer Influenced and Corrupt Organizations) statue, the abortion-rights activists may have bought themselves more grief than they bargained for. The RICO actions against clinic protestors helped fuel the rage of the antiabortion movement against the federal judiciary, with consequences that last to this day.

11. In a letter sent to doctors by the U.S. marketers of levonorgestrel at the behest of the FDA, it was noted that in 350,000 American users from 2000 to 2004, there had been 99 serious side effects, including 3 deaths.

12. It was widely reported that Father Reese was forced out of the high-profile job at the Jesuit publication for speaking out one too many times in contradiction of stated church opinions.

13. "Kerry and Hillary Clinton, among others, distanced themselves from the party's customary and straightforward enthusiasm for abortion on demand. Hillary Clinton was so bewildered by Kerry's defeat on moral issues that she even started speaking of a rapprochement with pro-lifers." George Neumayr, "Planned Politics,"*American Spectator,* July 2005.

14. Fox News Channel, *Hannity and Colmes,* July 27, 2005.

15. *Focus on the Family Radio,* James C. Dobson daily radio program, October 7, 2005.

16. Charles Babington, "Viewing Videotape, Frist Disputes Florida Doctors' Diagnosis of Schiavo," *Washington Post,* March 19, 2005.

17. *Gonzales, Attorney General et al v. The State of Oregon,* decided January 17, 2006.

18. Sam Hananel, "Stem Cell Research Divides GOP in Missouri," Associated Press, February 6, 2006.

19. *St. Louis Post-Dispatch* February 21, 2005.

CHAPTER NINE

1. Alfred E. Smith, "Catholic and Patriot: Governor Smith Replies." *Atlantic Monthly,* May 1927.

2. Charles Marshall, "An Open Letter to the Honorable Alfred E. Smith," *Atlantic Monthly,* April 1927.

3. Smith, "Catholic and Patriot."

4. *US News and World Report,* July 2000.

5. *Ladies' Home Journal,* August 2004.

6. John Kerry, *A Call to Service My Vision for a Better America* (New York: Penguin, 2004) p. 24.

7. Ibid, pp. 24–26.

8. American Life League ad, *Washington Times,* September 30, 2004.

9. *Dallas Morning News,* 2002.

10. *Philadelphia Inquirer,* September 21, 2005.

11. Ibid.

12. Rick Santorum, "Fishers of Men," *Catholic Online,* July 12, 2002.

CHAPTER TEN

1. George Barna and Harry R. Jackson, Jr., *High Impact African American Churches* (Ventura, CA: Regal Books, 2004).

2. Psalm 89:30–37 (Today's English Version): "If his descendants disobey my law, and no not live according to my commands, if they disregard my instructions and do not keep my commandments, then I will punish them for their sins; I will make them suffer for their wrongs. But I will not stop loving David or fail to keep my promise to him. I will not break my covenant with him or take back even one promise I made him." Psalm 97:10–12 (Today's English Version): "The Lord loves those who hate evil, he protects the lives of his people; he rescues them from the power of the wicked. Light shines on the righteous, and gladness on the good. All you that are righteous be glad because of what the Lord has done!"

3. The Los Angeles Lakers of the National Basketball Association and the Los Angeles Kings of the National Hockey League both left the LA Forum for the newly built Staples Center in downtown Los Angeles in 1999.

4. Bishop Harry Jackson, "Blacks Should Vote for George W. Bush," *Black America Today,* October 26, 2004.

5. Bishop Harry Jackson, "I Support George Bush!" elijahlist.com.

CHAPTER ELEVEN

1. Bureau of Economic Analysis, *Regional Economic Accounts* (Washington, DC: U.S. Government Printing Office, 2005).

2. *America's Health: State Health Rankings, 2004,* United Health Foundation, a nonprofit foundation established by the United Health Group.

3. Ibid.

4. Monique Oosse, *Rankings of State Life Expectancy at Age 65 for Non-White Males and Females: 1960–1990* (Washington, DC: U.S. Census Bureau, 2005).

5. *In the Matter of Roy Moore, Chief Justice of the Supreme Court of Alabama,* Court of the Judiciary Case Number 33, 2003.

6. This was not Moore's first brush with controversy over the Ten Commandments. In the late 1990s he fought to keep a wooden plaque with the Commandments on the wall of his circuit courtroom. That fight propelled him to statewide elected office and eventually to the chief justice's seat.

7. Roy Moore, "Our American Birthright," a poem composed for the August 16, 2003 rally in defense of the public acknowledgment of God nationwide.

8. Matthew 22:19–22 (King James Version): "Shew me the tribute money. And they brought unto him a penny. And he saith unto them, Whose is this image and superscription? They say unto him, Caesar's. Then saith he unto them, Render therefore unto Caesar the things which are Caesar's; and unto God the things that are God's. When they had heard these words, they marvelled, and left him, and went their way."

9. *The Bible and Public Schools: A First Amendment Guide* (The Bible Literacy Project and First Amendment Center, 1999).

10. Cullen Schippe, Check Steton, et al., "Why Study the Bible?" in *The Bible and Its Influence* (Fairfax, VA: BLP Publishing, 2005), 9–10.

11. In the 2002 opinion, Moore also called homosexuality abhorrent, detestable, and immoral, further asserting "[t]he State carries the power of the sword, that is, the power to prohibit [homosexual] conduct with physical penalties, such as confinement and even execution. It must use that power to prevent the subversion of children toward this lifestyle." Supreme Court of Alabama, 1002045, ex parte H.H., Moore concurrence.

Chapter Twelve

1. Gary Bauer, "Values Voters and the Left," *Washington Times,* November 21, 2004.

2. David Brooks, "The Values Vote Myth," *New York Times,* November 6, 2004.

3. Genesis 2:19–20 (King James Version): "And out of the ground the LORD God formed every beast of the field, and every fowl of the air; and brought [them] unto Adam to see what he would call them: and whatsoever Adam called every living creature, that [was] the name thereof. And Adam gave names to all cattle, and to the fowl of the air, and to every beast of the field."

4. John C. Danforth, "Onward, Moderate Christian Soldiers," *New York Times,* June 17, 2005; and John C. Danforth, "In the Name of Politics," *New York Times,* March 30, 2005.

5. *The IRS Goes to Church,* by the Rev. Ed Bacon, November 13, 2005. Sermon delivered at All Saints' Episcopal Church, Pasadena, Calif.

ACKNOWLEDGMENTS

St. Jerome translated the Bible into Latin in the enforced solitude of a cell. For a reporter 1,600 years later, especially one with a full-time day job, making a book as a solo act just doesn't seem possible.

All kinds of help and support made my work easier. My researcher Mike Melia helped me keep the project moving forward, running down facts and people as needed. Transcriber Deb Reeb turned hour after hour of conversation into text.

My editor Rene Alegria gave me a long enough leash to respond as new events and national debates forced their way onto America's political and religious agendas, by changing the outline. Over time, we migrated to a place far from the original proposal. Anyone immersed in a manuscript up to their eyes and teeth needs an editor who always sees the big picture, and I thank Rene for being exactly that.

It is a special joy to acknowledge all the people who talked to me about the debates, controversies, and ideas that make up the book, off the record and on, over the course of the last two years. From across the country's ideological, political, and religious divides, hundreds of people responded to my questions with an encouraging openness and a bracing candor.

It may strike you as funny, but I also have to thank the dozens of prominent people who refused to give me an interview for this book. Their excessive caution, evasiveness, and reluctance to engage with a key set of questions about our shared future was their choice. By ducking me, they forced me to dig deeper, think harder, and better understand what this book should be about. I was reminded of how uncomfortable many people are talking about these topics, and how much easier it is to just avoid them.

I wrote this book at my kitchen counter, in the midst of the daily comings and goings of a busy house. During the months of intense work in the winter and spring of early 2006, my wife and children did without my company and my help in keeping our home running, sane, and happy. The love and support of my wife Carole and my kids Rafael, Eva, and Isabel give me both the reason and the emotional wherewithal to work as hard as I do.

Finally, special thanks go to the people of St. Columba's Church in Washington, D.C. They are a lantern that gives light to the whole room, alive with the challenge of being a church in the twenty-first century.

JUNE, 2006. WASHINGTON, D.C.

INDEX

Index

Index

Index

Index

Index